THE HISTORY OF QUEBEC

A Patriote's Handbook

Battle of St.Eustache, 1837

By C.W. Jefferys*

* The reproduction in this book of pertinent historical drawings by the well-known Canadian artist, C.W. Jefferys, has been a matter of widespread discussion and controversy. The reader is referred for further information to Appendices II and III: publisher's statement regarding the C.W. Jefferys historical drawings; and the open letter to W.O. Twaits, Chairman of the Board, Imperial Oil.

The History of

QUEBEC

A Patriote's Handbook

by Léandre Bergeron

NC PRESS
1971

The cover shows the flag of the Québécois struggle. The Patriote flag of 1837 consisted of three horizontal bands, green, white and red. The gold star has been added to symbolize the resumption of the struggle for liberation of the people of Quebec in solidarity with all the oppressed peoples of the world who are throwing off the chains of colonialism.

Translated from the fifth French edition by Baila Markus and revised by the author.

First printing, August 1971
Second Printing, September 1971
Third Printing, November 1972

Printed by union labour

111

PRINTED IN CANADA

TO ENGLISH-CANADIANS

Quebec is spoiling the image Canada has of itself. Quebec is disturbing the comfort of a 'peaceful country going about its business.' Quebec is undermining the very foundations of a well-adjusted modern state. How awful can a province get?

Canadians have been told that their country was founded by two nations who decided one day to become partners in building a country, like two businessmen getting together to swing a deal. Canadians have been told that the French (that is, the Québécois) are less interested in commercial enterprise because of their Gallic origins and their educational system, that they are a gay, carefree people, keeping to themselves, and trying to keep alive centuries-old traditions. Canadians have been told things about the Québécois that reassured them and kept them away from the real issue: that the Québécois are colonized and that Canadians are accomplices of the colonizer.

For many Canadians this is an accusation of the vilest kind. Aren't Canadians just ordinary people who cannot imagine they have anything in common with Ian Smith and Voerster? Aren't Canadians just Canadians from coast to coast working hard to keep a nice big country together?

Canada is first of all the most cooperative colony the U.S. has ever had. Canadians are colonized economically, politically and culturally by the U.S. American companies dominate the economy of Canada and, by the same process, its political life. American T.V., American magazines, American professors spread American ideology systematically from coast to coast, from the 49th parallel to the North Pole.

But at the same time, the Canadian ruling class, the Canadian bourgeois class, which is giving away the country to the U.S. for immediate profits, is acting vis à vis the Québécois as a colonizer. It is members of that class who have organized the exploitation of Quebec. It is they who control the production in Quebec. It is they who hire and fire Québécois workers and decide where the products will end up. The vast majority of the Québécois are strictly labour power in an organization of production that is absolutely foreign to them. The capitalist mode of production was imposed on a people who had been isolated by military conquest.

And today the realization of this situation is the motive force behind the movement that is taking shape in Quebec. The movement is a general liberation movement. And no patch up job can stop it. The colonizer is always wrong, even when, in his own eyes, he is making great concessions. The colonized is right in all his attempts at breaking the colonial master-slave relationship.

This handbook is an attempt at explaining the historical process that has brought about the situation we have today. Official and traditional explanations are being exposed. Things that aren't very nice to say are printed in black and white. But it is better to see things clearly and know where things are at, although it hurts to find out, than to confuse the issues to comfort ourselves.

It is hoped that this handbook will help Canadians at large realize that the movement in Quebec is not directed against them, but in fact, against our common enemy. Canadians must realize that they have a liberation struggle to undertake if they want to survive and that this liberation struggle can be successful only if they co-operate with other such movements. They must first of all accept the Québécois' struggle for political and economic independence and secondly support it. Only on this basis can Canadians and Québécois relate to one another and become true partners in whatever they want to undertake together after that. An independent Quebec and an independent Canada can be friendly neighbours respecting each other as equals. Anything else will only perpetuate misery and hatred.

Léandre Bergeron
May, 1971

FOREWORD

Our elite has told us stories about our past but has not set our past in the context of History. The stories they told us were conceived to keep us, the Québécois, outside History.

The elite who collaborated with the English colonizer after the defeat of the Rebellion of 1837-38 behaved like the elites of all colonized peoples. Instead of fighting to rid Quebec of the colonizer, they turned back to a 'heroic' past to avoid facing the present. They went about glorifying the exploits of figures like Champlain, Madeleine de Verchères and martyred missionaries to make us believe that at a certain epoch we too were great colonizers and nation builders. Since we were colonized by the English we could find compensation in the fact that we had colonized the Red man. Our elite had us dreaming about the great French Empire of America of Frontenac's time to save us from the real humiliation of being a conquered people imprisoned in Confederation. Generations of Québécois were indoctrinated in this reactionary nationalism that defined us as a chosen people whose mission was to evangelize the world and spread French Catholic civilization throughout America.

With the American capitalist industrialization of Quebec, a more 'enlightened' and secular elite undertook to revise our past. Under the guise of 'objectivity' and of scientific research of 'historical facts,' historians in our universities accumulated many facts and documents. But there the work ended. This kind of historian places himself outside history. He is like an angel of knowledge rummaging through humanity's garbage dumps to extract material for neat obituary notices. In these terms our history is a long disinterment confirming, without admitting it, our defeat and subjection. In borrowing the Americans' research methods, these historians also borrowed their point of view; according to which American capitalism sets the supreme order, and the small nations, relics of another era, are marginal.

Recently, a few of our historians have been daring to interpret the facts, daring to orient their historical work within the context of Québécois ''ce, and daring to set themselves within the framework of the c   tion of the people of Québec toward their liberation.

The latter or   'ion characterizes this handbook of Quebec history. We Québécois are an imprisoned people subjected to colonialism. To change our situation we must first understand it. To understand it well, we must analyze the historical forces that brought it about. Once we have defined the forces that reduced us to colonial status, and those that keep us there today, we can identify our enemies correctly, study the relationships of forces carefully and engage in struggle more effectively.

This handbook does not pretend to be more than a short basic manual giving a general orientation and a broad outline. It does not purport to be complete, but simply re-examines the outstanding events in our history and places them in the struggle between oppressor and oppressed, colonizer and colonized, exploiter and exploited. It defines the general framework of this struggle in Quebec but does not hope to include every detail. This handbook will have achieved its goal if individual readers or study groups use it as a springboard to advance the study of our history and to better understand the mechanisms of colonialism, in order to channel our collective frustration into precise and effective acts of decolonization.

This handbook is on the course, the course of the School of the Street, for the man in the street, for the people of Quebec thrown into the street and dispossessed of their house, of the fruits of their work, of their daily life.

This handbook sets its sights on a repossession, the repossession of our history, the first step in the repossession of ourselves, in order to move on to the next step, the possession of our own future.

Léandre Bergeron

TABLE OF CONTENTS

TO ENGLISH-CANADIANS. v

FOREWORD. vii

INTRODUCTION. 1

PART ONE: THE FRENCH REGIME (1534-1759)

EUROPE'S CONQUEST OF THE WORLD. 3

FIRST ADVENTURES IN CANADA. 9
*the exploration of Canada – the compagnies take over trade –
exploitation of the White – a short-lived English conquest*

BEGINNINGS OF CANAYEN SOCIETY. 20
*the seigneurial system – founding of Ville Marie – the Iroquois
counter attack – Louis XIV reorganizes the colony*

THE PERIOD OF INTERNAL EXPANSION. 28
Frontenac and the brandy trade – the colony adrift

THE FINAL ROUND. 34
*the fall of Acadia – deportation of the Acadians – the colony on the
eve of the Conquest – the British Conquest*

PART TWO: THE ENGLISH REGIME (1760-1919)

THE ENGLISH ADMINISTRATION. 44
*reorganization of society – Treaty of Paris – the new government –
English policies – the English merchants formulate some demands –
the Quebec Act – reactions to the Quebec Act*

EFFECTS OF THE REVOLUTIONARY WARS. 53
*the American Revolution – arrival of the Loyalists – Constitution of
1791 – elections of 1792 – the French Revolution*

THE REBELLION IN CANADA. 61
*colonial economy of the early 1800's — education — evolution of the
political situation — American aggression 1812-14 — the crisis
resumes — the armed conflict — the metropolis investigates — the
rebellion in Upper Canada*

CONSEQUENCES OF THE REBELLION. 95
*the Durham Report — reactions to the Durham Report — the Act of
Union 1840 — the Union fails*

CONFEDERATION. 116
*economic interests underlying Confederation — the people's silence —
the population situation — the economic situation — Confederation —
the division of power — Riel and Manitoba*

BRITISH EXPANSIONISM. 158
*the Boer War — the naval question — World War I — French schools
in Ontario — the conscription crisis — the aftermath of war*

PART THREE: THE AMERICAN REGIME (1920-?)

THE GROWTH OF AMERICAN CONTROL. 171
*politics: more of the same — Quebec in depression — World War II —
the war economy — on the federal scene*

AFTER THE WAR. 191
*the Asbestos strike — apparent political structure — real political
structure — apparent social structure — the real social structure of
Quebec society — nationalities and social classes in Quebec*

RECENT EVENTS. 216
the fifties and sixties — 1970 before October

OCTOBER 1970. 230

APPENDIX I. 236
time table of history

APPENDIX II. 238
*publisher's statement regarding the C.W. Jefferys
historical drawings*

APPENDIX III 240
the open letter to W.O. Twaits, Chairman of the Board, Imperial Oil

INTRODUCTION

Our history can be divided into three parts:

The French Regime,[1] which dates from the first French explorations at the beginning of the sixteenth century to 1760, date of the Conquest of New France by Great Britain.

The English Regime, which begins with the Conquest of New France and continues until the beginning of the twentieth century when it gives way to the American Regime.

The American Regime, which begins with the invasion of American capital[2] at the beginning of the twentieth century and follows with an increasingly greater hold by American capitalists,[3]

first on our economy,[4] then on our politics,[5] and finally on our culture.[6]

1. *regime:* structure or organization of a society and its government at a given period of time.

2. *capital:* money invested in a business or enterprise which yields interest based on the exploitation of the labour power of the workers in the enterprise.

3. *capitalists:* individuals who have capital to invest in different enterprises in order to extract a maximum profit without concerning themselves with the interests of the workers.

4. *economy:* all human acitivity concerned with the transformation of material resources in order to satisfy the needs of the group, class or people that controls the resources.

5. *politics:* the general administration of a country; political power is the control exercised on society by those who have the country's administration in their hands.

6. *culture:* the personal characteristics of a people; a particular way for a people to express itself, to act on reality and to view the world. A nation's culture depends on its political and economic situation.

We can see that there has not yet been a *Québécois Regime,* that is, a Regime in which the Québécois would be masters of their destiny. It has always been the Regime of *the Others.* We, the Québécois, have always been under the domination of these 'others.' We have been colonized [7] in the past and are still being colonized. Yet one senses during the last few years a movement taking shape in Quebec which is demanding that we make it a *Québécois Regime,* that our economy belong to us, the Québécois, that Quebec become a sovereign[8] state, and that the Québécois themselves direct the politics of their own country.

7. *colonized:* the condition of a people who have been conquered by a foreign power and who are maintained in a position of economic, political and cultural inferiority. The relationship between colonized and colonizer is the same as that between slave and master.

The colonizer manipulates the colonized to serve his own interests. The colonized, defeated, stripped of his human dignity, submits to slavery and searches for escape in dreams, religion, or intoxicants , until the day when he realizes that he too has a right to personal freedom, and takes the steps necessary to rid his country of the colonizer.

8. *sovereign:* state of liberty and independence that allows a country to govern in the way it sees best, to make appropriate laws, and to deal with other countries on an equal footing.

PART 1 THE FRENCH REGIME (1534-1759)

Europe's Conquest of the World

In the fifteenth and sixteenth centuries Europe embarks on the conquest of the rest of the world. The Spanish, Portuguese, Dutch, French and English set out on the high seas to rob and plunder the natural resources of foreign lands. In these monarchical European countries, a class was developing that accumulated money by trade in consumer goods.

The social structure at this time in Europe resembles the following pyramid:

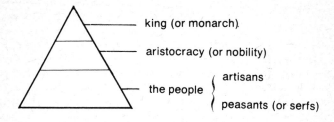

The top of the pyramid represents the person or persons who hold political power. The king is the supreme authority, the sovereign. Moreover, he tries to make the people believe that his authority comes from God. Under his domination are the nobles, who are really little kings, each in his own province. The

3

nobles in turn dominate the masses, the peasants, who work their seigneurs' lands in return for little more than bare subsistence. These peasants live in a kind of slavery. The seigneur is master with nearly absolute authority over them.

During this period, money (especially gold and silver coins) serves as exchange only for products and services. There are at this time very few people who accumulate money in order to lend it with interest, just as there are very few who buy products to sell at a higher price. The peasants of one domain produce what is needed for the entire population of that domain. As for the craftsmen who make tools, instruments, and other products of small industry, most of the time they sell their products directly to the consumer without a middleman.

At this time the Church plays an important role in European life. It is an institution which parallels the pyramid of secular power:

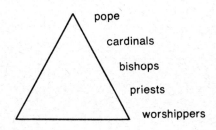

It is always competing with secular authority because it strives to establish its own domination over the people. The Church is rich. It owns huge territories. It is like a state within a state. It has the threat of hell or the promise of heaven at its disposal to extend and consolidate its power. At a time when man has a very weak conception of the laws and mechanisms governing the universe, the easiest explanation is the belief in a spiritual kingdom to which man can refer in order to dissipate all his fears of this world below. The Church exploits these fears for its own profit. It extends its power over all of Europe with the magical invocation of the sacraments, competing with kings and even trying to subject them to its own authority.

But, the misdeeds of its bishops and clergy arouse certain 'sincere' souls who launch the Protestant Reformation, thus causing a division in the bosom of the Church. In the sixteenth century the Wars of Religion between Catholics and Protestants covered Europe with blood. Frenchmen slaughtered each other, Englishmen slaughtered each other, Spaniards slaughtered each other, all in the name of God. But the secular powers themselves used religion to ward off the temporal domination of the Church. The creation of a Protestant England, for instance, allows the English kings to reduce Rome's influence on British politics in both domestic and foreign affairs.

The relation between the secular and clerical pyramids of power:

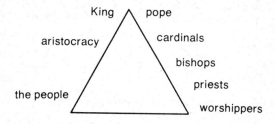

The sixteenth and seventeenth centuries add another class to this social pyramid, the commercial or bourgeois class, made up largely of serfs who purchased their freedom and regrouped in the towns (bourgs). These merchants, sprung from the people, make their money not in productive work, like the peasants and craftsmen, but rather by exchanging commodities produced by the labour of others. They grow rich by selling these things at a price much higher than what they paid for them. By exploiting the distribution of products they become a class of parasites. The peasants and craftsmen do the real work. They produce a commodity (wheat, flour, wine, clothing, dwellings, etc.), whereas all the merchant does is draw his profit from the exchange made between producer and consumer. He is essentially an exploiter. Without having to produce anything himself, he makes money by labelling products and finding a buyer.

These merchants trade not only in goods, but also in money. After accumulating a certain amount of money in trade they are now ready to lend it. But the correct word is not *lend,* as you might lend a book or a pen. They in effect *rent* money. The borrower must repay the amount *plus* interest, thus transforming the merchant's money into capital. Eventually they make money simply by lending it to kings and seigneurs who raise armies in order to extend their domination over foreign lands, or to other merchants who are willing to try their luck with huge shipments of exotic goods.

And in addition to commodities and money, these merchants also traded in human lives. They chartered ships to sail to the coast of Africa to abduct entire tribes, reduce them to slavery and *sell* them to the sugar, cotton, and coffee plantation *owners* who would work them harder than they worked animals.

In the fifteenth century trade in spices with the East (India and China) develops and drives kings and merchants toward the conquest of the producer countries. This rush to foreign wealth captivated every European country capable of putting a fleet together.

And thus, while searching for China and India, they come to America.

WORD TO BE ABOLISHED: DISCOVERY.

The explorers did not *discover* the Americas. Christopher Columbus did not *discover* the 'New World.' Jacques Cartier did not *discover* Canada. These territories were discovered by the first men who set foot on them. When the white explorers came to America, the land was already populated by *men,* men of a different colour, yes, but men all the same. To say that Columbus discovered America and Cartier Canada is to show the racism that has infected the white race for centuries. To say that Columbus and Cartier are *discoverers* is to say that only Whites can *discover* for the human race and that the Indians found on the continent were animals not much more evolved than apes. The white explorers did not discover anything. They *explored* territories and *conquered* them by force. They practised genocide [1] as barbarously as Hitler did against the Jews or as the Americans are doing against the Vietnamese.

---

1. *genocide:* systematic annihilation of a people, race or ethnic group.

The Spanish explorers, Christopher Columbus, Amerigo Vespucci, Hernando Cortez and others land in the West Indies, in Central America and in South America. They are welcomed and treated as distinguished guests by peoples of a different colour. Most of these peoples, like the Mayas of Mexico and the Incas of Peru have highly developed cultures, but have not reached the 'higher level' of European Civilization.

But the Spanish conquerors can see only the gold and silver that these people mine to decorate their temples, homes and utensils. It did not occur to them to trade for these precious metals. To the white European these people were inferior, and deserved nothing better than slavery or death.

They begin the systematic massacre and pillage which is to continue for many centuries. The Spaniards kill the tribal chiefs and all resisting elements. They rape the women, slaughter the children, and subject the survivors to forced labour in the gold and silver mines or on the sugar and coffee plantations. These people - who are called by the generic name of 'Indians' because the conquerors thought they were in India - are reduced to a sub-human, colonized condition by the brutality and greed of these international bandits, the 'Christian,' 'civilized' White man.

The Portuguese take what is now Brazil, and the Spanish the rest of South and Central America. The English and French each grab certain islands of the Antilles and reduce the populations to slavery. When the Indians die of misery or are so devastated by the white man's diseases that they can no longer work on the plantation, the English, French, Spanish, and Dutch merchants sail to the coast of Africa to buy Blacks, pack them into slave-ships tighter than they would crowd animals, and sell them to those other white bandits, the plantation 'owners.'

One cannot but see the profound racism of the Whites during this period. They considered themselves a superior race, the 'civilized' race, with their inventions like the compass and their formidable fire-arms, with their 'divine mission' and their all-conquering ambition, their expansionist aims and their aggressiveness. They held the Yellow, Black, and Red peoples to be deluded heathens, inferior, incapable of reaching the 'heights' of White 'civilization.' This racism still permeates much of White society, and will only disappear with the complete liberation of all non-White peoples.

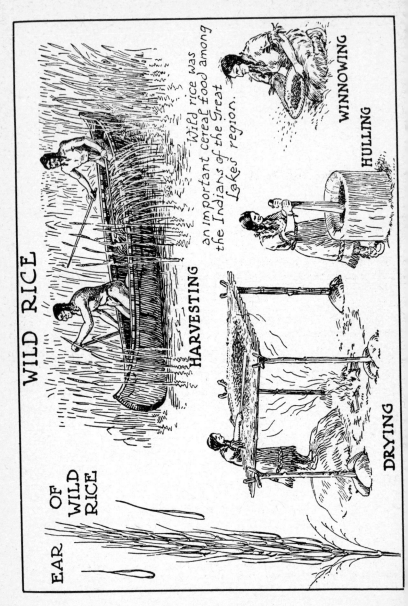

WILD RICE

EAR OF WILD RICE

HARVESTING

Wild rice was an important cereal food among the Indians of the Great Lakes region.

WINNOWING

HULLING

DRYING

First Adventures in Canada

The Exploration of Canada

In 1534, Francis I, King of France, sends out an explorer to North America to search for a passage to China. Jacques Cartier, arriving at what is now Gaspé Bay, *takes possession of the territory* in the name of the King of France without asking the Amerindians [1] if they are agreeable to having their country taken over by foreigners. The Red man, not understanding the significance of the planting of the wooden cross, warily and respectfully welcomes his guests. But the first words of the White man are a lie: Jacques Cartier tells the Red man that the cross merely serves as a beacon, a landmark for navigators. The White man - hypocrite, liar and crook - makes sport of the Red man's honesty and naiveté from the first. Later on, he will wonder why the Red man speaks of the White man's forked tongue.

Cartier carries his insolence to the point of asking the Chief of the Red men for permission to take his two sons away to France. Because of the Red man's generosity, Cartier's request is granted. He has not found the passage to China, but the returns to France with a hunting trophy — two Redskins.

1. *Amerindians:* generic term that can be given to all peoples living in America before the arrival of the White man. The word is derived from *America* and *Indian,* meaning the Indians of America, so as not to confuse them with the Indians of India. The correct word to use would be *El-nou,* which the Amerindians called themselves. However, we will use the term Red man just as we say White for the European, Black for the African south of the Sahara, and Yellow for the Asian.

For his second voyage in 1534-35 Cartier uses the two Red men as guides to explore the river now called the St. Lawrence. Donnacona, chief of the region which the Red men called Canada, receives Cartier in his canoe after boarding the French boat. They exchange gifts and courtesies. But Cartier is impatient to continue the expedition into the kingdom of *gold* and *silver*.

He reaches Stadacona (Quebec) and wants to move on to Hochelaga (Montreal), the Iroquois capital of Canada. Donnacona is beginning to feel that his guest is behaving more like a master than a visitor, and tries to prevent any further exploration of Iroquois territory. But Cartier refuses to take him seriously and continues up the river to Hochelaga; then returns to Stadacona where he spends the winter. The Red men are finding their visitors more and more irksome and, justifiably, begin to show their hostility.

Cartier, the very Christian White man, now has to deal with Donnacona. Consistent with his past treacherous behaviour, he takes advantage of a ceremony — the erection of a cross near the fort the French have built to protect themselves from the winter and their hosts — to seize Donnacona and four other Iroquois chiefs. Cartier makes Donnacona understand that he wants to take him away to France. An acquiescent Donnacona explains this to his irate blood-brothers to calm them down. In May, Cartier and ten Iroquois leave for France, where the Red men were added to his retinue as if they were wild animals the great hunter had tamed.

Donnacona died in France. Cartier returns to Stadacona in 1541 and lies to the Iroquois that 'their chief has not returned because he is so happy in France, so proud that he has become a big seigneur that he has no desire to come back to his own people.'

During this third visit, Cartier has another fort built this time at Cap Rouge (near Quebec). The Iroquois begin to feel they have had enough of these guests, who do not know when to leave but apparently intend to remain permanently and exploit their lands. Their hostility increases.

Cartier's obsession, however, is to find precious metals, and, near the post, he discovers what he takes for gold and diamonds. When he returns to France, his 'treasure' proves to be pyrite and mica. Cartier spends the rest of his days in St. Malo, a good bourgeois.

One of the results of these explorations is the interest French merchants take in the fur trade. The Norman merchants, in particular, wished to lay their hands on those reserves of pelts; however, it would take many years before they could organize their commercial activities. It isn't until 1600, almost sixty years after Cartier's last voyage, that Pierre Chauvin comes to trade with the Red man. He leaves sixteen of his men to spend the winter at Tadoussac (at the mouth of the Saguenay). Only five are still alive in the spring; and even these would have died if the Iroquois had not taught them how to find food in their climate. Once again the Red men display their generosity to the White men, who have only come here to exploit them.

The Companies Take Over Trade

The French kings, like the English and the Spanish, are well aware that colonial conquests will result in an increase of their power; but serious problems arise in the financing of their expeditions. So they appeal to the rising bourgeois class, which is accumulating capital and is prepared to lend it if profit seems likely.

Companies are created. Bourgeois merchants collaborate, each investing certain sums of money to launch the project of exploration that is intended to bring huge profits. The king officially recognizes the companies by granting them charters, while imposing certain conditions on them, such as the settling of the colonies. But, more important, he grants them privileges, including the rights to own land, to levy taxes, to administer justice and to keep troops and of course the exclusive right to trade – that is, a commercial monopoly. Consequently the company has no competitors, and is free to buy the colony's products

The Chain of Exploitation

	1 Red Man	2 Coureur- de-Bois	3 Company
ACTIVITY	producer of raw material	carrier and middleman	middleman
PRODUCTIVE LABOUR percent of total	65%	5%	0%
PROFITS TAKEN percent of total	.01%	4.99%	60%
SOCIAL CLASS	sub- proletarian	quasi- proletarian	bourgeois

Note:
1. Here, 'company' means the organization that amasses capital. Strictly speaking, amassing capital cannot be considered productive labour.

of the Fur Trade

4 Artisan	5 Merchant	6 Buyer
producer of finished product	middleman	consumer
30%	0%	
5%	30%	
autonomous worker	bourgeois	noble or bourgeois

2. Later, when the factory appears, the artisan is replaced by salaried workers whose labour power is bought by the owner of the factory. This owner is in the bourgeois class.

The first prescription in Canada, 1536

and export them to the metropolis., as well as to import products from the metropolis to the colony. This trade is duty-free and protected by the Royal Navy against attacks from other colonies. In addition to all this the governor of the colony is both the king's representative *and* the company's representative.

This arrangement clearly demonstrates that the king uses the merchants to extend his power overseas, while at the same time the merchants use the state (the king) in their pursuit of profit. Further on we will see how the merchants (the bourgeoisie) will overthrow the monarchy and take complete control of the state in the French Revolution. They will institute what they call a 'liberal democracy,' the form of government under which we still live, which is a dictatorship by this same class, the bourgeoisie.

As a means of colonization, the company system does not work. Despite all their privileges the companies do not fulfil their obligations. They have only profits in mind; they abuse the colonists, and they declare bankruptcy whenever it is to their advantage.

The companies concentrate on the fur trade, since it is easy to exploit. The chain of exploitation of this trade is the following: Red man – *coureur-de-bois* – company merchant – metropolitan manufacturer – salesman – European consumer. The real producer is the Red man, who hunts the animal and prepares the fur; he does the most work, but is the least paid. He is systematically robbed of his furs by the *coureur-de-bois* and the company. When they don't reward him with cheap objects like bits of mirror and common tools, they pay him with alcohol. The Red man was unaware of the existence of alcohol before the arrival of the White man. The more he is reduced to a slave of the Whites and loses his dignity as a Red man, the more he takes to drink.

1 *metropolis:* political, economic and cultural centre upon which other regions are dependent. The metropolis can be a country, a region or a city. Its dependencies can be other countries, regions or cities. In this case the metropolis is a country, France, and its dependency is the colony, 'New France.' This colony is subject to the political, economic and cultural decisions made in the metropolis. The metropolis ensures that the colony enjoys no existence for its own sake, but merely provides materials for the metropolis. If it does not serve the interests of the metropolis, the colony is dropped like a dead weight.

The companies also pay for tons of furs with fire-arms, but of course not with enough to enable the Red man to clear the White plague from his country.

The Red man is therefore the true producer and the biggest loser in the commercial chain. The second in line is the *coureur-de-bois*, an adventurer or ex-convict hired by the company to search for skins in the hunting grounds when the Red men no longer come to Quebec or Montreal. The *coureur-de-bois* is an intermediary who exploits the Redman, but is himself exploited at the same time. He robs the Red man in the name of the company: he is an exploiter who is ready for anything, even murder, if it means bales of furs for him. And yet by the fact that he merely carries out company orders in return for a salary, he is himself exploited.

The third link, the central link in the chain of exploitation, is the merchant, or rather the company itself, which directly or indirectly through the *coureur-de-bois takes* the Red man's furs. The company, under the protection of the Royal Navy, ensures the shipment of furs to Europe but does no productive work, as such, to change the product. All it does is supervise the shipment and delivery of the furs to a craftsman who will buy them at stiff prices to manufacture hats and clothing.

The final link is the merchant who buys the finished product and looks for customers among the bourgeoisie or nobility.

In 1603, a company expedition brings over a navigator named Champlain. While the company's agents 'trade' with the Red men, Champlain explores the region and makes friends with the Montagnais. This tribe is very pleased to have a powerful ally against its rivals, the Iroquois, who had extended their territory to the Saguenay in Cartier's time but now have been pushed south by the Hurons, Montagnais and Algonquins.

Instead of letting the Red men settle their own quarrels, the White man exploits their conflicts to consolidate his power. This is the colonialist tactic of divide-and-rule. The ruler nourishes or provokes quarrels among those he wishes to dominate. So long as they are quarreling they will not attack the real enemy, the colonizer. Soon we will see how the French colonizer becomes colonized in his turn when the English use the same tactic to dominate the French-Canadians after the Conquest.

The Montagnais, who feel they need the French to fight the Iroquois, invite them to settle and do all the fur-trading they wish. The French could not ask for a prettier invitation to justify their presence and colonization. Champlain can claim to be the saviour of the Red man, a chance he would not miss. He 'takes sides with' the Montagnais.

The following year, Champlain and De Monts explore the Atlantic coast and establish several posts including Port Royal. The colonization of Acadia begins.

But in 1606, the King of England, James I, concedes to English companies some coastal regions including a part of Acadia already taken by the French. This is the first round in the struggle between the two colonialist powers, France and England, for possession of North American territories. The English raze St. Sauveur and Port Royal, two French forts. The French destroy an English settlement on Cape Breton Island in 1629. It is a fight between two powers bent on conquering as much territory as possible, siphoning off its wealth and providing kings and merchants with huge profits. France and England can be compared to two merchants with a common understanding of fair play in their competition to exploit the same people. The biggest loser in this game can only be the Red man.

In 1608 Champlain returns to Canada *where the fur-trade is best*, on an expedition financed by Norman merchants. Without asking permission from the owners of the land, the Red men, he founds Quebec. He selects the site because of the promontory and the narrowness of the river, both of which provide *easy defense*.

The united Montagnais, Algonquins, Etchemins and Hurons ask for Champlain's help in fighting the Iroquois. Champlain calculates the odds and decides to support them. He has to since these tribes represent *cheap labour* for the French. He can afford to make the Iroquois his enemies, since they have already been driven back to Lake Champlain and weakened. So in 1609 Champlain, arquebus in hand, sets out with his allies to fight the Iroquois. In this famous battle, two hundred Iroquois confront sixty 'allies' and three Frenchmen. Champlain moves forward and pulls the trigger. This has the same effect as the atomic bomb on Hiroshima in 1945. The Iroquois are terrified.

The White man exploits his superior technology not to help the Red man but rather to reduce him to the rank of colonial servitude.

For the Frenchman, Champlain, the domination of the political and economic life of New France is not enough. To enjoy complete authority he has to also dominate its culture, manifest, in this case, in religion. According to the White man, the Red man has "neither faith nor laws... " is "without God, without religion, like a wild beast." This was the most shameful expression of White racism. The Red man had his faith, his laws, his gods and his religion. He was no more a "wild beast" than Champlain who used gunpowder to butcher him. The White man believed he was superior, that he alone had the truth, that his god was the only real god, that it was his duty as a 'Christian' and 'civilized being' to impose his beliefs and prejudices on the Red man. So, he had missionaries brought over.

The Recollets arrive in 1615, pleased to come at the expense of the company that robs the Red man. The Jesuits follow in 1625. The Christian religion will be used (here as in every country colonized by the White man) to justify *in the name of God* the systematic exploitation of peoples forceably subjected to colonialism.

Champlain meanwhile explores the Great Lakes with his 'allies' the Hurons. The Iroquois cannot put up with this. They inflict a defeat on the 'allies' in a battle in which Champlain himself is wounded. Champlain has miscalculated his alliances. The Iroquois, the most courageous of all the tribes, will for a long time courageously defend their threatened territory.

Exploitation of the White Man

The class of exploiters to which Champlain and the company belong does not limit itself to the exploitation of the Red man. The lower-class White man, like Louis Hébert, is also a victim. The *Company of Canada*, which has the commercial monopoly at this time, is supposed to be bringing over colonists to settle the land. Louis Hébert, who arrives with his family, will be employed by the company for two years. Everything he produces belongs to the company and he is absolutely forbidden to engage in the fur trade.

Louis Hébert is the real father of the Québécois. Exploited first by French merchants and nobles, then by the English and now by the Americans, the Québécois can trace their origins to these exploited settlers, composed of convicts, vagabonds and the 'king's daughters.' The Champlains, the French administrators, the French or English merchants with the complicity of the Clergy will exploit and maintain the people of Québec in a position of inferiority and a condition of subjection under every regime.

A Short-Lived English Conquest

In 1627 an English company is formed in London to settle the shores of the St. Lawrence. The Kirke brothers, who are hired by that company, capture Quebec in 1629. Sixty of the eighty French people in Quebec return to France with Champlain. But, this conquest is short-lived. England returns Canada and Acadia to France in 1632 by the Treaty of Saint-Germain-en-Laye. The Company of New France regains control of the fur trade but now leaves settling the lands to individuals who are given grants in the form of *seigneuries*.

Beginnings of Canayen Society

The Seigneurial System

The companies, the 'legal' owners of the land in the colony, grant *seigneuries* to individuals so that they will no longer be responsible for settlement. The recipient of a land grant becomes a *seigneur* but is not necessarily of the nobility. He is more often a company associate (a bourgeois) or a former officer. Religious orders are also granted *seigneuries*.

The *seigneurie* is usually a narrow strip of land fronting a river, the only means of communication at the time. The *seigneur* builds a manor for himself in the centre of his land and grants the rest to those wishing to become his *censitaires* [1].

The *censitaires*, sometimes about a hundred in one seigneurial domain, settle on a plot of land measuring two to three hundred yards wide by a mile or more long. They cultivate the land, pay a tax to the *seigneur*, and fork over 1/14 of the grain they grind at his mill. They have to work four or five days a year for the *seigneur* without remuneration, and are obliged to render him homage.

As for the *seigneur*, he has his own pew in church and takes 'precedence over the people.' He collects rents, taxes and grains. His obligations are to build a house and live in it from time to time, to construct a mill, to settle the *seigneurie* by granting

1. *censitaires:* from 'census,' as these tenants pay the seigneur their dues at the time of census-taking.

Tenants paying their yearly dues, in money or in produce, to their Seigneur

On receiving his grant of land the Seigneur, bareheaded, without sword or spurs, kneeling at the Governor's door, swore to be faithful to the King.

C.W. JEFFERYS

21

plots to *censitaires*, to pay 'faith and homage' to the governor and to show his accounts to the authorities.

One of the first *seigneuries* is granted to Robert Giffard de Moncel who receives ten square miles of land near Quebec and settles about forty *censitaires* on it from his native province, Le Perche. After Giffard, the Jesuits and Sulpicians are granted several *seigneuries* and thus find themselves in the *seigneurial* class, ready to exploit the Quebec people with the complicity of the *Company* merchants.

This class of *seigneurs* we will call the 'land-owning class.'

1641

White population of Canada . . . . approximately 300
White population of 'New England' 50,000

The Founding of Ville Marie (Montreal)

The wars of religion between Catholics and Protestants, which tore Europe apart in the sixteenth century, brought about a religious revival closely linked with the growth of capitalism.

Many Protestants, known as Puritans, left England because of persecution and settled in 'New England' in 1620. They were to become the colonists and merchants who, by accumulating capital, provided the necessary stimulus to the fantastic growth of American trade.

In France, mystical fervour gripped entire communities; religious orders were founded. People were seeking the most glorious way to do God's Will. What could be better than to bring the Divine Word to the 'barbarians' of America? One must sacrifice oneself for God, fight for Him, perhaps even become a martyr for Him. But, at the same time, this mystical action has to take place in the context of capitalist expansion!

Thus, Jean-Jacques Alier (future founder of the religious order, the Sulpicians), Maisonneuve, Jeanne Mance and Angélique de Bullion found the *Société de Notre-Dame de Montréal* in

22

1639 with capital of £200,000. This religious and economic society buys the island of Montreal from Jean Lauzon who had appropriated it when he was principal director of the *Company of 100 Associates*. Father Lalemant makes the purchase in the name of the *Société Notre-Dame*, but soon after, the *Company of 100 Associates* decides to keep the island and to grant it to the *Société* as a *seigneurie*. Consequently, the *Société Notre-Dame* finds itself working directly in the service of the *Company*.

In the spring of 1642, Maisonneuve, Jeanne Mance and their group arrive on the island without asking the Iroquois if they are welcome. A religious ceremony justifies their taking possession. Despite the Iroquois 'threat' the site is well chosen. There could not be a better place to exploit the Red man who is willing to sell his furs. The company proceeds to take advantage of him while Jeanne Mance busies herself founding her hospital, and Marguerite Bourgeoys, her school. Maisonneuve, as governor of the island, watches over its morals.

However in 1663, the *Société Notre-Dame*, which is £100,000 in debt, hands the island over to the Sulpicians, and is itself dissolved. Three hundred acres have been cleared and about fifty families have settled there.

The Iroquois Counter Attack

The Iroquois watch as the French and their 'allies,' the Hurons and Algonquins advance into their territory. They trade furs for guns with the Dutch at Fort Orange (Albany), and soon feel strong enough to counter-attack. They advance on Trois-Rivières and Ville-Marie. The French suffer heavy losses while their 'allies' the Hurons, are weakened by smallpox caught from the French.

Montmagny, the French governor, forbids the sale of guns and alcohol to their 'allies' for fear that they may turn against the White population. The Iroquois on the other hand are not afraid to demand more arms for fewer furs from the Dutch to continue their attacks on the French posts. Father Jogues, French 'ambassador' to the Iroquois, is one of the first to be wiped out.

The French even consider abandoning Montreal, since the Iroquois now control both shores of the St. Lawrence. Caught short, Montmagny looks to the English of 'New England' for help in checking the Red man. His alliance with the Hurons has broken down and he is forced to seek other allies, even White competitors, to crush the Red man. The governor is ready to make a commercial agreement with the English - an understanding between White men - to exploit the Red man together. But the English are too well satisfied with their commercial relations with the Iroquois and are not prepared to help the French. On the contrary, they would rather see the French disappear from the continent, just as they will force the Dutch to disappear a little later.

In 1658, Iroquois guerilla warfare resumes with still greater intensity. The French fortify Quebec, Trois Rivières, and Montreal. Two years later Dollard des Ormeaux thinks he and his men can check the Iroquois and at the same time seize a sizeable amount of booty in order to pay their debts. These seventeenth century cowboys are all slaughtered. In 1662, Ville-Marie nearly falls.

The Iroquois onslaught lost strength not from fighting the French as much as from the smallpox they caught from blankets left behind by White men who had used them to cover their sick. (You can see that bacteriological warfare was not invented by the Americans.) In addition, widespread famine and the arrival of one hundred French soldiers shook Iroquois morale.

	1663
White population of Canada.	2,500
White population of New England.	80,000

Louis XIV Reorganizes the Colony (1663)

On ascending the throne of France, Louis XIV instructs his minister Colbert to reorganize his colony, New France: it appears to be costing the royal treasury more than it is worth. Successive company merchants have, while exploiting the fur trade, taken advantage of the privileges granted them without due regard for the interests of the French state.

The result is that Louis decides to intervene more directly in the affairs of the colony. From this date forward, it is the monarch, and no longer the company, who will name the governor. The governor's duties are to administer the colony's external relations and to command the army. More direct administration of New France is to be in the hands of another civil servant, the intendant, also named by the king. He will be responsible for trade and settlement, cultivation of the land, control of finances, and administration of justice.

And so, King Louis created a Sovereign Council composed of the governor, the intendant, the bishop and five councillors appointed by the governor and bishop. Its main function is to administer justice and, especially, to settle cases submitted to it by the intendant. In fact, it becomes the scene of political rivalry between the governor and the bishop.

What appears to be direct interference by the king in the affairs of the colony does not imply, however, that private companies are now to be replaced by Crown Companies.[1] Quite the contrary, for Louis XIV issues a charter to *The West India Company* permitting it to exploit every French colony in America and Asia. The company becomes the owner of all these territories, is still handed a trade and navigation monopoly, and continues to propose nominations for governor. Its only obligations are to subsidize missions and to see to colonization.

Ultimately, the only changes Louis XIV brought to New France were better organization of its colonization, and military reinforcements – by the Carignan-Salières regiment consisting of 1300 men.

The presence of these troops means that repression of the Iroquois can resume with renewed vigour. The French soldiers burn Iroquois villages, scatter the population and destroy huge supplies of corn, the Red man's staple food. In fact what happened was a systematic destruction similar to the current American aggression against Vietnam, Laos and Cambodia.

1. *Crown Company:* a business enterprise financed, organized and administered by the state.

After the massacres the French sing a *Te Deum* on the smouldering ruins and butchered bodies of the Iroquois. They thank God for having given them the strength to carry out this genocide.

After these 'glorious' expeditions there will be seventeen years of peace, enabling the Intendant, Talon, to develop the colony's economy. To make New France self-sufficient and perhaps even capable of exporting some wheat, Talon concentrates on agricultural development. He introduces flax, hemp and barley but is forbidden by the king to grow tobacco for fear that it may hinder trade with French colonies in the Antilles. This is an example of how the economic life of the colony is controlled by and for the metropolis, and how the colony exists only to be exploited for the profit of the metropolis.

Talon increases the number of cattle to 3,400 in 1668, imports horses and ploughs, and brings over 2,500 settlers.

Who are these settlers?

The poor whom Louis XIV wants to get rid of, the *'King's Daughters,* illegitimate offspring of grand French ladies, orphans and prostitutes (by necessity); these 'outcasts' and 'rejects' are sent to New France to found the Québécois stock. There are also the soldiers who settle, after the massacre of the Red man, marry the newly-arrived young girls, and sire many children. Families of ten or more children receive allowances from the King. Talon encourages young marriages – men from 18 years and women from 14. Bachelors are obliged to pay additional taxes.

White population of Canada in 1672. 6,700

Louis XIV (as well as Talon) wants a self-sufficient colony, the colony must not depend on the metropolis for its daily bread. For the metropolis, France, the colony is a milk-cow that must find its own hay. The metropolis wants to spend as little as possible on the colony and at the same time to extract maximum profits. Thus Talon encourages agriculture and settlement not so much for the good of the colony and its inhabitants as to make profits for the metropolis.

This relationship between metropolis and colony is classic. We find it in every country that has been subjected to colonialism. England, France, Spain, Portugal, Holland, in fact every colonial power has sought to extract all possible natural resources from the colony in order to grow rich and powerful — to the detriment of the colony. Europe was able to develop its wealth and consolidate its power over the rest of the world by systematically plundering Africa, Asia, and America. One of these colonies broke its chains very early and became a colonial power itself. This is the United States, which became a metropolis, a *power*, at the beginning of the 19th century and today exploits its colonies in Latin America, Africa, part of Asia, Canada, and of course, Quebec.

At first glance it would seem that France was really generous to Canada, that she gave men, women, and material resources to her colony. In point of fact, France got back one hundred times as much as she put in, by plundering its wealth and making huge profits riding the backs of the Red men and the lower class Whites, the poor colonists who thought they could make their fortunes within this system of exploitation.

Even by establishing a brewery at Quebec, and also shoe and clothing factories and a ship-building industry, and by attempting to develop mines (coal on Cape Breton Island, copper around Lake Superior, iron at Trois Rivières), Talon served the interests of the metropolis more than the colony. The inhabitants of New France got just enough to subsist, so that they could produce and serve the metropolis.

In spite of all this, Louis XIV was not satisfied. The returns on New France were not going to realize his visions of grandeur. His interest faded and Talon's plans fell by the wayside.

The Period of Internal Expansion

Frontenac and the Brandy Trade

Frontenac who became governor in 1672 was obsessed with the fur trade. It was the easiest way to make profits. And this old soldier was saddled with debts. Thanks to his wife's charms, Louis XIV had given him this post.

But, no sooner does Frontenac arrive than he begins to quarrel with Bishop Laval who thinks it's immoral to trade brandy for furs. Frontenac argues that, since it's not beneath the morals of the English from New England to entice the Red man with rum, the French must do so with brandy. Bishop Laval remains firm and even goes to France to try to persuade the king to recall Frontenac.

It may appear that Bishop Laval was very *moral* in his condemnation of the brandy trade, one of the most shameful kinds of exploitation; in reality he was condemning neither the exploitation of the Red man as such, nor the massacres of the Red man, nor the degredation of the Red man to a state of near slavery. He was merely condemning *excessive* exploitation and so, was hardly more moral than Frontenac who was at least frank enough to admit being an exploiter. (All the while denouncing the Jesuits' evangelical work as yet another means to enslave the Red man, exploit him more efficiently, and, not incidentally, to increase the Jesuits' power in the colony!)

Under Frontenac, expeditions continue into the Great Lakes region where trading-posts are established. In 1673 Jolliet and Father Marquette paddle down the Mississippi as far as the Arkansas River. A few years later, Lasalle repeats the journey and reaches the mouth of the great American river. He names this region 'Louisiana' in honour of Louis XIV and claims it for France.

These explorations are not pleasure trips. Their purpose is strictly commercial. The French, at all costs, want to prevent the English from gaining control of the western fur-trade. The English, for their part, encourage the Iroquois to harass the French and their Amerindian 'allies.' In order to accomplish their goals, these commercial rivals, the English and French, use the Red man as cannon fodder. The English supply the Iroquois with arms for the massacre of Lachine. The French reply by terrorizing the English colonies.

In 1690, Admiral Phipps confronts Quebec with thirty-four warships. Frontenac refuses to surrender. They battle it out, but as winter approaches the English withdraw. Lemoyne d'Iberville takes back Acadia, Newfoundland and the Hudson Bay posts from the English. But by the Treaty of Utrecht of 1713, Hudson Bay, Acadia (except Cape Breton Island) and Newfoundland are restored to England. By the same treaty the Iroquois become British subjects.

It is quite clear that the fate of the colonies was decided in the metropolis. The colonists could try as much as they liked to get a hold on the land, but ultimately territorial gains depended on palace intrigues in Europe and on trading patterns designed in the metropolis. By the end of the seventeenth century the metropolis, saturated with beaver pelts, had lost interest in Canada and was even prepared to give up part of it for other interests in Europe.

	1689	1715
White population of Canada.	15,000	18,500
White population of 'New England'. . . .	200,000	434,000

The Colony Adrift

Following the Treaty Of Utrecht, the French colony in America consisted of present-day New Brunswick, Quebec, Ontario, the valley of the Mississippi and Louisiana. The colony could boast an immense expanse of territory but was sparsely populated, badly organized and suffered from the disinterest of the mother country.

In the next few years, an attempt to fortify the colony will prove quite fruitless. The construction of a fortress at Louisbourg on Cape Breton Island in 1718 is still not completed in 1745 when the English capture it. Quebec and Montreal are fortified and forts are constructed along the Mississippi, the Great Lakes and Lake Champlain. The administrators of the colony encourage LaVérendrye to explore the West and to trade directly with the Red men so as to prevent them from going to Hudson Bay to trade with the English. Between 1731 and 1742 LaVérendrye senior, financed by Montreal merchants, explores and constructs trading posts in the region of what is today Manitoba and Saskatchewan. His two sons make their way to the Rockies in 1743.

Between 1713 and 1739, the White population in New France increases from 18,000 to 43,000 inhabitants. This is largely due to the high birth rate. There is little immigration, and what little does take place is the result of coercion. Convicts and prisoners are brought over.

The metropolis now conceives of the colony as a huge camp where it can isolate 'undesirables.' In 1722, eighty prisoners are freed in New France. In the 1740's, 648 convicts are enumerated. When the seasoned criminals begin to make trouble they are of course locked up again. As for those petty criminals, convicted of minor offenses like hunting on the king's lands, they are eminently *exploitable* in the colony. These poor buggers who have 'robbed' the king simply in order to eat are prepared to do honest work over here. But, they are to be exploited by the merchants and *seigneurs,* and assimilated with the other exploited *habitants* already settled here. These are the people to whom the Québécois trace their real ancestral lineage.

At this time, three-quarters of the population is engaged in agriculture. Enough wheat is produced to feed the colony and occasionally there is a surplus for export to the French Antilles. Hemp is cultivated for the manufacture of sail-cloth and rope, both needed for the ship-building industry established in Quebec in 1732. Flax is grown for cloth manufacture. In 1721, defying a prohibition dating from Talon's time, 48,038 pounds of tobacco are harvested. Wooden planks are exported to France from the fifty-two saw-mills that have been established in Canada by 1734. At the same time, the authorities forbid the manufacture of hats, and even demand the destruction of any establishment producing fur hats or coats.

It is quite evident that an iron law governs the colony:

ALL PROFITS FOR THE METROPOLIS

● Raw materials must go directly to the metropolis to be converted in its workshops and manufactories. For example, furs. If clothing workshops were created in the colony, it would mean competition for the metropolis. Thus the manufacture of finished products is forbidden.

● If the metropolis has a surplus of certain raw materials, the colony must stop producing them. Such, at a given period, was the case of furs; which explains France's subsequent disinterest in the fur-trading colony.

● The colony must support itself and not rely on shipments from the metropolis. That's why cattle-raising, the cultivation of hemp and flax, the brewing of beer and the manufacture of utensils from iron ore refined in the furnaces of St. Maurice was encouraged.

● The colony must not compete with another colony belonging to the same metropolis. Thus, tobacco production was forbidden to prevent competition with the French Antilles.

To sum up: the colony is purely tributary, giving a great deal but receiving nothing. If it does receive something, it must repay the mother country tenfold. All its wealth is siphoned out. The colony has nothing but obligations while the metropolis has nothing but rights.

The balance of trade rarely favours the colony. The value given to what enters the colony is always greater than the value given to what leaves. And yet we know that tons of furs left the colony for France every year (150,000 beaver skins in 1740 alone) and only a few utensils, tools and agricultural implements entered. But the cards are stacked against the colony. The real value, that is to say the value in *labour-time*, for fur production was very often greater than the value in labour-time of the objects imported from the metropolis. However, the merchants do not measure the value of a product in labour-time, but rather in what it costs them to rob the Red man. Thus tons of furs of 'little value' leave the colony. They cost the merchants next to nothing, perhaps a few trinkets or a bottle of brandy. But, once landed in France as they pass into the hands of the manufacturers, these furs are suddenly worth 100 or even 1,000 times more. It is the merchant who *gives* them this value according to market possibilities. And so the beaver skin that cost the company crook half a cent is suddenly *worth* five or six dollars. Somebody must have manufactured the 'value' along the way!

The tools or implements entering the colony are priced very high, as much as one would pay in the mother country plus transportation costs. Thus, the workers who actually do the work, who produce in the colony, have the products of their labour taken from them for almost nothing, and are forced to buy tools they need at prices twenty times higher. The workers in the colony are always in the red, whereas the exploiters, that is the merchants and administrators, reap double profits. They make money on goods entering as well as on goods leaving the colony.

This relationship between imperial centre and colony still exists today. Latin America (except for Cuba) is a huge colony of the imperialist United States. American capitalists invest in the extraction of raw materials (petroleum, minerals etc.) in these Latin American countries. That is to say, they take the products for practically nothing because they have the power and technical means to do so. The raw material is then sent on to the United States where it takes on a new 'value.' It is sold to manufacturers who convert it into finished products by exploiting the labour-power of American workers. These finished products are then sold at exhorbitant prices in the U.S. and in other countries including Latin America itself.

The same phenomenon occurs in Quebec. Was not the St. Lawrence Seaway constructed for American ships to go directly to Sept-Iles for iron ore and take it straight back to Pittsburgh? There are, of course, factories that convert raw materials in Quebec. Noranda owns our copper mines and factories here that convert copper into semi-finished and finished products. But the establishment of American control over our secondary industry only makes us more colonized and more dependent.

The Final Round

The Fall of Acadia

The whims of European kings dictate the fate of the colony, whether it is to live in peace or go to war. The peaceful years between 1713 and 1740 give way to years of war because the Emperor of Austria, Charles VI, has no male successor. The European countries (or rather the ruling classes of these countries) are immediately at each others' throats trying to get their hands on Austria. These quarrels among power-thirsty kings bring with them, as always, hardships for the people. This time, New France, a colony of 85,000 souls is to be snatched up like some pawn on the chessboard of their royal highnesses, the European monarchs.

In 1745, Louisbourg, the French fortress on Cape Breton Island that had been built to protect the entrance to the St. Lawrence, fell to the English. To retaliate, France decided to take back Acadia and even considered invading New England.

But, Louis XV, now King of France, signs the Treaty of Aix-la-Chapelle in 1748, rendering Louisbourg back to the French. This infuriates the New England colonials. Yet by the same treaty, the rest of Acadia remains in English hands, which in turn infuriates the colonials of New France.

NORTH AMERICA
1755-1760

FRENCH ∷∷∷∷∷∷

BRITISH ▒▒▒▒▒

SPANISH ///////

UNEXPLORED

HUDSON
BAY

RUPERT'S LAND
HUDSON'S BAY
COMPANY

CANADA, OR NEW FRANCE

BRITISH COLONIES

ATLANTIC

OCEAN

LOUISIANA

NEW
SPAIN

GULF
OF
MEXICO

PACIFIC

OCEAN

CARIBBEAN SEA

SOUTH
AMERICA

35

The Deportation of the Acadians

The administrators of the English part of Acadia wanted to get rid of the Acadians settled there. So an oath of allegiance to the British monarch was demanded of those who chose to remain. In addition, it was hoped that by flooding the colony with English immigrants the French could be made to disappear. Halifax was founded for this express purpose in 1749. If the French were unwilling to assimilate quickly, they were to be deported.

In 1755 the governor of Halifax, Charles Lawrence, decides that the Acadians have not become good British subjects since they refuse to sign the oath of allegiance. To his mind, they are no help to British trade and they are occupying fertile lands that the English could cultivate. Solution: DEPORTATION. That year, 7,000 Acadians are packed into ships like animals and dispersed along the American coast. (The White man had usually applied his barbarism to the Red man, but here we see that he could practice it on his fellow Whites as well).

Some Acadians eventually manage to return to Acadia. Others settle in various American centres particularly in New Orleans where, along with the earlier French settlers, they comprise the ethnic group the Americans call *Cajuns* – a corruption of the French word *Acadiens*.

Again in 1755, there were clashes between the English and French in the Ohio valley, and around Lake Champlain. A few more years and New France would pass into English hands.

The English continued deporting the Acadians up until 1762, four years after the conquest of the rest of Acadia. By then they had completed the 'house-cleaning' of Nova Scotia.

	1754
White population of New France.	85,000
White population of New England.	1,485,634

The Colony on the Eve of the Conquest

Before discussing the conquest, let us take a closer look at the composition of society in the French colony in Canada.

THE SOCIAL STRUCTURE OF EARLY QUEBEC

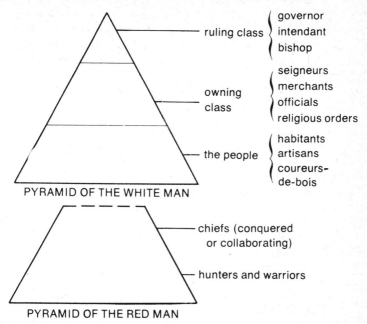

ruling class { governor, intendant, bishop

owning class { seigneurs, merchants, officials, religious orders

the people { habitants, artisans, coureurs-de-bois

PYRAMID OF THE WHITE MAN

chiefs (conquered or collaborating)

hunters and warriors

PYRAMID OF THE RED MAN

The principal characteristic of human society in New France was the domination of the White population over the Red population. As the diagram shows, the Whites dominated, oppressed and crushed the Red man. The Red man was done away with if he rebelled against this domination. Yet if he submitted to White law and order, he would be exploited as a fur-trapper or as cannon fodder to fight the English and their allies, the Iroquois.[1] The Red man was by far the most exploited man in the colony. White oppression grew so devastating that he soon found his very race degenerating, isolated in concentration camps called *reserves*. He would become passive – the condition of all colonized people before their struggle for liberation – and he would be at the mercy

---

1. The seigneurs and the religious orders had the right to keep slaves. These slaves were the subjugated Red men or else Blacks bought from slave merchants in English colonies.

of the 'generous colonizer' to whom he owed his 'survival.' The slow genocide of the Red race is another crime on the conscience of the White ruling class, be it French, English, Spanish, Portugese or Dutch.

The White colonial society that exploited the Red man had a class structure and a system of exploitation similar to that of the metropolis.

At the peak of the pyramid was the governor, representing the king. He was of the French nobility, and very often a *former military officer*.[1] Next to him was the intendant, a civil servant of bourgeois origin or *noblesse de robe*.[2]

A third personage, the bishop, had to compete with the first two for power. He of course, was of nobility.[3] As we have seen, he represented an institution, a kind of state within the state that continually sought to extend its power over the whole of society. The bishop and his parish priests were in constant conflict with the administrators (the governor, the intendant, and civil servants). The Church had already succeeded in forbidding Protestants from settling in New France, yet its religious monopoly was not enough. The height of its ambition was the establishment of a theocracy, a government in which the clergy exercises its authority, without rival, in the name of God.[4]

1. *former military officer:* in feudal times, army officers were always of the nobility. The rank and file were always of the peasantry. An army's structure always corresponds to the social structure it serves. In present bourgeois society, most officers are of the bourgeois or petit-bourgeois class, while simple privates are still of the peasant or working class.

2. *noblesse de robe:* a title of nobility conferred by the king on certain bourgeois who had served him particularly faithfully.

3. In feudal times the structure of the Church was similar to that of the army as described above. The higher clergy, such as cardinals and bishops, were of the nobility. Aristocratic families would buy these positions and the property that went along with them. The simple parish priests were of the peasantry, seldom from the bourgeoisie. This was the Lower Clergy, much closer to the people. We shall see that some priests were indeed so close to the people that they made common cause with them, as in the Rebellion of 1837.

4. Summoned to appear in court, the Reverends Fénelon, de Francheville and Rémy of the Montreal Seminary refused to appear, saying that they were subject only to the laws of the Church and not to civil laws.

Certainly, the Church had the means to realize its ambitions. First, it prospered from three sources of income: its own direct taxation, the tithe; a subsidy from the Company; and the income from the seigneuries granted to the church. Secondly, the Church had the knowledge and the contacts. The parish priest was often the only educated person in the community. Lawyers were at this time forbidden so priests performed the function of lawyer and notary.

Finally the Clergy controlled education. The parish priests still selected the children fit to be educated. The Seminary of Quebec, founded in 1663 by Bishop Laval, prepared the most gifted young men for the priesthood.

Under this threefold leadership were the seigneurs, merchants and religious orders, who constituted the land-owning and entrepreneurial class.

Seigneurs [1] were rarely of the nobility. They were more often merchants, civil servants or former officers. A few of them gave themselves titles in order to climb a bit higher. Occasionally, habitants could become seigneurs. Religious orders too were part of the land-owning class, since economically and politically they participated in it. They owned several seigneuries in their own right and under cover of missionary work accumulated capital, received land grants, carried on trade and exploited the Red man every bit as much as the poor White – the habitant and the craftsman.

But the soul of this class was incarnate in the merchant, the bourgeois. He was the agent of the company. whose only interest was to reap profits from the fur-trade. He was an exploiter through and through. He robbed the Red men, exploited the coureur-de-bois, hoarded capital, had seigneuries granted him and used his influence with the governor to obtain favours, titles and prestige.

The third class, the people, was made up of craftsmen, habitants and coureurs-de-bois. The craftman and the habitants were the workers in the White society, the real producers of consumer goods. Forced to sell their labour-power to the seigneur, merchants and religious orders, they were completely at the mercy

1. Less than four hundred seigneurs owned 5,888,716 acres of land at the end of the French regime.

of the upper classes and without voice in the government of the colony. The coureur-de-bois did productive work only insofar as he carried the furs from the Red trapper to market. As a middleman he too was an exploiter. Yet he remained at the bottom of the White social scale because he was at the mercy of his employer, the merchant.

Nevertheless the roots of the people were firmly planted in the colony, and they had begun to have a sense of themselves as *Canayens*.[1] Their administrators, the Higher Clergy, the merchants and many seigneurs on the other hand were in Canada only to govern and exploit the people. They were French and they stayed French. They were Metropolitans[2] in the colony and could be distinguished from the Canayen people not only with respect to their dominating role but also by their 'aristocratic' manners, their frills and laces, their refined language and their receptions in the best tradition of 'high society'.

1. *Canayen:* The word *'Canadien'* is ambiguous. Under the French regime it referred to people of French origin born in Canada. After the Conquest it denoted the conquered people, the 70,000 French men and women who remained in Canada. A little later when England created Upper and Lower Canada the Canadien was robbed of his name, for 'Canadian' now included the English of Ontario. With Confederation and the creation of the Dominion of Canada, Canadians of French origin were obliged to call themselves *French-Canadian* to keep their identity. Today *'Canadian'* refers to the inhabitants of Canada from sea to sea. The *French-Canadian* who refuses to accept British, U.S. or Canadian colonialism any longer, who is conscious of a homeland of his own, must call himself *Québécois.*

In order to avoid confusion, we will use *Canayen* when referring to those 70,000 French people of Canada and their descendants. We will use *French-Canadian* to identify those Canayens who sold out to the English. Who collaborated with the colonizer. This, of course, includes those who still feel that Canadian federalism has something to offer to the Quebec people. The *French-Canadian* is the Canayen who licks the boots of the English or American colonizer. He is like the American Negro who tries to escape from his identity and hopes to be integrated into White society. But the *Québécois* is the Canayen who rejects colonialism, who fights it, who struggles against the Anglo-American-Canadian domination of Quebec in order to establish Quebec as his country and homeland. In this regard he is like the Black American who rejects integration into White society, who refers to himself as *Black*, not as *Negro* - and who struggles for the liberation of all Black Americans from the oppression of American society.

2. *Metropolitans:* Those people in the colony who were still French-based and whose allegiance was to France rather than to the colony.

Despite his oppression, the Canayen of that time managed to keep his spirits high. He cared little for hard work, and rejoiced in an independent spirit. He was restless and would sometimes leave the seigneurie to become a coureur-de-bois, free as a wild animal. The Clergy tried to tie him down, drag him to church, impose strict rules and keep him from reading the Encyclopaedists[3] and Molière, but all to no avail. The Canayen seldom worried about what tomorrow would bring. He ate the fruit of his labour, had fun, sang and enjoyed life. The opposite was true of the English Puritan[4] in 'New England' who led an

---

CHURCH PROPERTY IN 1763

	acres
The Ursulines of Quebec.	164,615
The Ursulines of Three Rivers.	38,909
The Recollets.	945
The bishop and the Seminary of Quebec.	693,324
The Jesuits.	891,845
The Sulpicians.	250,191
General Hospital, Quebec.	73
General Hospital, Montreal.	404
Hôtel-Dieu, Quebec.	14,112
The Grey Nuns.	42,336
	2,096,754

These figures amount to one quarter of all lands granted. Source: Report of Lieut.-Gov. Milnes, to the Duke of Portland, Nov. 1, 1800. Canadian Archives, - Series 8, Vol. 85, p. 228. Cited by Myers, *History of Canadian Wealth*, Chicago (1914) p. 17.

---

3. *Encyclopaedists:* a groupe of eighteenth-century authors who drafted an encyclopaedia consisting of a compilation of contemporary scientific knowledge. Their research challenged the absolute truths of the Church. The Clergy's reaction was hostile, since they challenged the monopoly of the Church on intellectual life. Among the Encyclopaedists were Voltaire, Rousseau, Diderot, Montesquieu and Condillac.

4. *Puritanism:* in general the tendency among some Protestants to lead an austere ife. In this view, all sensual pleasure is regarded as the work of the devil. Hard work is the only commendable activity, second only to reading the Bible. But such work must be very profitable; it must produce pennies to be saved and accumulated as capital to be invested in further profit-making enterprises.

austere life, hoarded his goods, spent cautiously and worked doggedly. This kind of discipline and austerity was foreign to the Canayen. To forget his poverty and the exploitation he was subjected to, and to show others that he did not live in utter misery, he would put himself into debt to buy a carriage - just like the poor American Black who buys a Cadillac.

The Conquest (1760)

New France in 1750 formed a huge arc encompassing the entire St Lawrence valley, the Great Lakes, and the valley of the Mississippi to the Gulf of Mexico. This immense territory was very sparsely populated (about 85,000 inhabitants) and contained only a few cities and trading-posts.

By contrast, New England, squeezed into an area one-twentieth the size of New France (between the Atlantic Ocean and the Appalachian Mountains) had a population of one-and-a-half million.

In Europe, the French are at war with England's allies, the Prussians. The English take advantage of this by concentrating their war efforts on the seas, to win naval superiority and consequently to gain new colonies. The British bourgeoisie has already obtained a voice in government by a series of small revolutions. The English monarch has delegated to the bourgeoisie the task of exploiting the colonies and spreading British rule over America, Asia and Africa. A further factor in its rush for colonies is England's scarcity of natural resources. The exploitation of her colonies is absolutely indispensable for her development.

In France, however, the evolution of the bourgeoisie is still being held back by feudal structures. It does not control the government. The French Revolution (1789) will be necessary for it to take power. Moreover, with the exception of furs, New France has very little to offer French merchants by way of natural resources. The French Antilles are much more attractive.

France and England, then, hold divergent views on America. The great difference in the strength of the military forces they station on this continent clearly indicates the direction each colonial power intends to take. In 1756, the French send Montcalm, Lévis, Bourlamaque and 450 soldiers to defend New France. The English on the other hand, prepare a regular invasion. The final confrontation is at hand.

In 1758, the French win a victory at Carillon (Ticonderoga). Thirty-five hundred French and Canayen soldiers repel General Abercromby and his 15,000 men.

However, the English soon take Louisbourg on Cape Breton Island and Fort Duquesne in the Ohio Valley. In 1759, Fort Niagara on the Great Lakes and Fort Carillon and Fort Frederick on Lake Champlain fall into English hands. Then Wolfe, with 30,000 sailors and 9,000 soldiers, lays siege to Quebec City. On the 13th of September, the English disembark and wait for the French on the Plains of Abraham — Quebec falls.

The following year, Montreal surrenders. New France is no more.

END OF THE FRENCH REGIME

PART 2 THE ENGLISH REGIME (1760-1919)

The English Administration

For the Canayens the shift from the French regime to the English regime means little more than *changing masters*. Under the French regime they were exploited and controlled by French colonialists. Now it will be the English colonialists.

The most pressing problem for the Canayens is the economic situation. English soldiers have burnt their farms, stolen their cattle and destroyed the harvest. Card money[1] is greatly devalued, since the English, now masters of the colony's entire life including finance, value the French notes at next to nothing. English money can buy anything – and at ridiculous prices. French administrators are leaving for France with their pockets bulging with money; like Intendant Bigot, who had manipulated the economy at the end of the French regime to make himself rich. The small merchants, seigneurs and habitants, on the other hand, are ruined. A few Canayens had been killed in battle; sixty thousand remain to face the hardships that follow the years of war.

The battle between the two colonial powers in America is over. The Canayens are now prisoners on a continent ruled by England. But in Europe, the war goes on. Thus the colony must wait under military occupation; its future depends on the outcome in Europe.

1. Currency adapted from playing-cards had been used by the Canayens due to scarcity of hard cash in the colony.

The French administrators (governor, intendant, civil servants in high office), merchants and officers go back to France. Their work is done. It is all over now. Who remains? The Canayens; that is, those who now feel themselves Canayen. They are the habitants, the soldiers, the seigneurs, a few merchants who stay despite the bankruptcies — and the clergy.

Quick to grasp how it can profit from the political situation, the Church remains. The French have been replaced by English administrators who require an intermediary between themselves and the Canayens. This is the role the Church takes it upon itself to play. It becomes the spokesman for the Canayens, their official representative to the Conqueror. It becomes the colony's *Negro-King*.[1]

Shortly after the surrender of New France, the Ursuline Sisters were already knitting woollen socks for Scottish soldiers. The parish priests were collaborating with militia captains to make habitants sign an oath of allegiance, and confiscating their guns. The Vicar General Bishop Briand declared, like a typical *Negro-King,* "Is it not now evident that these noble conquerors, once they became our masters, forgot that they were our enemy and now only want to look after our needs and find means to satisfy them?" The Conqueror allowed 'free choice of religion' to guarantee the collaboration of the clergy until the Canayens could be assimilated into the 'higher civilization' of Protestantism by means of massive English immigration.

English merchants come to New France after the Conquest to exploit both the habitants and resources of the conquered territories. They are to be the ancestors of our contemporary Anglophone exploiters settled in Westmount, Hampstead and the Town of Mount Royal.

As for the Red man, the Conquest speeds up the theft of his territory. No longer faced with French competition, the English merchants eagerly carry out this wholesale robbery. The Red

1. *Negro-King:* The conquest of Africa by White colonialism advanced in two stages: first, a brutal military conquest and destruction of any nest of resistance, followed by an appeal for collaboration. While ostensibly maintaining their traditional position as leaders, certain tribal chiefs became, in fact, mere puppets of the colonialists. Such indigenous collaboration effectively camouflaged the extent of colonial domination.

man, however, fights back. Led by the Algonquin chief, Pontiac, a federation of tribes takes almost all the forts in the region of the Great Lakes, from Sault Ste Marie to Pittsburgh. But English power is not to be shaken, and Pontiac's rebellion is put down in a bloody battle at Detroit in 1763.

After the Conquest, the social structure of the communities along the shores of the St. Lawrence looks like this:

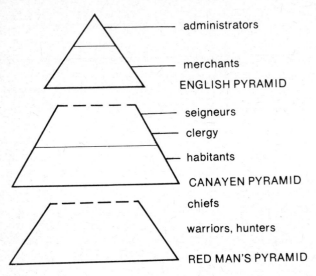

The Red man is almost entirely crushed by Pontiac's defeat. To isolate him from the Canayen who might stir him to further hostilities against the English, the whole western part of the colony is made into a huge reserve.

Although Canayen society is now entirely dominated by the English, its structure remains feudal. The nature of the exploitation of the habitant stays the same, except that the ruling class now speaks English and clerical domination intensifies. It is a hard life.

The small merchant who opts to stay in New France is soon faced with bankruptcy. Some become simple habitants.

Life does not change much for the seigneur after the turmoil of war. The Conqueror asks him to carry on as before, to put the

46

habitant to work. He can keep his privileges on condition that he collaborate with the new regime. Most seigneurs willingly accept.

Under the new regime the Church actually improves its position. It becomes the ruler of Canayen society, governing the Canayens in the name of the Conqueror. In return for services rendered, the Conqueror allows it to set up a virtual theocracy in Quebec.

English society in Quebec, the society of the Conqueror, is divided into administrators and merchants. The administrators, the military and the nobility take their orders from the British metropolis and govern in its name. Merchants like McTavish, McGill, Todd, Frobisher and Patterson found the *North West Company,* which boasts an annual profit of £200,000 sterling after only ten years in operation. These merchants deeply scorn the Canayens whom they consider as cheap labour to be exploited. Privately they refer to them as 'born slaves.'

The Treaty of Paris (1763)

From 1759 to 1763, New France languished under a military occupation headed by General Murray. Its fate depends on the outcome of the Seven Years' War between France and England. Finally, the Treaty of Paris confirms the military conquest. France loses Acadia, Canada, Newfoundland, Cape Breton Island and all the territory east of the Mississippi. She keeps only two tiny fishing islands, St Pierre and Miquelon. The *Province of Quebec* (the new name given to the colony) is now reduced to a rectangle bordering the St Lawrence River from Anticosti Island to the Ottawa River. Any Frenchmen or Canayens wishing to leave Quebec have eighteen months to do so. If they want to sell their possessions, they can sell only to the English.

The New Government of the Colony

The governor is both a civilian and military leader. He has dictatorial powers – to make the people swear an oath of allegiance, to decree whatever laws he wishes, to reverse all Council decisions, to establish courts of justice, to appoint judges, reeves, bishops and priests, to raise troops and grant lands or concessions.

A council is created to assist the governor in his work. It is composed of Lieutenant-governors in the cities, judges and other influential English people.

General Murray is appointed first Governor of the Province of Quebec.

English Policies

The British Metropolis finds that it must try to dispose of the Canayen problem. What means can be used? Deportation is out of the question. So assimilation must be the answer. One must 'civilize' the Canayens, make them adhere to the Protestant religion, and let them enjoy English laws. British colonists in large numbers must be urged to settle in Quebec to sink the Canayens in an English sea. Lands are reserved for Protestant ministers 'so that the habitants may "embrace the Protestant religion."

The Metropolis demands an oath of allegiance to the British crown. The Canayens comply.

The Metropolis also demands an oath of belief (repudiation of the Pope, of Transubstantiation and of the Cult of the Virgin) from every civil servant in the colony. However, the governors do not apply this decree for fear of jeopordizing their alliance with the Catholic clergy. Both Rome and England agree to the appointment of Bishop Briand as Bishop of Quebec with the title of Superintendant of the Roman Church.

The English Merchants Formulate Some Demands

The English merchants in Montreal are immediately dissatisfied with their lack of representation in the colonial government. They want an elected Assembly to be consulted by the governor, like those in other colonies. For them of course, there is no question of electing a Canayen to this Assembly, nor even that the Canayen might have the right to vote for its members. François Maseres, a civil servant, writes: "An assembly so constituted, might claim to be representative of the people in the province, but in truth it would be representative of only the six hundred new English settlers, and in their hands, an instrument of domination of the 90,000 French."

The British government is not prepared to concede this Assembly, for fear that the English merchants might really take advantage of their privileges and so incite the Canayens to revolt. Moreover, London has no desire to grant an Assembly that might lead to the election of Canayens. Obviously these Canayens would use such an Assembly to struggle against the Conqueror. Better to postpone the Assembly for the present so as to bring about, as Maseres puts it. "This coalition of the two nations, or rather the absorption of the French nation by the English, which in matters of language, patriotism, law and religion is evidently what is most desirable and could perhaps be realized in one or two generations if appropriate measures are adopted to this end."

Carleton replaces Murray as Governor in 1766. He regards the clergy and the seigneurs as the real leaders of the Canayens and uses them to keep the Canayens in their place. An aristocrat, he does not want an Assembly that would give the Montreal merchants too strong a voice. He prefers a council where a few Canayen notables can be mixed in with the others. He is in favour of the restoration of French civil law and wants to give the Catholic Church free reign to keep it on his side.

The Quebec Act (1774)

Fourteen years after the Conquest, a constitution, the Quebec Act, is imposed on the Canayens. The following are some of its main clauses:

1. The province of Quebec is expanded. Previously a small rectangle, Quebec now consists of the entire valley of the St Lawrence, the islands of the Gulf of St. Lawrence, Labrador and the entire region of the Great Lakes down to the Ohio River.

The western 'reserve' of the Red Man is absorbed. No longer do the British fear that the Red Man will be stirred up by having Canayens among them. The absorption must be accomplished, since the exploitation of the fur trade can be facilitated by integration of the hunting territories into the province. The eastern expansion brings control of the fishing grounds in the Gulf of St. Lawrence. These territorial gains in no way benefit the Canayens. They are solely in the interests of the Montreal merchants.

2. The administration of the colony has not changed. It has a governor with dictatorial powers and a 17 to 23 man legislative council.

The council is 'legislative' in the sense that it helps the governor make his laws. The members, English or French notables, are to be nominated by the Governor himself. The Council can levy taxes only for roads or public buildings. Any of its decisions can be rejected by the Governor.

The merchants are not granted their cherished Assembly. The Metropolis is not about to make the same mistake it made when it granted assemblies to the New England colonies, where merchants' agitation against the imperial government is already growing strong.

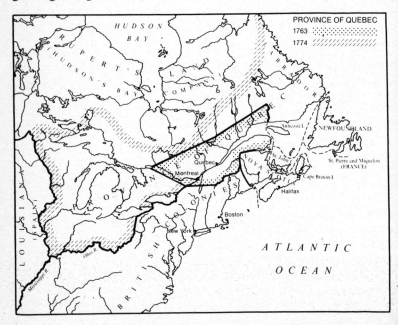

As far as the Canayens are concerned, they do not insist on an Assembly since they never had one under the French regime. They see it only as a discussion centre for the merchant exploiters.

   3. Conflicts relative to civil matters and property are to be regulated under French civil law. As for criminal acts, they will be judged by the English criminal code.

Conceding French civil law to the Canayens is a way of placating them and keeping them down. When they engage in lawsuits among themselves, they are allowed to proceed in court according to French feudal laws. But when criminal acts are judged, English laws come into play. The Conqueror judges serious offenses according to his own laws.

The seigneurial system is retained for the Canayens because it works well at keeping the habitants in their place. Notably, the Conqueror reserves the option to distribute lands in "free and common tenure" rather than in fiefs. This means that the English settlers who wish to cultivate the land can buy it without submitting to a feudal 'contract'. The liberties that the English take in respect to land ownership also extend to wills and testaments. Even if wills come under civil law, the English can draft them and apply them according to English laws.

We can see that the Conqueror makes only those concessions that bind the Canayens to feudal structures while at the same time reserving rights for himself that permit him greater freedom to exploit the habitants and the resources of their country.

   4. *Serment du Test* (Oath of Belief) is withdrawn. Catholics are allowed to become civil servants without having to renounce their religion. The Church can continue to collect the tithe. The Bishop retains the rights he enjoyed under the French regime.

Clearly, the Conqueror has found his *Negro-King*. The priests will know how to keep the Canayens down and he makes concessions to them. As long as it closely collaborates with the Conqueror, the Church has the English king's blessing to extend its domination over all of Canayen society. The Church is elated; it extends its blessing. There is to be only one minor inconvenience: the financial power of religious communities is restricted. The Conqueror will allow it to exploit the Canayens and the natural resources of Quebec as long as it does not compete with the British merchants. The Sulpicians, for example, will have to wait until 1839 for the Conqueror to approve their right to vast tracts of real estate.

Reactions to the Quebec Act

The English merchants are dissatisfied with the Quebec Act. They did not get their Assembly and consequently have no say in public expenditures.

The Church is well satisfied. It is free to dominate the Canayens and establish a theocracy in Quebec.

The seigneurs are also satisfied for the seigneurial system is intact and they can continue their exploitation of the Canayens.

The Canayens are not the least bit satisfied with the Quebec Act. Their servitude is confirmed, nothing is to change for the habitant. They have to pay the tithe; they have to pay taxes to the seigneur; they have to swear the oath of allegiance, now to the King of England. Theirs are the obligations. The Clergy, the seigneurs, the English merchants and the officials have the privileges. Privileges the habitant makes possible.

The Red man does not respond. He has been stunned by the repression following the uprising of Pontaic in 1763. In his own native land he is hunted down, exploited and murdered. To him the very proper constitutions voted by the British Parliament are nothing but bits of paper pledging him to extinction.

The Effects of the Revolutionary Wars

The American Revolution

The thirteen colonies of New England are peopled by Puritans who had sought refuge from the reign of the Stuarts, and by Catholics who fled Cromwell's England. They settled along the coast and in the cities of New York and Boston gradually driving the Red man back as they moved inland. They developed agriculture and traded furs, rum and wheat. Their population increased rapidly to about three million.

Most have little affection for the mother country. They feel more American than English and resent England's meddling in their affairs.

The Conquest of New France brings almost all of North America into the British Empire. The task is now to organize the administration of these vast territories. They have limited the power of the colonists in Quebec by refusing to grant them an Assembly. Why not do the same in New England? The British Parliament attempts to levy duties on paper, glass, dyes and tea imported into the Thirteen Colonies from other countries, to defray the cost of the Conquest of Canada, and to stop the colonies' trade with all countries but itself.

The Thirteen Colonies refuse to pay the new taxes. In 1767, the British Army occupies Boston. The conflict escalates. The more the imperial centre pressures the Colonies, the more they resist until in 1774, they feel strong enough to break the colonial tie. Representatives of the Thirteen Colonies hold their first convention in Philadelphia and denounce British imperial policies. They want to levy their own taxes, build their own army, and boycott British goods. It is at this Convention that they prepare an "Address to the Habitants of the Province of Quebec", calling upon them to unite with the Thirteen Colonies in their struggle for freedom, representative government, an Assembly, and an end to economic persecution.

The Canayen people listen to the call and understand that joining the Americans would mean an end to the Clergy, the seigneurs and the Conqueror. But, the Clergy, the seigneurs and the Conqueror, of course, lose no time in launching a systematic anti-American propaganda campaign. The English merchants, however, support the Americans and try to win the habitants to the cause of American independence.

Carleton, the Governor of Quebec, calls out the militia by giving orders to his *Negro-King,* Bishop Briand, to summon his flock to arms to fight the American rebels. Briand does not object because, after all, England has just granted the Canayens "the practice of our laws, the free exercise of our religion and the privileges and advantages of British subjects." The Canayen is threatened with the denial of the sacraments if he does not take up arms to defend the Conqueror against the "rebelling British subjects."

The habitant may well be ready to join the Americans and see the end of tithes and seigneurial dues, but he lacks organization and a leader to rally the people to the liberation struggle. And so he chooses passive resistance. He refuses to enlist in the militia, and denounces the Clergy for actively defending British interests. Some Canayens severely criticize the *Negro-King*, Bishop Briand, who they say should spend his time training priests, not soldiers. At Terrebonne, Verchères and Berthier, the habitants rebel against the seigneurs who are pushing them into the militia.

The American army launches an invasion of the province of Quebec hoping to drive the British imperialists out of the St. Lawrence region. It quickly overruns the region south of Montreal. In the next few weeks, while advancing on Montreal, the Americans recruit two Canayen regiments.

On the other side of the lines, Carleton had recruited 1,200 inhabitants to 'defend' Montreal, but they have gone home for the autumn harvest. Carleton, disguised as a habitant (naturally) flees to Quebec. Montreal falls to the American rebels.

The American general, Montgomery, having taken Montreal, moves on Quebec where he is supposed to join his comrade Benedict Arnold and more troops. Quebec resists. An English fleet led by General Burgoyne arrives in the spring of 1776, drives out the American troops and pursues them into their own territory, only to be defeated at Saratoga and shipped back to England in 1777.

Those Canayens who were tempted to join the Americans soon realized that the 'freedom' they were offered was in reality only the freedom to become subjects of the new American republic. They knew only too well that they would be just as colonized under the American regime as under the British. Liberation for the Canayen could come only from the Canayens, themselves.

The Americans issue their Declaration of Independence on July 4, 1776.

France is overjoyed to see an English colony rebel. During the war, she had supplied the Americans with huge quantities of gunpowder and arms. France immediately recognizes the independence of the Thirteen Colonies which are now called the United States of America. In fact, the French would have liked to take back Quebec, but the United States sees no advantage in having France to the north as it has Spain to the south.

In 1783, England is forced to recognize the independence of the U.S. The border between Quebec and the new country is drawn along a line that cuts across the Great Lakes, Superior, Huron, Erie and Ontario.

Canayen population in 1784. 113,000

The Arrival of the Loyalists

When the United States declares its independence, one-third of the population is opposed and remains loyal to England. The American government takes away their citizenship rights and drives the Loyalists, as they are called, out of their homes. By the end of the conflict, 100,000 Loyalists leave the United States. Many go back

55

to England, others to the British West Indies. Thirty thousand come to the maritime provinces and six thousand to Quebec. These latter settle on the north shores of Lake Ontario and Lake Erie on fertile lands and receive sizable subsidies as payment for their loyalty to the English king. From the time of their arrival, they will have nothing to do with the Canayens, their seigneurial system or their French civil law. The Loyalists demand a separate district where British law and tenure would prevail. London grants it to them immediately. Upper Canada will be carved out of the Province of Quebec.

The Constitution of 1791

Canada requires a *new* constitution; firstly, the Loyalists demand their own district and an Assembly; and secondly, the Montreal merchants, who already own 90% of the Quebec economy, also want an Assembly but not a division of the province which would separate them from the English-speaking Loyalists.

After the American War of Independence, some Canayens realize that an Assembly could very well help them escape from their position of inferiority. The Clergy and the seigneurs oppose any change. They are well satisfied with their deal with the Conqueror.

The Constitutional Act of 1791 divided the Province of Quebec into Upper and Lower Canada. The border was the same as the present-day border between Ontario and Quebec. Upper Canada is the Loyalists Province; Lower Canada, the Canayen colony. A Governor-general, nominated in London, is to preside over the administration of the two Canadas.

Each Canada is to have a Lieutenant-governor, also nominated in London, an executive council nominated in London, a legislative council nominated in London – and an elected Assembly.

The Governor still has dictatorial powers. The Executive Council is composed of notables who assist the governor. The Legislative Council is composed of notables who are supposed to check the decisions of the Assembly. The Assembly, whose members are to be elected representatives, has the right to 'recommend' certain laws.

The Governor, the Executive Council and the Legislative Council represent the nobility and its feudal and aristocratic values. The Assembly represents the interests of the bourgeois class – the growing merchant class – hungry for more power. The people have no representatives. They are to be dragged along by the bourgeoisie and used to provide them with votes and political power.

The Elections of 1792

In the elections of 1792 in Lower Canada, thirty-five French-speaking and fifteen English-speaking representatives are elected – an unbelievable disproportion when it is taken into account that the English made up only one-fifteenth of the population. Those elected are mostly seigneurs, lawyers, notaries and English merchants. Few are habitants. First session debate centres on what language is to be used : of course, the official language will be English. French will be permitted as 'the language of translation'.

In the Legislative Council, nine out of sixteen members are English notables; in the Executive Council, five of nine. The Canayens in all cases are in an inferior position even though they make up the majority of the population. The creation of the Assembly, 'British democracy', as it manifests itself in colony, benefits only the English merchants.

The French Revolution

The Conquerors keep a watchful eye on the Canayens. The French Revolution has shaken Europe and is even making itself felt in the colonies. The French bourgeoisie is finally overthrowing the remnants of feudalism in France. Louis XVI loses his head. The aristocracy loses its privileges and flees the country and the guillotine. Even the Higher Clergy is stripped of its privileges, parish-priests are forced to swear an oath of loyalty to the revolution. Laggards are dealt with appropriately.

Rumour spreads in Quebec that a French fleet is on its way to the St. Lawrence. There is mounting agitation. Habitants try to invade the Montreal prisons. There is talk of overthrowing the government. A ship carrying 20,000 muskets destined to arm the Canayens is intercepted in the English Channel.

The Clergy, the seigneurs and the Conqueror are in a panic. In 1793 Bishop Hubert, a good *Negro-King*, writes a letter to his priests advising them that the ties that had bound them to France are now completely broken and that all the loyalty and obedience they previously owed to the King of France, they have owed for some time now to His Majesty, the King of Great Britain. It is their duty to drive the French from Quebec.

The following year, the Bishop and some other notables sign a Loyalist manifesto condemning "the seditious attempts lately made by wicked and evil-intentioned persons in circulating false and inflammatory writings, in exciting by false rumours the fears and doubts of our compatriots against the laws and power of the government".

In 1796, Bishop Hubert again writes to his Clergy : "It does not suffice that we be loyal and faithful subjects. If the habitants who are confided to our care allow themselves to be seduced by the enemies of peace and good order; if they lose sight of the rules of dependence and subordination that the Christian religion pre-scribes for them and that are responsible for their special happi-ness and for the maintenance of harmonious relations between subjects and ruler : then, we believe it to be more than ever our duty to impress upon the people, either in public instructions or in private conversations, how closely they are obliged to uphold the loyalty they have sworn to the King of Great Britain, to prompt obedience to the laws, and to avoid any spirit which might inspire them with the ideas of rebellion and independence, which have caused such sad ravages in recent years, and from which it is so much to be desired that this part of the globe ever be preserved".

In 1794, Father Plessis, then parish-priest in Quebec City, praised the Conqueror at Bishop Briand's funeral : "Generous nation. . . industrious nation. . . charitable nation, which has res-cued with such humanity the most faithful and most maltreated subjects of the kingdom to which we formerly belonged; kind nation, which gives each day proofs to Canada of your liberality; no, no, you are not our enemy, neither of our rights, which your laws protect, nor of our Holy Religion, which you respect. Pardon this early distrust in a people who had not until now the happiness to know you. . ."

The Conqueror could scarcely find a better *Negro-King!*

This same parish-priest, and future bishop (we can see why) went so far as to claim that Bishop Briand considered the Conquest a blessing to the Catholic Religion.

In 1799, the Assembly in Lower Canada (English merchants and Canayen notables) vote £ 20,000 sterling to aid England against France and Napoleon. In 1801, Canayen notables and the Clergy subscribe to 'patriotic' funds to help England defeat France.

Clearly, our elite of those days was more attached to its social class than to its mother country. The notables and Clergy would rather obey a foreign sovereign who granted them freedom to exploit the people under the cover of the seigneurial system and the Catholic religion than see the French bourgeoisie stir up the Canayens against them.

The only Frenchmen London allowed to enter Lower Canada were about fifty priests who had fled revolutionary France and were only too happy to settle in Canada and preach against the 'bloody revolutionaries'. They did not lose any time. They helped open seven classical colleges from 1802 to 1832 and numerous arch-Catholic and arch-Loyalist schools to indoctrinate the people against any form of rebellion or revolution which might challenge the divine right of the nobility and the Clergy to exploit them.

Despite these measures, unrest persisted among the habitants. Captains of the militia continued to be elected in each village — something the Canayens had learned from the Americans during the invasion of 1775-76. This primitive form of people's demo-cracy was the beginning of a strong movement that was to challenge the established order and demand important changes. The habitants opposed the military law of 1794 that set up compulsory service. The Assembly notables, under the instigation of Governor Dor-chester, passed the law. Those excluded from compulsory service, of course, were the Clergy, judges and other persons 'indispens-able to civilian life' — in other words, the notables and their friends.

The habitants also opposed the Roads Act of 1796, which was to create a road network by a system of forced labour. Offenders re-ceived fines and penalties. The habitants refused to have roads built with forced labour and fines imposed on them. Riots broke out and agents of the government were beaten up. The 'ringleaders' were arrested, order was restored, and the law was enforced.

The Seigneurs and the Church gradually lost the confidence of the masses. The Clergy increased its threats of excommunication. The seigneurs gradually pulled out of the Assembly and took refuge in the comfortable and remunerative posts of the Executive and Legislative Councils.

Members of the liberal professions : lawyers, notaries and doctors, and some habitants, were elected to the Assembly. They were beginning to make up a *petit-bourgeoisie* within Canayen society. This petit-bourgeoisie was neither a merchant nor an owner class. It considered itself the elite of the Canayen people, an elite that, as in the American Revolution, could lead the people in the struggle to break colonial ties and assume their own economic and political destiny. It got its inspiration not only from the Americans but also from some French authors like Voltaire and Rousseau, and from leaders of the French Revolution. The aim of this petit-bourgeoisie was to establish a regime in Quebec where it could gain political control and then take over the economy. The struggle in the Assembly had now begun.

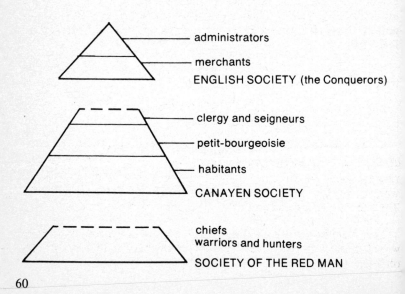

administrators

merchants

ENGLISH SOCIETY (the Conquerors)

clergy and seigneurs

petit-bourgeoisie

habitants

CANAYEN SOCIETY

chiefs
warriors and hunters

SOCIETY OF THE RED MAN

The Rebellion in Canada

The Colonial Economy of the Early 1800's .

The fur trade is of diminishing importance. Lumbering now takes first place due to increased demand in the British metropolis. In fact, England is at war with Napoleon and her lumber supply from Scandinavia is cut off by an economic blocade. She is dependent on her Canadian colony for lumber and fixes a special or preferential tariff. The imperial headquarters removes custom duties on lumber imported from Canada. Quebec is the port of loading.

Who produces the lumber and who makes the money in the lumber trade?

The habitant-turned-lumberjack cuts the wood. His wages are a mere pittance. Enough for subsistance.

By bribing members of the Council, Montreal's English merchants grant themselves huge lumbering concessions. They get the raw material for nothing. Their only outlay is the lumberjack's wages and the cost of shipping the lumber across the Atlantic. Their buyers in England pay well. Profits are exorbitant.

The majority of the habitants, on the other hand, must still work the land to live. They produce their own food and clothing on the seigneuries.

The Chain of Exploitation of the Lumber Trade

	1 Canayen	2 English Merchant	3 English Worker	4 English Government
ACTIVITY	cutting and shipping the wood	middleman	shipbuilding	purchasing ships
PRODUCTIVE LABOUR percent of total	60%	0%	40%	
PROFITS TAKEN percent of total	5%	90%	5%	
SOCIAL CLASS	proletarian	bourgeois	proletarian	

Education

The schools which the Clergy had established in a few cities were nothing more than preparatory institutions for the most gifted to enter the seminary. The masses of the people were kept in medieval ignorance. However, the Conqueror did not believe that the Quebec people could be adequately assimilated in this way. In 1801, the Anglican Bishop, Mountain, attempted to pass a law to establish free primary schools with English teachers "to suppress ignorance, to stimulate industry (that is, the desire to work), and to confirm the people's loyalty by the gradual introduction of English ideas, customs and sentiments."

This anglicization campaign was led by the *Chateau Clique* composed of the English administrators and the 'sell-out' seigneurs. The English merchants naturally supported the campaign, but there was immediate opposition from the habitants who made it known to their 'representatives' that they had not intention of being anglicized. The Clergy let the bill pass, without saying a word, when it was modified to assure the independence of religious and private schools and to allow the population of each parish to decide on the creation of English schools.

Evolution of the Political Situation

The representatives of the British government hold all the power. The British merchants would like to at least share it with the administrators in the same way as the bourgeois of Great Britain share it with the king through parliament. The only means they have is the Assembly (the equivalent of the English parliament). No longer can they obtain a majority in the Assembly where most members are Canayen. It is a waste of money to buy the votes of the seigneurs since they cannot constitute a majority. Moreover the petit-bourgeoisie are now being elected and it is they who are setting the pace. The Assembly is clearly divided into two parties: the *Tory* party on one side, rallying the governor, civil servants, English merchants and the sell-out seigneurs; on the other, the *Parti Canadien* composed almost entirely of Canayen representatives. The Clergy does not overtly engage in politics but it is forever active in back-stage manipulations. In the forthcoming conflict it will of course take the side of the Tories.

In 1807, elections are held. Despite its numerical victory, the Parti Canadien feels threatened because some of its representatives cannot take their seats for lack of funds. It presents a bill compensating those members of the Assembly who come from afar. Judge De Bonne (a Tory) opposes the Bill. The Parti Canadien counterattacks by voting a bill excluding judges from the Assembly. The Legislative Council blocks the bill to check the Parti Canadien. The governor then calls a new election, hoping to use his influence to get an English majority in the Assembly.

The newspaper *Le Canadien*, founded in 1806 (the English have long had two newspapers, the *Montreal Gazette* and the *Quebec Mercury*); enters the campaign and smashes the arguments of the English 'to bring the Canayens to their senses'. It explains to its readers that the Constitution of 1791 gives the Canayens the right to elect representatives and gives these representatives the right to convene a party representing their interests.

Without beating around the bush, *Le Canadien* denounces complicity between influential persons, particularly the governor and the English members of the Assembly. It firmly denounces speculation on public lands. In fact the governor had allowed his friends from the Chateau Clique to make huge profits on the sale of new lands to the English whose votes could counteract Canayen strength in the Assembly.

This is just one example: four English merchants with connections obtained a concession of two million acres in the Eastern Townships. Advertisements were placed in American newspapers and the land sold to Americans. As early as 1805, this region was settled by 5,000 farmers of American origin. They were encouraged to raise large families and thus outnumber the Canayens. Soon they were brought into the Assembly to oppose the Parti Canadien. Patronage always benefits the English businessman. He and the governor contrive to swamp the Canayen — all within the bounds of their 'liberal' constitution!

Le Canadien tells the truth: truth intolerable to the English. Governor Craig, nominated in 1807, speaks of "a seditious and libelous publication that is actively disseminated throughout the province and which is expressly calculated to vilify his majesty's government, and to create a spirit of dissatisfaction and discontent among his subjects, as well as a spirit of disunion and animosity between the two parts of which they are composed".

The Parti Canadien again wins a majority in the elections and again takes up the issue of the expulsion of judges. Craig dissolves the Assembly.

In 1810, elections are again held. Again the Parti Canadien wins a majority and again it votes for the expulsion of judges. The Legislative Council feels obliged to approve the Bill but adds an amendment protecting Judge De Bonne (the worst sell-out!) for the duration of his mandate. The Assembly votes for his exclusion.

Governor Craig is at the end of his rope. In his eyes, the Assembly, led by the Parti Canadien, has overstepped the limits of its power. He decrees its dissolution. A few days later, he seizes *Le Canadien's* printing press and throws its printer in jail. At his order the streets are patrolled and mail service is suspended. He sends three of the founders of *Le Canadien,* the lawyers Bédard and Taschereau, and Dr Blanchet, all of whom are members of the Assembly, to jail without trial. Craig issues a proclamation denouncing "instigators of sedition" and exonerates himself from any acts of oppression.

The Canayens are not intimidated by Craig. New elections take place and again the Parti Canadien wins a majority; Bédard and Blanchet, who are still in jail, are re-elected. Craig is furious. He sends his secretary to London with suggestions for a 'solution to the Canayen problem.'

First, the province must be anglicized. This can be achieved through massive American immigration and by a political union of Upper and Lower Canada. The Canayens would be completely swamped by the English majority.

Secondly, to check the Parti Canadien, the Assembly must be abolished. Or alternatively, only landowners should be permitted to be representatives. Further, there must be larger representation from the Eastern Townships, by now predominately English.

Thirdly, to control the expansion of the Catholic religion, the governor, rather than the bishop, ought to nominate parish-priests.

In effect, Craig is attacking the Constitution of 1791 in favour of a return to the regime of 1763.

In his dispatch to London, Craig writes: "the great mass of the people are completely infected." Further the leaders of the Parti Canadien "publicly declare that no officer of the Crown is to be trusted or to be elected to the House. These, together with all as their own Seigneurs, are entirely proscribed." He adds, "This spirit of independence, this total insubordination, and this freedom of conversation by which they communicate their Ideas of Government, as they imbibe them from their Leaders, all of which have increased astonishingly within the last five or six years, owe their origin entirely to their House of Assembly, and to the intrigue incident to Elections."

He goes on to express scorn for the colonized people. "It really, My Lord, appears to me an adsurdity that the Interests of certainly not an unimportant Colony, of a not inconsiderable portion of the Commercial concerns of the British Empire, should be in the hands of six petty shopkeepers, a blacksmith, a miller, and fifteen ignorant peasants, who are indeed members of your present Assembly, and a doctor or apothecary, twelve lawyers and notaries, and four people who are at least respectable enough not to keep shops, together with ten English members 'now complete the list. There is not one person among them who could be described as a gentleman."

Mountain, the Anglican bishop, sees Catholic domination, papism, as he calls it, spreading over the entire population. He tries to persuade the British government to reduce the powers of the Catholic bishop. As far as he is concerned, the Clergy, Quebec's *Negro-King*, had tried to grab too much power and was not sufficiently oriented toward the colonizer.

The British government takes note of all this but feels that the time is not right to deal too severely with the Canayens. A war is brewing with the Americans and the use of repressive measures may turn the Canayens towards them as almost happened during the American War of Independence in 1774-6. Again the Canayens take advantage of the American threat to stall for time under sentence of death. For the Canayens are a people living on borrowed time. Their annihilation has been decreed – but a certain event will allow them to survive a little while longer.

American Aggression (1812-1814)

The young American nation to the south is experiencing growing pains. It feels strong, it is dynamic and eager to extend its
power as quickly as possible over all of North America. To the
south, it wishes to assimilate Florida which is a Spanish possession; to the west, it wants to overcome the resistance of the
Red man and extend its frontiers over the fertile plains; to the
north, its ambition is to control the St. Lawrence River, an important
commercial waterway. On all sides, America's enemy is the English, the alley of the Spanish in the south, the Red man to the west
and the master of the Canadians in the north.

A naval incident provides the excuse for the American declaration of war against Great Britain.

	1812
American White population.	7,500,000
Canadian White population.	500,000

In 1812, the Americans attack Upper Canada. There are battles
at Detroit and Queenston. Both sides retreat. In 1813 the Americans raid York (Toronto), and burn part of the city, including the
parliament buildings (the assembly of Upper Canada). Two American defeats follow: at Chateauguay where de Salaberry becomes
a small-time hero, and at Crysler's Farm on the St. Lawrence
in Upper Canada.

In 1814, there is a battle at Lundy's Lane near Niagara. Then
the British counterattack violently at Chesapeake Bay. Then attack the U.S. capital, Washington, and burn the government buildings. The Americans manage to drive off the English invaders.

In 1817, The Treaty of Ghent (in Belgium) returns the conquered
territories to each side.

In 1818, England and the United States establish the border between British and American America at the 49th parallel, from
the Lake of the Woods to the Rockies.

And where do the Canayens stand in all this?

In 1811, Prevost had replaced Craig as governor. The new
governor, a Swiss Huguenot (Protestant) is most conciliatory,

and has no intention of provoking the Canayens. When the war breaks out the Canayens are not anxious to join the Americans because they fear the expansionist and imperialist aims of this young nation, and have no sympathy for their brothers who came to settle in the Eastern Townships in order to swamp them. The Americans are also *maudits Anglais* in the minds of the Canayens.

The governor exploits this feeling. He asks the Clergy to rally the Canayen people against the Americans. The Assembly votes $928,000 for the enrollment of 6,000 men. De Salaberry recruits the first Canayen regiment, the *Voltigeurs canadiens,* in a few days.

In order to assure the loyalty of the Clergy during the war, the British government's orders to Prévost are, "the salary of the Catholic Bishop of Quebec shall henceforth be increased to the sum recommended by you of 1,000 sterling per annum, as a testimony to the appreciation which His Royal Highness has for the loyalty and good conduct of the gentleman who now occupies that post, and of the other Catholic clergy of the Province."

The Crisis Resumes

Let us review the situation in the two Canadas.

In Upper Canada, the population of 125,000 souls is White and all English. There are three classes: petty nobility, bourgeoisie and the people.

The petty nobility, consisting of the governor, the lieutenant-governor, the Anglican Bishop and other important civil servants, has control of the Executive and Legislative Councils as in Lower Canada. This group calls itself the *Family Compact,* equivalent of the *Chateau Clique* in Lower Canada. These are influential people and big landowners.

The class of merchants, lawyers and doctors who get elected to the Assembly demand more power in the government of the province. They severely criticize the *Family Compact* for their practices of land speculation and patronage and for their despotic government.

The people, colonists and craftsmen, consider the bourgeoisie their elite and support their demands.

SOCIAL STRUCTURE OF UPPER CANADA

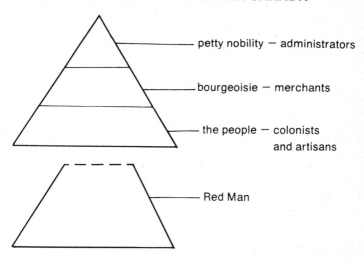

petty nobility — administrators

bourgeoisie — merchants

the people — colonists and artisans

Red Man

On the other hand, in Lower Canada, the situation is more complex because of the conflicting ethnic groups. The White population consists of 420,000 of which 80,000 are English and 340,000 are Canayens.

There are conflicts within the English group. The merchants, seeking to increase their power, pressure the administrators. They are in the extreme minority, but their presence is keenly felt in the Assembly. They push for more governmental control by the Assembly whenever it serves their economic interests.

The English colonists in the Eastern Townships consider the English merchants to be *their elite* and support their demands.

The Canayens are not without their own conflicts. The petit-bourgeoisie challenges the role of the seigneurs and the Higher Clergy, whom they consider sell-outs. Their ambition is to replace them as leaders of the Canayen people. They would like to rally the Canayen people against these oppressors and against the English. Every legal resource the Assembly can offer is to be

69

exploited. The people are receptive. They will accept its leadership and even go one step forward: the Rebellion of 1837-38.

SOCIAL STRUCTURE OF LOWER CANADA

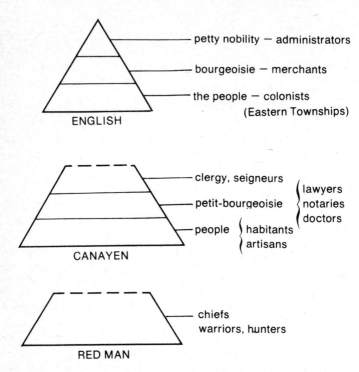

petty nobility — administrators

bourgeoisie — merchants

the people — colonists
(Eastern Townships)

ENGLISH

clergy, seigneurs

petit-bourgeoisie { lawyers
notaries
doctors

people { habitants
artisans

CANAYEN

chiefs
warriors, hunters

RED MAN

The primary conflict, however, is between the English and the Canayens. The Canayens refuse to be assimilated. They are determined to survive as a people and are ready to exploit every possible avenue so that they can take state power.

The Conqueror's weak spot is Parliament, the institution he himself has created. The bourgeoisie in Great Britain gradually assumed a certain amount of power in the government. When it was elected to Parliament it was successful in limiting the king's powers and taking them to itself, for example, control of public expenditure. In the colonies, the English bourgeoisie demanded the same rights and was granted an Assembly, the equivalent of the British Parliament in the two Canadas. The Assembly is elected by the people and, in addition to proposing laws to the governor and the Executive Council, it has the right of taxation (sales taxes, customs duties and tavern permits).

But what annoys the English in Lower Canada is that the very institution the English bourgeoisie demanded to give themselves power is now under the sway of the majority, the Canayens. The Canayens are in the majority in the Assembly for the simple reason that, since they make up 5/6 of the White population, they have no difficulty in electing a majority to the Assembly, in spite of all the English intrigues and underhanded attempts to influence the vote.

The English are caught in their own *democratic* game. We have seen how Governor Graig tried to keep the Canayens down. No way. The succeeding governors are all annoyed and baffled, one as much as the other. Prévost, Drummond, Sherbrooke, Richmond - whether they use the stick or the carrot all fail to break the determination of the Canayens to liberate themselves.

The Assembly has accumulated money from the taxes it levies. In 1795, it lends some to the governor and his Executive Council to cover the increasing costs of administration, which England has no intention of paying. This situation gives the Assembly a powerful lever. The governor and his Executive Council become its debtors. In exchange for the loans the Assembly demands control of the expenditures of the colony, not only for roads, canals, army, etc., but also for the *salaries* of the members of the Council and of civil servants. For obvious reasons, the British government refuses to grant such control. The governors do not know how to go about getting the money they need to balance their budget without allowing the predominantly Canayen Assembly to exercise control of public expenditures. The Assembly holds fast. Each year it becomes more aggressive and more watchful.

In 1820, Governor Dalhousie tries to have the budget passed in the Assembly by studying it chapter by chapter rather than in its entirety. He thinks that the members will have the impression of really exercising their right of examination and will easily pass it. But then the members discover £96,000 missing. The Attorney-

General, Caldwell, has helped himself to the public treasury to speculate on crown lands. (We know where today's politicians learned to rob the population through patronage). The Assembly howls its indignation and more than ever claims its right to ex-. amine all the public expenditures.

From the viewpoint of the English administrators, merchants and colonists of the Eastern Townships, there was only one way to control the finances of the Assembly without leaving it in the hands of the Parti Canadien: make the Canayens a minority in the Assembly.

But how?

The solution: unite Upper and Lower Canada. A bill for such a proposal is sent to the English Parliament: a single assembly would have sixty deputies each from Upper and Lower Canada. They figure that in Lower Canada the English would elect about 20 representatives. Upper Canada would elect 60. That would make 80 English deputies against 40 Canayens. In this way the English, representing a population of 200,000, would have an elected majority against a Canayen population of 300,000. *Beautiful English democracy!*

	1820
White population of the United States.	.9,637,000
White population of Lower Canada.	420,000
White population of Upper Canada.	125,000
White population of the Maritimes.	200,000

According to this Bill, the official language would be English, and every member of the Assembly would be required to own at least £ 500 sterling in property.

The British government tried to rush the Bill through but opposition in Parliament put the brakes on. Meanwhile, the Canayens got wind of it. One can well imagine their reaction!

Louis-Joseph Papineau, lawyer, notary's son (therefore of the petit-bourgeoisie) and an Assembly member since 1808, spearheads Canayen opposition. His second-in-command, John Neilson, is a Scot of radical sentiment who founded the *Quebec Ga-*

zette in 1796 and was first elected to the Assembly in 1818, is also a member of the Parti Canadien.

Papineau and Neilson leave for London with a petition bearing 60,000 names. The British government welcomes them and a Parliamentary Committee is formed to prepare a Report. It recommends that the budget of the colony be put under the control of the Assembly except for the salaries of the governor, the members of the Executive Council and the judges. Judges are no longer to be members of the councils.

It is 1828. Governor Dalhousie is recalled and replaced by the more conciliatory Sir James Kempt who immediately approves the nomination of Papineau as President of the Assembly. The Parti Canadian (also called the *Parti Populaire)* wins a round. A temporary calm settles in Quebec. The governor, using this conciliatory tactic, goes so far as to invite Papineau and Neilson to become members of the Executive Council. Both refuse to be bought off.

It is to be noted that the colonial strategy is to systematically alternate between a tyrannical governor and a conciliatory one. Now, one should not be lured into believing that it was an 'error' in the first case and 'goodwill' in the second. Both were part of the strategy of British imperial domination. It's the old carrot-and-stick routine. If the carrot, the candy, does not work to 'win over' the colonized, let's try the stick. This technique is well-known in Quebec, especially during periods such as this when Canayens relentlessly fight their oppressors.

In 1830, Aylmer becomes governor. He is ready to put the budget before the Assembly for approval so long as it agrees not to ask for the right of examination of the salaries of the governor and judges and of *certain pensions*. The Assembly refuses on the grounds that it does not conform to the Report of 1828. Neilson proposes some moderate resolutions: Papineau takes a more radical position. This difference between the two leaders of the Parti Canadien divides it into *Moderates* and *Patriotes*.

Aylmer modifies his proposal and reduces the raise in the salaries of the governor, magistrates and other civil servants. The Patriotes still refuse to approve the budget. The British Government is obliged to consent to everything they have been demanding since 1818.

However, for the Patriotes the battle has just begun. They are not interested in mere concessions from the imperial power. They must go farther. The people demand it. They must become a sovereign state. The Canayen people have the right to a Canayen state. Why not independence, the creation of a State of Quebec that would negotiate commercial relations with the Empire?

The petit-bourgeoisie founds the *Banque du Peuple* and boycotts the *Bank of Montreal* (the bank founded in 1817 by the merchant-crooks of Montreal, John Molson and Peter McGill). The Assembly's duty is to restrain British commerce in Lower Canada and to limit the profits of the English capitalists who exploit the people. People can have political freedom only when they control the economy.

The domination of the Clergy must also be limited. The Patriotes strongly support a motion that would place possessions of the Clergy under the control of *parish councils* elected by the people. Neilson, the moderate, opposes the motion. As an English protestant he would favour the Catholic Clergy rather than give power to the Québécois. This is the 'moderate' anglophone who supports the power of the *Negro-King* to the detriment of the people who want to be liberated. (This type of English 'moderate,' or 'liberal,' our enemy masked in liberalism, can be found throughout our history. Today we still find those who are sympathetic to our cause provided we 'do not go too far.')

Despite the 'moderate' Neilson, the motion is carried, but it is blocked in the Legislative Council. The English notables and sell-out Canayens in the Legislative Council have the same frame of reference as Neilson, that is, to keep Quebec in a colonial position with the Clergy as *Negro-king*.

At a by-election in 1832 in Montreal, things get rougher. The Canayens organize demonstrations. English soldiers fire into the crowd and kill three Canayens. The two officers responsible for this action are acquitted, and Governor Aylmer approves the verdict. The Canayens are enraged and the newspaper *Le Canadien* expresses their anger.

When the Assembly re-convenes, the Patriotes vote a motion of censure against the governor and a motion to make the Legislative Council elective. The session ends without a vote for the budget. The governor is going to have to use illegal means to pay his and the other notables' salaries in the Chateau Clique. For example, he takes £47,000 from the Jesuit possessions' net income of £49,000 which had been destined for use in education (according to the Report of 1828).

Tension mounts. The yearly immigration of up to 50,000 Anglophones[1] into the country angers the Canayens, who do not care to be inundated by a tidal wave of Anglo-Saxons.

In addition, cholera breaks out. The Canayens are sure that England is responsible, since thousands of immigrants are sent over under poor hygienic conditions. In one year alone, in 1832, 3,000 persons are victims of cholera in the city of Quebec.

In the 1832-33 session of the Assembly, the same conflicts come to the fore: the budget and the conversion of the Legislative Council into a council elected by the people. Aylmer is stubborn. In addition, the *British American Land Co.* formed in London buys 500,000 acres of land in the Eastern Townships. Governor Aylmer intends to settle 600,000 British here and in the Ottawa region.

In the 1834 session, the Patriotes propose 92 resolutions which constitute a résumé of the grievances and demands of the Assembly. The Legislative Council should be elected. The Assembly should control the budget and have the same powers, privileges and immunities as the British parliament. Threats of independence for Quebec and annexion to the United States can now be heard.

The 92 resolutions are adopted by the Assembly despite reformists[2] like Neilson voting against them.

In the elections of 1834, the Patriotes win a crushing victory while the reformist moderates like Neilson lose their seats.

The economic situation is very bad. It is the beginning of a depression. In 1833, there is an economic scare in the United States that has its repercussions among Montreal merchants. Papineau drives the merchants to the end of despair when he asks the Canayens to boycott English goods and to withdraw their deposits from banks controlled by these merchants. The Canayens

---

1. *Anglophones:* English-speaking people. They comprise the English and other groups such as Scottish, Irish and Welsh who had the English language imposed on them in their own countries by British rule.

2 *reformists :* those who favour patching up the system rather than radical changes.

withdraw their savings from the *Quebec Bank* and the *Bank of Montreal*. The Tories (the English party) meet to define a strategy that would destroy the *Parti Canadien*. The Patriotes recalling how the Tories called upon bouncers to intimidate the voters at the last elections, know that a strategy calling for physical violence has been defined at this meeting. They themselves *see the need to resort* to arms. The line is drawn. Armed conflict is inevitable.

The Armed Conflict

Gosford replaces Aylmer in 1835. His mission is to inquire into the situation in the two Canadas, "to maintain the peace and integrity of the Empire and to act as mediator between the two parties." He got the idea of trying to conciliate the moderate Canayens, by taking them into the government, hoping thereby to neutralize and quietly eliminate the Patriotes. Divide and Rule. And always call on the moderates when the rebels can't be bought.

The 1835 session of the Assembly begins with a call for peace and harmony from Gosford. Papineau has the budget passed for six months only. Nothing can be done: the parties are irreconcilable.

LEGISLATIVE BUILDINGS

Quebec. Built 1833. Burnt 1854.

But Gosford keeps trying. He dissolves the British Rifle Corps, a gang of armed Englishmen in Montreal who want to defend English 'rights.' They cannot depend on the British army because the mother country is too conciliatory. A contemporary equivalent of this little army is the OAS in Algeria during the Algerian War of 1954-62. The OAS *(Organisation de l'Armée Secrète)* was made up of French colonialists in Algeria determined to keep Algeria French and deny the Algerians their right to independence and sovereignty.

Gosford's tactics of 'moderation' succeed up to a point. The Patriote Bédard and a few others go over to the ranks of Neilson's moderate reformists. Gosford has managed to reduce the Patriotes from a majority position to a single seat when, thanks to a rebel from Upper Canada named Mackenzie, they finally realize that London had instructed Gosford to use these very tactics of conciliation to destroy the Parti Canadien and assimilate the Canayens. The Patriotes come to their senses.

The 1836 special session of the Assembly lasts 12 days and simply confirms the conflict. The Montreal merchants increase their verbal attacks against the Canayens and call for armed confrontation.

The harvest is bad. Unemployment rises. There seems to be no end to the economic depression. England herself badly hurt by the crisis cannot relieve the colonial economy and pacify rebellious feelings.

In 1837, Lord Russel submits his recommendations for the 'solution' to the problem in Canada: no elected legislative council; no executive council responsible to the assembly (control of the budget by the governor if the assembly refuses to pass it); and confirmation of the legal title of the British American Land Company.

Now, the Patriotes get organized. They hold public meetings in the cities and villages. On the Richelieu at St-Ours an assembly of 1,200 adopts 12 resolutions prepared by the Patriotes' Permanent Central Committee, denouncing the British government as an 'oppressor power,' and denouncing the machiavellian tactics[1] used by British colonialism since the conquest. The fifth

---

1. *machiavellian tactics:* exploitation of all possible means, regardless of the people's welfare, to attain and maintain power.

resolution recognizes the friendship of the United States. The seventh states that the Canayens are tied to the English government by force only. The eighth calls for a boycott of imported products such as tea, tobacco, rum and wine, and asks the people to buy only Canayen products. This same resolution *legalizes* smuggling. The tenth resolution asks all the Canayens to rally "round a single man," Papineau and create the "Papineau Tribute," a kind of tax levied by the Patriotes for the fight against the oppressor.

The Patriotes' newspaper *La Minerve* and the Irish sympathizers' *Vindicator* widely publicize these resolutions. Despite Gosford's prohibition, the popular assemblies of the Patriotes continue to meet. Meanwhile the Governor is busy helping the English party organize meetings which they call 'constitutional assemblies.' The repression begins.

Gosford calls on the Negro-kings to use their influence on the rebellious people. At the consecration of Bishop Bourget, Bishop Lartigue reminds his audience, composed mostly of parish priests, "that it is never permitted to revolt against supreme authority nor to transgress the laws of the country; that we will refuse absolution to anybody who teaches that one can revolt against the government under which we have the good fortune to live, or that it is permitted to violate the laws of the country, in particular those that forbid smuggling."

The Clergy -- which has repeatedly told us that it's thanks to them that we have survived -- showed again in 1837 that the Church is *against* the people's liberation and *for* colonial domination. During the rebellion, the Clergy's anti-Patriote mouthpiece was its newspaper *L'Ami du peuple*.

In the summer of 1837, Queen Victoria assumed the British throne. The *Te Deum* was sung in all the churches in Quebec but everybody walked out when the parish priests intoned the 'hymn of joy.'

It is now August. Gosford convenes the Assembly to make yet another offer of 'conciliation.' The Patriotes refuse to be drawn in and Gosford dissolves the Assembly.

Some young Patriotes, André Ouimet, Amédée Papineau (Louis Joseph's son), and Thomas Brown (born in New Brunswick and raised in the United States) organize a para-military group, th

Docteur Jean-Olivier Chénier

Fils de la Liberté. The *Doric Club* is the para-military association of the English.

The Patriotes now push for parallel institutions. The Committee of the Two Mountains decides to elect its own justices of the peace, and an assembly of habitants does so on October 15th. "The Revolution Has Begun!" announces the anti-Patriote newspaper *Le Populaire.* On October 23rd, 5,000 people assemble in St Charles. But the leader begins to waver: Papineau advises them against taking up arms. He talks about keeping the struggle "constitutional" and limiting the action to boycotting English goods.

Doctor Wolfred Nelson, an English petit-bourgeois gone over to the Patriotes, retorts "the time has come to melt down our tin plates and spoons to make bullets." The popular assembly asks the citizens of the six Richelieu counties to elect their justices of the peace and their military officers. Next day, the delegates call for a meeting of a Convention, that is, of an elected assembly that would draw up a new constitution for Quebec.

In Montreal, the *Fils de la Liberté* swear an oath of loyalty to their native land for victory or death. At the same time in another part of the city, Peter McGill is presiding over an anti-Patriote constitutionalist rally.

Bishop Lartigue publishes a pastoral letter that supports Gosford all the way and puts every Catholic on guard against complicity with the "rebels". The letter provokes demonstrations throughout the province. In Montreal, 1,200 Patriotes march in front of St. James Cathedral; in Chambly, Bishop Bourget is booed off the steps of the church. The Patriotes say that the reactionary attitude of the Clergy will hasten the revolution, and they sing the *Marseillaise.* Bishop Lartigue is running scared and offers his resignation to Rome. The Clergy's system of propaganda just goes on preaching loyalty to the British Monarch and respect for the laws – in other words, submission to colonial power.

The newspaper *Le Canadien,* which had formerly supported the Canayen struggle, is getting more and more anti-Patriote. Its owner, Etienne Parent, now defends the bishops' position. *La Minerve* in Montreal is the Patriotes' mouthpiece, as well as *Le Libéral* in Quebec (a bilingual newspaper).

The Patriotes now know precisely who are their enemies : the English merchants, the seigneurs, the Clergy and the *chouayens* (cabbagehead-Canayens), the Canayens who have sold out to the English.

On November 6th, some members of the Doric Club, the English para-military organization, decide to 'nip the rebellion in the bud' and attack the *Fils de la Liberté* as they leave one of their meetings. The *Fils* fight back as well as they can, but they are outnumbered. The English band wins the scuffle and proceeds to ransack the printing office of Doctor O'Callaghan's Irish pro-Patriote newspaper, the *Vindicator*. From there they go on to attack Papineau's house. The armed guards the authorities have patrolling the streets let the Doric Club boys do their thing, while they keep a close watch on the *Fils de la Liberté*.

Gosford writes to London asking for authorization to suspend *habeas corpus*[1] and proclaim martial law[2]. He then calls for reinforcements from the Maritimes and Upper Canada. Regiments of violently anti-Patriote Englishmen volunteer in Montreal, Quebec and the Eastern Townships. The commander-in-chief of this army of repression is Sir John Colborne.

On November 12th, all assemblies and processions are forbidden. On November 16th, warrants are issued for the arrest of 26 Patriotes on the charge of treason. Papineau, O'Callaghan, Desrivières, T.S. Brown and Ovide Perreault escape to the Richelieu. André Ouimet, president of the *Fils de la Liberté,* is thrown in jail. The same day, the Montreal Volunteer Cavalry from St Jean hunts down the doctor, Davignon, and the notary, Demaray. But it falls into an ambush between Chambly and Longueuil set up by Patriotes under the command of the movement's local leaders, Bonaventure Viger and Dr. Timothée Kimber. The Patriotes fire; the Montreal Volunteer Cavalry flees, abandoning Davignon and Demaray.

This is the first victory for the Patriotes. They organize, regroup, and arm themselves as best they can. In command of the

---

1 *habeas corpus:* a law that prevents prolonged imprisonment of a person without a hearing.

2 *martial law:* dictatorial powers that the government uses in times of crisis to systematically repress any revolt. This is the legal justification which the government uses to crush any popular uprising.

Patriote troops at St Denis is Dr. Wolfred Nelson; at Montreal, T.S. Brown.

The *chouayens*, the sell-outs, provide Colborne with a good espionage service. He knows the Patriotes' comings and goings well. He sends Lieutenant-Colonel Wetherall with an infantry regiment, a Montreal volunteer cavalry troop and two cannons to join Colonel Gore at St Denis. Gore has five companies of regulars, a volunteer cavalry troop, and a cannon believed to have come from Sorel.

On the night of November 22nd, Gore veers off the road to avoid St Ours, which is held by the Patriotes. Thus the surprise attack on St Denis, planned to take place in the middle of the night, turns into a battle in full daylight between exhausted and frost-bitten soldiers and a village well-prepared for combat. For five hours the fighting is desperate. Young Georges-Etienne Cartier (who later sold out Quebec in Ottawa) is one of the most relentless Patriote fighters. The Patriotes kill six soldiers and wound 18 more. Gore retires to Sorel and counts his men: one hundred and seventeen missing - where did they go? The Patriotes count eleven dead and seven wounded.

Where is Papineau, the 'leader' of the rebellion? He left for St. Hyacinthe with O'Callaghan right at the beginning of the battle. From there they fled to the United States. Papineau was against the armed uprising. When it took place despite his protests, he could not assume the leadership of the revolutionary movement.

But the people understood that power is in the barrel of a gun. The people understood that only an armed revolution could liberate them from Anglo-Saxon colonialism. The habitant logic was simple and powerful: "We are oppressed by a class of English exploiters and by their puppets, the seigneurs and the Clergy. This class uses the army to maintain its domination over us. Therefore the only way to overthrow the oppressor class is by armed struggle. To arms, Patriotes!"

Papineau did not understand this simple argument. His reasoning was more round-about. Although he realized that the English were an oppressor class, he also believed that the English oppressor would cease being an oppressor if the oppressed made explosive declarations and threatened economic boycott, separation, and annexation to the United States. Papineau did not understand the nature of imperialism. He believed in the English and in a 'gentleman's agreement.' He did not understand that the liberation of a people subjected to economic colonialism can only be accomplished through armed struggle. The fact is, Papineau was bourgeois, and he never changed. He remained a 'gentleman', a man it is easy to get along with if he is granted a 'gentleman's privileges.' In short, Papineau did not really want a revolution that would bring the habitants to power. He wanted an *evolution* that would give the Canayen petit-bourgeoisie the same rights and privileges that the British and American bourgeoisie had. In fact, he wanted a French Revolution in Quebec, a bourgeois revolution, but without recourse to arms.

Papineau's treason to the cause of the people of Quebec led to a split in the Patriote movement, and weakened it. The leader had run away. How could the struggle go on? It had to be improvised.

While Seigneur Debartzch sought refuge in Montreal, the Patriotes under T.S. Brown fortified his manor at St. Charles. The house was held by 200 men with about 100 guns in bad condition.

Here we must criticize the Patriotes for their lack of military strategy. They thought in terms of well-fortified towns and of pitched battles à la Napoléon. They made their stand in manors (as at St. Charles) or in churches (as in St Eustache later on) and were perfect targets for the well-armed, well-equipped, well-supplied colonialist army. It would have been better to adopt the guerrilla strategy[1] which had succeeded for the Spanish and the Russians more than 25 years earlier when Napoleon's great, 'invincible' army invaded Spain in 1808 and Russia in 1812. The Patriotes were on home ground; every habitant was a Patriote. They held the countryside. By contrast the English army was in foreign, hostile territory. The Patriotes should have left the villages, faded into the background and systematically harassed the colonialist troops with hard, stinging little jabs to demoralize, decimate and destroy them. One year of guerrilla warfare could have liberated Quebec from British colonialism and imperialism. The strategy of classic warfare was the mistake the Patriotes made.

[1]. *guerrilla:* Spanish word that means 'little war.' It is the strategy of surprise attack and ambush by small armed bands.

On November 24th, Wetherall, well-equipped and reinforced, advances on St Charles. He is preceded by Bonaventure Viger, leading a small group, who slows down the enemy by destroying bridges and attacking reconnaissance squads (Viger seems to be the only Patriote with any idea of guerrilla warfare, as he demonstrated also on November 16th at Longueuil).

Wetherall burns the village and concentrates on the manor. He sends the classic message to the beseiged Patriotes that if they disperse they will not be molested. Brown replies in kind: he offers the English troops free passage to Sorel if they consent to lay down their arms. Wetherall then attacks the manor with his artillery, and sends in his soldiers, bayonets fixed. They clean out the place in no time. Viger escapes by swimming across the Richelieu.

Brown tries to rally his troops, but it is no use. He flees to St. Denis.

The battle was very unequal: two colonialist soldiers for each Patriote. The score: Patriotes killed, 40; wounded, 30; taken prisoner, 30. Colonialist troops killed, 3; wounded, 18.

Wetherall triumphantly returns to Montreal with his prisoners and the liberty mast of St Charles.

On December 1st, Gore returns to St Denis, the site of his defeat. Everything is peaceful. The Patriotes have deserted the village. In the Richelieu he finds the body of an English soldier killed by the Patriotes as he tried to escape from being held prisoner. English fury is suddenly unleashed. The English soldiers desecrate the church, loot and burn the village where, the week before, the habitants had been caring for the wounded the English had abandoned.

The Patriotes taking refuge in the United States have received a warm welcome but only verbal support. On the 6th of December, a troop of 200 Patriotes attempt to rally volunteers and return from American territory. Mailhot and Bouchette are their commanders. But the Missisquoi Volunteers, under Captain Kent, push them back across the border. The wounded Bouchette is taken prisoner, and Wolfred Nelson and Bonaventure Viger are captured and imprisoned in Montreal. During the next few months, the exiled Patriotes in the U.S. split into two factions quite distinct from each other. Papineau speaks of peace and conciliation, but Robert Nelson (Wolfred's brother), Côté, Rodier, Mailhot,

Gagnon and Duvernay (founder of the St Jean-Baptiste Society in 1834) favour armed struggle unto final victory.

It is important to mention the role played during this time by the sell-out Hippolyte Lafontaine. As soon as the conflict became serious he turned against the Patriotes, beseching Gosford to convene a 'moderate' assembly. When he was refused he left for London to make the same request. A warrant was then issued for his arrest and he fled to Paris. After the repression of the rebellion, this fine gentleman played an important role as a Negro-king.

On December 5th, Gosford decrees martial law. The Patriote leaders now have a price on their heads and the habitants are summoned to surrender their arms. The authorities are counting on the Church to pacify them. The priests need no encouragement. From the pulpit and the confessional come threats of hell for the Patriotes and their sympathizers. The few priests who sympathize with the Patriotes are soon relieved of their duties. Bishop Bourget, co-adjutator to Bishop Lartigue of Montreal, is sympathetic to the Patriotes but doesn't show it.

The Patriotes organize north of Montreal. On November 29th, Jean Chénier, a doctor, and Amury Girod, a Swiss agriculturist and adventurer, lead 200 Patriotes into the Hudson's Bay Company's stores at the Indian mission at Oka and pick up guns, ammunition and a small cannon. They establish their headquarters in a newly-constructed convent at St Eustache.

The parish priest Paquin, a hard-bitten anti-Patriote, denounces them violently and is put under house arrest by Chénier. However Chartier, the priest from the St. Benoit parish, wholeheartedly supports the Patriotes. Gorod musters 1,000 Irish and Canayens, but they are undisciplined and spend their time drinking and quarrelling instead of training.

On December 13th Colborne begins to advance on St. Eustache with three regular regiments and two volunteer cavalry, plus artillery: a total of 2,000 well-equipped men. The next day he arrives at the town where 250 Patriotes have taken refuge in the church, the presbytery, the convent and in the home of an English sympathizer, Scott. Cannons bombard the front of the Church. Soldiers set fire to the back of the church and to the presbytery. The Patriotes jump out the windows and are shot down one after another. The victims include Chénier and 70 other Patriotes. About ten more burn to death in the church. One hundred Patriotes are taken prisoner.

The enemy counts one soldier killed and nine wounded.

Girod flees to St. Benoit and commits suicide four days later. Reverend Chartier escapes to the United States. The colonialist army pillages and sets fire to the village, does the same thing the next day at St. Benoit, meeting no resistance. The army burns all the farms along the way home to Montreal.

The Metropolis Investigates

On February 10, the British Parliament suspends the constitution of Lower Canada and names Lord Durham governor-general and high-commissioner to inquire into the rebellion. The son of a wealthy coal-mine owner, Durham is a leader of the reformist Whigs[1] He arrives with a royal retinue and straight-away dissolves the special council Colborne had set up when he replaced the sick, discouraged Gosford.

The *chouayens* and Moderates come out of hiding to pay homage to the new governor. Etienne Parent publishes a laudatory poem by François-Xavier Garneau in *Le Canadien*.

Durham's first problem: what to do with the Patriotes in jail? A trial with a Canayen jury would acquit them. But, with an English jury, they'd certainly be condemned to death. So he decides to do without a trial. He gets eight of the Patriotes, including Wolfred Nelson, Bouchette, and Bonaventure Viger, to write him a letter placing them at his mercy. Then he exiles them to Bermuda. Sixteen other leaders who have fled the country, including Papineau, O'Callaghan, Robert Nelson, Rodier, Brown, Duvernay, Chartier, Gagnon, Cartier, the two John Ryans, Perrault, Demaray, Davignon, and Gauthier, are forbidden to return to Canada. The other prisoners are freed on condition of good conduct.

Durham makes his inquiry and draws up his report. Meanwhile,

1. *Whigs:* political party with liberal tendencies, made up of the rising industria English bourgeoisie of the 1830's.

news reaches England of the measures taken against the political prisoners. The governement and the Lords are aroused because they feel that a condemnation without trial is contrary to English tradition. Durham, hearing of this reaction, feels offended, and decides to leave Canada. On November 3, five months after his arrival, he returns to England.

Meanwhile the Patriotes who took refuge in the United States are very active. Robert Nelson had already proclaimed the *Republic of Lower Canada* on February 28, 1838. The document proclaims the independence of Lower Canada (Quebec): separation of church and state; suppression of the tithe; abolition of seigneurial dues; freedom of the press; universal suffrage for all men including the Red man; a secret ballot; nationalization of crown lands and lands of the British American Land Company; election of a constituent assembly; and the use of both languages in public affairs. Robert Nelson is president of the *Provisional Government of Lower Canada.*

Nelson and Côté begin organizing a liberation army called the *Frères Chasseurs* in the bordering American states to prepare for their invasion of Canada. Two hundred thousand persons in Canada and the United States are reported to support this army.

Before his departure, Durham speaks of "elevating the Province of Canada to a profoundly British nature," of "raising Lower Canada's faulty institutions to the level of English civilization and liberty," of "removing all obstacles to the progress of English ventures in that province," and of "dealing with old laws and customs as though they were deeply-rooted abuses." This foretaste of Durham's report provokes violent reactions. Every Canayen can see in it the extinction of his nation. The Moderates at last understand that the extremists are right, and many join the other side. The Clergy, fearing its own extinction if the Canayens are to disappear, revises its position to some extent. But this doesn't prevent the Patriote press from accusing Bishop Lartigue of high treason against the Canayen nation. This gentleman hides away in Quebec for fear of being judged and hanged by a people's court; once again he submits his resignation to Rome.

The Liberation Army foresees an invasion at the beginning of November and is counting on popular uprisings throughout Lower Canada. There are uprisings in Quebec, Sorel, Chambly, and

Montreal but only the area south-east of Montreal answers the call. At Beauharnois, 400 men seize the manor of the English merchant Ellice, and 150 men capture the steam-boat *Henry Brougham* near Lachine. Then, Chateauguay Patriotes disarm some Scottish loyalists and try to take the Iroquois' arms at Caughnawaga, but they themselves are captured. At St Charles, St Denis and St Ours, Patriotes await in vain the promised arms and their leaders. Finally they disperse.

On November 4, Nelson joins Côté and 3,000 assembled Patriotes at Napierville. The arms at their disposition: 250 guns, some forks and picks and pointed sticks. Côté tries to return to the border to pick up a waiting cargo of arms but a detachment of volunteer loyalists gets in the way.

Four days later, Colborne, who has replaced Durham, advances on Nelson with an army of 6,000 men. Nelson is waiting for him with 1,000 men at Odelltown near the border. But the village garrison gives him a hard time and some of his men mutiny. Next day, Nelson flees across the border as his men withdraw to Napierville, leaving 50 dead and 50 wounded behind them. Later, Colborne's troops pursue the Patriotes into the town and put them to flight.

At the same time, the Glengary Volunteers (Scottish volunteers from Ontario) disperse the Patriotes at Beauharnois and burn the village. The home of every known Patriote is burned.

Colborne had proclaimed martial law on November 4th and suspended *habeas corpus*. By November 9th he can claim 753 prisoners, who are all court-martialled[1]. No Canayen lawyers are permitted to defend them. Ninety-nine are condemned to death. Adam Thom of the *Montreal Herald* demands they be executed immediately. He claims, "it would be ridiculous to feed them all winter only to bring them to the gallows later." Colborne orders the public execution of 12 Patriotes in front of the Montreal Prison at the *Pied-du-Courant* (at the corner of Notre-Dame and DeLormier streets).

---

1. *court-martial:* military court which *usually* judges only soldiers and officers guilty of desertion, espionage and other such offences. The judges are military men. There is no jury.

The 12 Patriotes publicly executed by Dictator Colborne:

- Joseph-Narcisse Cardinal, 30, notary, member of the Assembly, married, 5 children
- Joseph Duquette, 22, law student, bachelor.
- Pierre Théophile Decoigne, 27, notary, married, 2 children
- François-Xavier Hamelin, 23, farmer, militia lieutenant, bachelor
- Jacques Robert, 54, farmer, militia captain, married, 5 children
- Ambroise Sanguinet, 38, farmer, married, 2 children
- Charles Sanguinet, 36, farmer, married, 2 children
- Amable Daunais, 21, farmer, bachelor
- François-Marie Thomas Chevalier de Lorimier, 30, notary, married, 3 children
- Pierre-Rémi de Narbonne, 36, painter and bailiff, married, 2 children
- François Nicolas, 44, teacher
- Charles Hindelang, 29, of French nationality, in the military, bachelor

Amongst the others sentenced, 58 were deported to Australian penal colonies,[1] two were banished from the country and 27 were freed on bail.

The Tories were hollering for more blood. The Canayens denounced Colborne's "blood-thirsty tyranny."

It is to be noted that those whom Colborne executed were not among the leaders of the Rebellion, but simple militants. While the tyrant had been heard to say that executions were necessary 'to set an example,' he did not dare execute the Patriote leaders for fear that popular indignation would turn to violence. By executing rank-and-file Patriotes, he was able to resolve this contradiction.

In February 1839, Papineau left the United States for France where he wrote a *History of the Insurrection of Canada.* He was to return in 1845 and sit in the Canadian Parliament from 1847 to 1854.

Lafontaine, Morin, Cartier and Taché were destined to become prime ministers. Wolfred Nelson would be re-elected to the Canadian Parliament in 1844; T.S. Brown would return to his business

1 In this period Australia is an English colony used as a concentration camp for criminals and political prisoners of the British Empire.

and write his memoirs; and Bouchette would become customs collector in Ottawa. Robert Nelson and O'Callaghan remained in the United States.

The Rebellion failed. Many Canayens were discouraged. Some left Quebec for parts of the United States like Massachussetts where industrialization was creating employment, particularly in the textile industry. Half a million Canayens went to the U.S. between the years of 1837 and 1910. Why did they not stay on the farms? There were no farms left. All the arable land in the province had been cleared. The harvests were bad. There was no 'future' in Quebec. For a good number of Canayens the defeat of the Rebellion meant perpetual English colonialism and the domination by the Clergy that went with it. Many chose emigration to the 'States.'

The Rebellion in Upper Canada

We mentioned in an earlier chapter the social classes found in Upper Canada and the developing conflict between the Anglophile petty nobility and the rising local bourgeoisie supported by the settlers. We will now look at the development of this conflict in that colony.

This petty nobility with its feudal ideology was responsible to England for the administration of Upper Canada. At the same time it had a great deal of economic power because of the large estates it had granted itself. An example is Colonel Thomas Talbot, member of the Legislative Council who had 'acquired' 60,000 acres north of Lake Erie.

Closely tied to that petty nobility was the upper clergy of the Church of England which grabbed one-seventh of all surveyed land automatically by law. These lands were called the 'Clergy Reserves.' In 1828, three million acres were in the blessed hands of this 'religious aristocracy.'

On the other hand, there was a growing bourgeoisie, comprising people of the liberal professions as well as shopkeepers and small business men who felt they were Canadian and were vying for political power.

90

Rebels drilling in North York in autumn, 1837.

On the bottom rung of the social ladder were thousands of settlers, clearing the land, sowing cereals, raising cattle, plus growing numbers of workers in burgeoning enterprises (grist mills, saw mills, tanneries, foundries etc.) The settlers and workers were doing the real productive labour while the local bourgeoisie was 'helping' them exchange goods and services. The petty nobility was just cashing in on the lot.

The rising bourgeoisie was straight-jacketed by the colony-metropolis relationship that forced it to trade only with the mother country and to use solely British ships to do so. It wanted greater freedom to trade with the U.S. and other countries. At the same time, it was aware of the frustrations the settlers were accumulating against the big land-owners and felt it could channel the resentment of all true Canadians into a movement of general reform. Agitation spread in the 20's and 30's.

As in Lower Canada, the Reformists started their struggle as a legal one in the Assembly. William Lyon Mackenzie became their leader. In 1828, they won a majority and promptly passed a vote of non-confidence in the Executive Council. But they lost the 1830 elections to the Tories who had organized a smear campaign insinuating their opponents were infiltrated by 'foreign agents' and U.S. annexationists. As always, the British-appointed Governor retained his power of veto.

Mackenzie who had retained his seat was expelled from the Assembly for "scandalous and malicious libel." He was promptly re-elected and promptly re-expelled. Five times the people elected him and five times the pro-England Tories expelled him. The Reformists then started organizing meetings.

As in Lower Canada there developed two wings of the Reform movement: one, moderate, stressing the need for responsible government (that is, greater autonomy for the colony), and the other, more radical, demanding outright independence.

The moderates found their support mainly among the petit-bourgeoisie proper, while the Radicals and Mackenzie found theirs mainly among the farmers (then called yeomen) and the workers.

The Radicals spoke of a Canada independent of England. In 1834, they formed the Canadian Alliance Society, a political organization that was to develop political education among the masses.

In 1834, Mackenzie becomes the first mayor of Toronto and the Reformists win back the majority in the Assembly. They demand responsible government. But Lieutenant-Governor Sir Francis Bond Head dissolves the Assembly in 1836, calls an election and gets his majority with the help of goons and smear experts.

When the Rebellion starts in Lower Canada in 1837, the Patriots pledge their support to the *Patriotes*. In July of 1837, the Radicals call for a convention that would in fact proclaim the independence of Upper Canada. They start organizing district committees and action groups.

Almost every blacksmith shop in Upper Canada is turned into a small-arms factory. Most of the guns and bullets used by the rebels are home-made. Samuel Lount, a blacksmith, supervises this work.

A declaration of independence is issued. All over the province, armed meetings are held. Local militia groups begin regular drilling.

In November, they prepare the take-over: a march on Toronto, the seizure of 4,000 guns, the arrest of Bond Head, the declaration of independence and the calling of a Convention.

The execution of the plan on December 3 is another thing. Some leaders [1] chicken out, communications are bad, discipline is worse, military competence is scarce. The great march fails. Mackenzie sees the collapse of his forces and takes refuge in Buffalo. On December 13, Mackenzie with a small band takes over Navy Island in the Niagara River and hopes to rally support on both sides of the border. *A Provisional Government of Upper Canada* is declared. But organization is poor.

Two leaders of the uprising, Samuel Lount, a worker, and Peter Mathews, a farmer, are executed by the colonial authorities on April 28 despite 30,000 signatures begging for clemency.

During 1838, guerrilla warfare goes on sporadically against the English. At the same time, Canadian refugees in the U.S. plan

---

1. The most notorious of these is Dr John Rolph who panicked and called out his troops three days too early. When his men were confused by this, he simply disappeared. The March on Toronto was met outside the city limits by a small delegation sent to stall the revolutionary army. The head of the delegation was Dr Rolph, as fearful as ever.

further attacks. In late 1838 and 1839, attacks are launched at Windsor and Kingston.

The British win both the Battle of Windsor and the Battle of the Windmill. The U.S. army helps them by drawing up along the border to prevent any aid from reaching the rebels -- and also by turning over some Canadian refugees in the U.S. Mother England shortly thereafter thanks Uncle Sam by giving him a few choice pieces of Canada.[2]

Colonial repression is ugly. Twenty-one prisoners of war are executed. There are 885 arrests in Upper Canada (nearly one per cent of the entire population) -- and Canadians are deported wholesale to Tasmania.[3]

The last eleven are executed in December, 1839 in Kingston. After two years of desperate struggle, the rebellion is finally crushed.

2. The Webster-Ashburton Treaty of 1842 drove a deep U.S. enclave into Canadian and Quebec territory. The British gave the U.S. navigation rights on the St John River, carved out the northern end of Maine from New Brunswick, Rouse's Point and the north end of Lake Champlain from Quebec and Isle Royale from Ontario. Saint John, N.B., was cut off from direct communication with Montreal.

3. Workers made up nearly half, and farmers over 40 per cent of the victims of repression.

Consequences of the Rebellion

The Durham Report

In February, 1839, Durham hands in his report to the Commons in London. His two main recommendations are (1) the union of the two Canadas, and (2) responsible government.

The first recommendation represents the 'solution' to the 'French-Canadian problem.' In uniting Upper and Lower Canada, in making them both into just one big province with a single assembly, one governor, and one executive, the Canayens would become a minority and, eventually, be assimilated. The second recommendation would give the elected assembly control of the budget and, consequently, power over the executive council and the governor himself. The first would satisfy the Tories of Upper and Lower Canada. They would no longer have to worry about Canayen nationalist and separatist aims. The second would satisfy the reformists of Upper Canada who had visions of possessing administrative control over the colony.

As for the Patriotes, the real Canayens, the recommendations serve as a death notice.

Durham is an imperialist, a racist and a liberal. He is an imperialist to the extent that the solutions he proposes serve the interests of the Metropolis: get rid of the Canayens and let the English colonialists participate in government to tighten the ties with the Empire. He is a racist according to the nature of his solution for the Canayen problem. He considers the English race superior and sees an opportunity for the Canayens to raise themselves to the level of a civilized people through assimilation. He is a liberal in as much as he grants responsible government to the *English* colonialists.

This is clearly demonstrated in excerpts from his report:

"The French appear to have used their democratic arms for conservative purposes, rather than those of liberal and enlightened movement; and the sympathies of the friends of reform are naturally enlisted on the side of sound amelioration which the English minority in vain attempted to introduce into the antiquated laws of the province."

Here he is blinded by his racism. He says the Canayens were aiming at conservative goals. There is nothing less conservative than wanting to overthrow the colonial regime and install a republic such as Nelson proposed in the Proclamation of 1838. In fact the Tories were the conservatives since they wanted to keep the Canayens in a state of inferiority under a colonial regime where they, the ruling class, could exploit them as they pleased. Durham, the racist, decides right from the start that nothing progressive or constructive can possibly come from the Canayen people. Only the English have a sense of progress and freedom.

He says, "the contest that was represented as a contest of classes was, in fact, a contest of the races." However, in the minds of the Canayens, it was not a struggle between the English and Canayens. If it had been, Canayens never would have accepted Wolfred Nelson, Robert Nelson, O'Callaghan, Brown and the two John Ryans into their ranks, let alone into leadership positions. Neither would they have attacked the seigneurs who were Canayens, the Clergy which was Canayen, and the *chouayens* who were Canayens.

The Patriotes' struggle was between a class of *exploiters* - English administrators, English merchants, Canayen seigneurs, the Negro-King in the robes of the Canayen Clergy - and the *exploited* class - the habitants and their enlightened elite. Even though the exploited group consisted in fact of two classes, the habitants on the one hand and the liberal professions of the petit-bourgeoisie, the doctors, lawyers, and notaries, on the other, there was a feeling of solidarity and common cause against the exploiter class. If Durham had accepted the fact that this was a class struggle, his liberal principles would have led him to recognize the legitimate demands of the exploited class, the majority of which was Canayen. But the racist in him was much stronger than the liberal, and hiding the reality of class conflict behind the smoke-screen of racial strife, he could resolve the problem by invoking Anglo-Saxon 'superiority.'

Durham's view of the Canayens is as follows: ". . . a race of men habituated to the incessant labour of a rude and unskilled agriculture, and habitually fond of social enjoyments, congregated together in rural communities, occupying portions of the wholly unappropriated soil, sufficient to provide each family with material comforts . . . under the same institutions they remained the same uninstructed, inactive, unprogressive people . . . The higher classes, and the inhabitants of the towns, have adopted some English customs and feelings; but the continued negligence of the British government left the mass of the people without any of the institutions which would have elevated them in freedom and civilization."

He praises British imperialism, saying that "the active and regular habits of the English capitalist drove out of all the more profitable kinds of industry their inert and careless competitors of the French race . . ." The English "have developed the resources of the country; they have constructed or improved its means of communication; they have created its internal and foreign commerce. The entire wholesale, and a large portion of the retail trade of the Province, with the most profitable and flourishing farms, are now in the hands of this numerical minority of the population. Therefore the mass of workers is French in the employment of English capitalists."

Without taking into account his own imperialist and scornful attitude toward the colonized, Durham reports, "The French could not but feel the superiority of English enterprise; they could not shut their eyes to their success in every undertaking in which they came into contact, and to the constant superiority which they were acquiring. They looked upon their rivals with alarm, with jealousy, and finally hatred. The English repaid them with a scorn, which soon assumed the same form of hatred."

He pays tribute to the Clergy for "their eminent services in resisting the arts of the disaffected," during the Rebellion. He says, "in the general absence of any permanent institutions of civil government, the Catholic Church has presented almost the only semblance of stability and organization, and furnished the only effectual support for civilization and order." The Negro-King did a good job for the colonizer. Understandably, Durham recommends that "the feelings and interests of the Catholic Clergy and population should invariably meet with due consideration from the Government."

He conceives of assimilation in these terms: "I entertain no doubt of the national character which must be given to Lower Canada: it must be that of the British Empire; that of the majority of British America; that of the great race which must, in the lapse of no long period of time, be predominant over the whole North American Continent. Without effecting the change so rapidly or roughly as to shock the feelings and trample on the welfare of the existing generation, it must henceforth be the first and steady purpose of the British Government to establish an English population, with English laws and language, in this Province, and to trust its government to none but a decidedly English Legislature."

This racist despot could not be more condescending than when he says, "It may be said that these are hard measures for a conquered people; that the French were originally the whole, and still are the bulk of the population of Lower Canada; that the English are newcomers, who have no right to demand the extinction of the nationality of the people, among whom commercial enterprise has drawn them . . . It may be said, that, if the French are not so civilized, so energetic, or so money-making a race as that by which they are surrounded, they are an amiable, a virtuous, and a contented people, possessing all the essentials of material comfort, and not to be despised, or ill-used, because they seek to enjoy what they have, without emulating the spirit of accumulation, which influences their neighbours."

In other words, Durham is saying that only the English are gifted with a sense of capitalist exploitation. But why feel scorn for the Canayens if they do not possess this quality? The greatest virtue in Durham's scale of values corresponds to that of the bourgeoisie - accumulation of capital through exploitation. According to Durham, the Canayens do not possess this 'virtue.' Instead, they tend to enjoy what they have.

To justify the extinction of the Canayen people, Durham relies on commercial reasons: "The pretensions of the French Canadians to the exclusive possession of Lower Canada would bar the yet larger English population of Upper Canada and the Townships from access to the great natural channel of that trade which they alone have created, and now carry on.

"The possession of the mouth of the St Lawrence concerns not only those who happen to have made their settlement along the narrow line which borders it, but all who now dwell, or will hereafter dwell, in the great basin of that river." According to Durham the Canayens are settled on the shores of the St Lawrence 'accidentally,' for no reason at all. He does not wish to recall the commercial reasons which brought the French over and are now used to justify not only the English Conquest but also the extinction of the "uninstructed, inactive and unprogressive" Canayen people.

The fastest way to swamp the Canayens is "by immigration from the British Isles, or from the United States . . . The whole interior of the British dominions must, ere long, be filled with an English population, every year rapidly increasing its numerical superiority over the French . . . The English have already in their hands the majority of the larger masses of property in the country; they have the decided superiority of intelligence on their side; they have the certainty that colonization must swell their numbers to a majority; and they belong to the race which wields the Imperial Government, and predominates on the American Continent."

Besides, Durham asks, "Is this French Canadian nationality a nationality? . . . I know of no national distinction marking and continuing a more hopeless inferiority."

"It is to elevate them from that inferiority that I desire to give the Canadians our English character." Now it's clear. We are inferior. The way to cast off our inferiority is to become English.

Durham, the colonialist, wants our extinction because he loves us. "I desire it for the sake of the educated classes, whom the distinction of language and manners keeps apart from the great Empire to which they belong . . . I desire the amalgamation still more for the sake of the humbler classes . . . If they attempt to better their condition, by extending themselves over the neighbouring country, they will necessarily get more and more mingled with an English population; if they prefer remaining stationary, the greater part of them must be labourers in the employ of English capitalists . . . The evils of poverty and dependence would merely be aggravated in a ten-fold degree, by a spirit of jealous and resentful nationality, which would separate the working classes of the community from the possessors of wealth and employers of labour."

English colonialism dispossessed us, reduced us to a state of inferiority, poverty and dependence. So that we may escape from this mess, the 'generous' colonizer is offering us the opportunity to become good English workers who speak English for English capitalists in a heaven of English bliss and harmony.

"They are a people with no history and no literature." Durham, the racist, considers us a bunch of hopeless fools. "Their nationality operates to deprive them of the enjoyments and civilizing influence of the arts."

This racism is not limited to the individual man, Lord Durham, Her Majesty's Governor. He merely expresses the racist attitudes of international colonialism in every period of history. This racism, a natural outcome of capitalist exploitation, is demonstrated in our century by the French in Algeria, Indochina and Black Africa; by the English in India, the Middle East, and Africa; and by the Americans in the Phillipines, Latin America, Vietnam, Thailand, and in their own country with respect to the Black population.

Reactions to the Durham Report
The Canayen Reaction

The Report decrees the death of the Canayen people. As a Canayen how could one not be against it? The reaction is unanimous. Even the sell-outs are against it.

The Clergy, represented by Bishop Lartigue, the anti-Patriote, overtly declares itself against the report. This is understandable; the Clergy became *Negro-King* and took sides with the colonizer in order to establish a theocracy within Canayen society. Now if the colonizer decides to get rid of this society, there will be no place for the Clergy and its theocracy. Therefore the Clergy opposes the report.

The seigneurs, sell-outs that they are, timidly oppose the report saying that perhaps it's going a bit too far, after all!

The Canayen petit-bourgeoisie, divided between defeated Patriotes and 'moderates,' unanimously condemns the extinction of the Canayen people. The Patriotes no longer have the influence they had before their defeat, so their voice will not be heard. Therefore the spokesmen for the Canayen petit-bourgeoisie are the compromisers, the 'moderates,' like Cartier, Lafontaine & Co. who gave up before things went too far. They will launch a systematic campaign against the assimilation of the Canayens.

As for the habitants, Patriotes all, they are unhappy about the report. But what can they do, now that they have been put down by force of arms? Passive resistance. Those who do not go into voluntary exile will resist assimilation with unbounded stubbornness.

The Colonizer's Reaction

In London, the report is met with approval and part of it is to be applied immediately: the union of the two Canadas, or in other words, Canayen extinction. As for responsible government, there's plenty of time for that.

The colonial administrators in the Chateau Clique are quite happy with the first recommendation - no more 'damned Frenchmen.' But they are not too pleased with the recommendation of a responsible government which would give the assembly control of the budget, since this means the members elected by the people would be keeping a close watch on their handling of public affairs.

The English merchants are euphoric. The report solves the whole 'French-Canadian problem' and what's more, by creating responsible government, grants them a voice in the administration of the country.

Aftermath of the Rebellion

Before going on to examine the applications of the Durham Report we must look at the effects of the defeat of the Rebellion on Canayen society.

The Rebellion was an attempt at a French Revolution here, an attempt to bring Quebec into contact with the historical evolution of the western world. In France, England and the United States the bourgeois class, where it did not completely assume power succeeded at least in sharing it with the monarchy.

In England, the bourgeoisie shared power with the king within the framework of a constitutional monarchy. In France, the French Revolution swept away the royalty, brought in first Napoleon's dictatorship and then a constitutional monarchy in which the middle class shared power with the Bourbons between 1815 and 1830, and with the kings of the House of Orleans until 1848. In the United States, the bourgeoisie came to power when the Thirteen Colonies declared their independence from England.

In Quebec, the petit-bourgeoisie, especially those in the liberal professions, also wanted to enter the historical current of the time by making a bourgeois revolution. To accomplish this it would have had to mobilize the people, reduce the role and influence of the Clergy, declare independence, overthrow the colonial power, and establish itself as the bourgeoisie, at the head of the Canayen state. Between 1800 and 1837 the conflicts in the Assembly were attempts at seizing power gradually and by legal means. The Rebellion was an attempt at taking power by armed struggle, when all legal means had failed.

This petit-bourgeoisie succeeded in mobilizing the people, and in rousing them against the colonial power and its puppets, the Clergy and the seigneurs. However, it would not lead the struggle to final victory because it did not have the economic power necessary. It didn't have at its disposal the industries and the trade of the French, English or American bourgeoisie. Moreover the seigneurs and the Clergy weren't its only enemies. The enemy was, above all, the English bourgeois class represent here by the colonial administrators and especially by the English merchants of Montreal. At this time, the British bourgeois class was the most powerful in the world. Proof of this is its expansionism during the entire 19th century.

How could a petit-bourgeoisie made up of a few thousand individuals, without commercial, financial or industrial backing think of fighting and defeating this English bourgeoisie? The Canayen petit-bourgeoisie counted on support from the American bourgeoisie but was mistaken. The Americans were prepared to give moral support but no more because they had good commercial relations with the English bourgeoisie. Despite their quarrels during the American War of Independence of 1774 to 1776, these "Anglo-Saxon cousins" could not see themselves divided by the aspirations of a small conquered people on the shores of the St Lawrence. Van Buren, then President of the United States, reassured Durham that the annexation of Canada was "contrary to the interests of the United States."

This Canayen petit-bourgeoisie with its bourgeois aspirations was bound to lose. Its only chance for victory lay in a People's War, a war of liberation. It is clear that the people, the habitants, fought in the Rebellion and many were killed. Their whole-hearted participation made it a people's war. But the Patriote leaders as a whole never conceived of a struggle which would lead to a revolution where the people, the habitants, would take power and establish a real people's democracy. What they did see was habitant support for the struggle of the petit-bourgeoisie to attain power and establish itself as the elite of the Canayen people. The Patriote leaders, in fact, exploited the habitants for their own ends.

The Patriote leaders lacked confidence in the habitants. They took refuge in the United States, and used it, intead of the Quebec countryside, as a base area. Had they carried on a people's war, the leaders would have begun their struggle from a habitant base. By working together, the two would have become politicized; they could have undertaken a common struggle against the colonizer and by rural guerrilla warfare, the Canayen people could have liberated themselves from English domination.

Instead of relying on the Canayen people, the Patriote leaders counted on the American bourgeoisie. This mistake cost them the resounding defeat. The habitants who had spilled their blood felt deeply deceived and betrayed. They withdrew into themselves, resigned to the fate of a colonized people, to being hewers-of-wood and drawers-of-water. Their effort during the Rebellion was so great and their defeat so disheartening that its effect was felt for a whole century.

Many, disgusted by the outcome, chose to emigrate to the United States or to the West. The rest accepted a hard life of medieval farming in the countryside, a life of fear, mistrust and passive resistance.

The failure of the Rebellion sounded the death knell of the Canayen petit-bourgeoisie. The most unyielding of the Patriotes did not return to the country. Others, less stubborn, came around later on. The 'moderates', those who left the movement before the actual Rebellion, came to share the leadership of Canayen society with the Clergy under the more rigid control of the colonial power. The economic and political aspirations of the Canayen petit-bourgeoisie were completely destroyed and all that was left for these 'moderates' to do was rally round and collaborate with the colonizer. In the years to come, Canayen society under the direction of the colonizer would be dominated by the clerical-bourgeois class, a class composed of the Clergy and the collaborating Catholic petit-bourgeoisie. No longer would the Clergy reign alone as *Negro-King*.

The Clergy is at first delighted at the failure of the Rebellion. Its rival for power, the radical and anti-clerical petit-bourgeoisie has been crushed. The Patriotes have been defeated; the parish-priests can resume their exploitation of the people. The perfect *Negro-King,* has well played its pro-colonialist role and it anxiously awaits its reward.

However, the colonizer has had to send in troops and has seen his soldiers shot down. His solution is to get rid of the Canayen people.

The Clergy's reward is its own death sentence, along with the Canayen people. Its reaction is to align itself with the 'moderates,' the lay elite, and to continue to collaborate with the colonizer, all the while trying to resist assimilation. This clerical-bourgeois group, will welcome the union of the two Canadas but at the same time try to keep their hold on the Canayen population.

This sell-out elite, like that of every colonized people, will try to forget and make the people forget the reality of their defeat, and their subservience by fabricating the myths[1] that will become the official ideology[2] propagated among the people.

The Clergy will exploit Canayen defeat and dejection to make people believe that their mission in life is not material dealings that should be 'left to the less civilized like the English' but rather in spiritual matters, such as the propagation of the Christian and Catholic faith, and the conversion of the heathen world to Christianity. The Clergy, which controls Canayen education and which founded classical colleges to recruit candidates for the priesthood, will inculcate in this conquered people the myth that they are the chosen people, called upon to convert the world. While the people, twice-defeated, live in poverty and are economically exploited by English merchants. the Clergy are sending our most gifted young people to Africa, Asia and to the Arctic as missionaries. Our best minds learn Greek, Latin, Catholic philosophy, and medieval theology in order to perpetuate White colonialism in China, Basutoland and the land of the Eskimo. The college graduates who managed to escape the Clergy's grasp will enter the liberal professions, medicine and law, only to work hand in hand with the Clergy as a lay elite, so great is their guilt over not going into the priesthood. In 1867, the same year that the colonizer legalizes his occupation of our national territory for an indefinite period of time, the Clergy will succeed in mobilizing 135 men to join the Zouaves to defend the Pope's temporal possessions in Italy.

The lay elite was to pursue a vocation too: spreading 'French civilisation' in America. We are economically, politically and culturally colonized yet our elite dreaming in technicolour, imag-

---

1. *myths:* in the political sense, imaginary explanations of situations and phenomena that are dished out to the people to keep them in a state of subjugation.

2. *ideology:* a scale of values of a group or class plus all the myths and justifications invented by it; frequently imposed by the ruling class to present a reassuring image and hide its self-interest.

ines itself the heir of French civilization and takes on the role of French civilizer in America. And, after all, France 'the eldest daughter of the Church' no longer has the right to the title because she made a nasty revolution which persecuted the Clergy. In fact, this lay mission won't go beyond elegant nationalistic speech-making in which the sell-out elite tries to make itself look good.

The elite will preach the glories of farming to the habitants. It will declare from the pulpit that the ideal man, next to the parish-priest, is the habitant who works hard, raises a large family, goes to mass every Sunday, represents the priest in his family, gives a son to the Clergy and a few daughters to the religious communities and dies of exhaustion... whereupon he may go to heaven and sit by the right hand of the Eternal Father!

The role of the Canayen woman is to step straight from innocent girlhood to motherhood, raise a large family and work alongside her husband in the fields when she is not in labour.

The clerical-bourgeois elite continues to preach land clearance and the planting of the Lord's wheat, despite the fact that there is not a single arpent of arable land left. It will, however, promote land clearance in areas such as the Gaspé Peninsula and the Laurentians so that the Canayens can cultivate -- stones. We now know that these areas, which should be reforested, can be used for their timber, not for their agricultural produce.

The three vocations of the Canayens -- *missionary, civilizer, farmer* – will be so inculcated by propaganda in the schools and churches that the people will live in medieval darkness and on the fringes of history for one hundred years before they are able to take their destiny into their own hands.

The Act of Union (1840)

In Lower Canada, the new Governor, Thompson (the future Lord Sydenham) approves the Act of Union in a special council set up by Colborne and composed of Englishmen and a few sell-out Canayens. The Canayen people are not consulted, naturally; but neither is the Clergy.

106

In Upper Canada, the situation is somewhat different. There, the people are English and their opinions count. They demand and are granted a larger representation in the Assembly than Lower Canada although their population is smaller. They want land tenure based on English law, restricting seigneurial tenure to the banks of the St Lawrence. Further, English must be proclaimed the official language. As soon as they realize that by the Act of Union, Upper Canada's debt of £1,200,000 sterling will be settled by Lower Canada, which has the stronger economy, they quickly agree.

The Act of Union (1840), then, established the *Province of Canada* with:

- a legislative council nominated for life
- an elected Assembly comprised of 42 members from each of Upper and Lower Canada
- English as the only official language in the Assembly
- property requirements of £500 for Assembly members
- public revenue controlled by the Assembly except for £45,000 sterling, the salaries of the governor and the judges, and £30,000 the salaries of senior civil servants.
- a right of veto reserved for the governor
- the right to block a bill for a maximum of two years reserved for the British monarch
- the right to create counties and nominate representatives accorded to the governor.

The English, by granting themselves larger representation, dominate the Assembly. This runs counter to their own 'democratic principles.' We can easily see that their democracy was tailor-made on the spot to serve their interests and not those of the Canayens. Ever since then, they've preached about how they brought us democracy and how, we, alas, never understood how to apply it -- insinuating that we are too stupid to understand the marvellous workings of the bourgeois democratic process!

	1840
White population in Upper Canada	450,000
White population in Lower Canada	650,000

We said above that the Canayen people were not consulted, where the population of Upper Canada was. The Canayen elite then presented a petition with 10,000 signatures to the British parliament. In vain. The conquered had dared to rebel: they were going to be put in their place. A further example of colonial despotism.

The intervention of one of the ministers of the British government was also instrumental in the rapid adoption of the Act of Union. His finance company Baring Brothers, was Upper Canada's main creditor and, as Lower Canada had 'agreed' to assume this debt, Baring would be reimbursed.

The young Pierre Chauvreau denounced this underhanded financial scheming with a poem:

> *The Bankers are having their day now!*
> *Tomorrow will be ours!*
> *Today oppression, tomorrow liberty,*
> *Today a weeping people is beaten,*
> *Tomorrow a people will be in arms,*
> *Today the felony, tomorrow the vengeance,*
> *Today gold commands*
> *Tomorrow it will be steel.*

The Act of Union was passed. A United Canada assured the English minority a majority and condemned the French to a minority role. Thus, Lord Durham's first recommendation had become law.

The second, responsible government, will be delayed. What exactly is 'responsible government'? It is the control by the Assembly, over the government, here, the Executive Council. Until now, decisions were made and carried out by the governor and the Executive Council which he nominated under a system of patronage. In effect, the governor and his Council had dictatorial powers. The power which the elected Assembly had won over the budget was not enough. It wanted the Executive Council to be answerable to the Assembly (bourgeois democracy) and not to the governor (feudal dictatorship).

Therefore, the Assembly demands that the governor be stripped of executive powers and that members of the Executive Council be nominated from the Assembly. As the Assembly is made up of political parties (in Lower Canada, Tories and Reformists) they must be nominated from among members of the majority party. Thus the majority party in the Assembly will occupy executive posts in the Executive Council, or Cabinet as it is called today.

The first Governor of United Canada, Sydenham, opposes responsible government. In the first election, he supports the Tories as they are not as sold on responsible government as the Reformists. He even changes county limits in Montreal and Quebec City to promote his own candidates. When this does not work he uses bouncers to intimidate Canayens who want to vote Reformist and against the Act of Union. Sydenham's tactics succeed : nineteen of his own candidates are elected out of forty-two in Lower Canada. (The birth of the electoral tactics we are so familiar with in Quebec? Duplessis didn't invent anything; he was simply the star pupil of our English 'masters'!)

Lafontaine, the timid 'moderate,' the Patriote-turned-collaborator, sees his chance as sell-out leader of a vanquished people. He decides to run for office and issues a proclamation cleary indicating that he will lick English boots. He speaks of a Canada, homeland of French Canadians but, also the adopted country of the English. Our happiness is to depend on social equality and political freedom!

He denounces the Union, all right, but agrees to play ball with the English. Instead of refusing to collaborate with the regime, as a self-respecting Patriote would do, he urges the Canayens to participate, to vote, to accept the 'democratic game.' Lafontaine behaves just like the obedient *Negro-King* who knows that he will never rule in his own right but hopes against all hope for a few crumbs from the colonizer.

Lafontaine runs in Terrebonne. Sydenham sends out several hundred bouncers, Englishmen from Montreal and Scotsmen from Glengarry (Ontario), to 'support' his candidate. Lafontaine withdraws from the contest proclaiming that "there are defeats more honorable than victory." Oh honour! This tendency of our elites to place their honour far 'above' election campaign riots permits them to keep their heads in the clouds so as not to see themselves grovelling on their knees.

Etienne Parent, of the anti-patriote newspaper *Le Canadien*, and Augustin Morin are elected. They agree completely with Lafontaine: play the English game and get close to the Reformists of Upper Canada because they are for responsible government which could give the Canayens a voice. During the session, the Reformists carry on their struggle for responsible government but Sydenham systematically blocks them. He dies shortly after and is replaced by Bagot.

It is now 1842. Lafontaine, who maintains good relations with Baldwin, the Reformist in Upper Canada, is elected to represent Toronto (!) thanks to Baldwin's help. Bagot asks Lafontaine and Baldwin to assume the posts of attorney general, the former for Lower Canada, the latter for Upper Canada. In effect, (but not in law) Bagot grants the reformists responsible government.

But Bagot dies in 1843. Metcalfe replaces him and once again Sydenham's methods are tried — with the result that Metcalfe is forced to dissolve the Assembly. Elections follow. Twenty-eight Reformists are elected in Lower Canada, eleven in Upper Canada. The Tories, who have the majority, favor government by the governor. When the Assembly meets in Montreal, the new capital, several bills are passed including £40.000 sterling compensation for losses sustained by Upper Canada during their Rebellion of 1837. Lafontaine timidly protests but no indemnity will be given to Lower Canada.

Finally, Responsible Government

In 1845, Metcalfe dies to be replaced in 1846 by Lord Elgin. The Whigs (Liberal Party) have come to power in England and call upon Elgin to grant Canada responsible government. In the 1847 elections, the Reformists win a strong majority and Baldwin and Lafontaine are invited to form the new government.

Henceforth, the majority party in the Assembly will govern the colony. The governor will simply be the Queen's representative and the liaison officer between metropolis and colony. The *Colonial Office* (the minister in the British Government who looks after the colonies) however, reserves for itself all powers relating to commerce, foreign affairs, defence and constitutional amendment.

England can easily grant responsible government to her Canadian colony now that there is no longer any Canayen threat. The Canayens have been definitively defeated; their leaders play the parliamentary game, speak English on command and integrate themselves into British institutions. A few concessions are even in order -- to bind them all the more strongly to the colonial masters. The French language becomes official in 1849.

Everything has been well planned. Colonial principles well-applied can prevail over the Canayens. The foremost is *divide-and-rule*. Lord Elgin conceals nothing in his letters to Grey at the Colonial Office: "I believe that the problem of how to govern Canada would be solved if the French would split into a Liberal and a Conservative Party and join the Upper Canadian parties bearing the corresponding names. The great difficulty hitherto has been that a Conservative Government has meant Government by Upper Canadians which is intolerable to the French and a Radical Government has meant a Government by the French which is no less hateful to the British. . . The national element would be merged in the political if the split to which I refer were accomplished."

The Assembly is now called *Parliament*.

Papineau returns in 1845. He publishes a manifesto openly critical of Great Britain, the Act of Union, Responsible Government and every existing institution. Nonetheless, he accepts his election by acclamation to the new Parliament and takes his seat next to Lafontaine and the other Reformists.

In 1848, revolution breaks out again in France. There is a rumbling in Italy. In Ireland, the struggle against English colonialism takes on greater proportions. Afraid that Papineau may exploit this agitation and arouse the people, Lord Elgin is ready to buy him off with a ministerial post. He needn't have worried.

The Reformists themselves fear Papineau's influence and move to combat it. Bishop Bourget plays his part and says in a pastoral letter: "For we are all children of the same Father who is in Heaven; we all live under the same Government which has no other end but the welfare of its subjects, and which must take its glory from ruling peoples speaking all the languages of the world;

111

we all have the same rights; we are all members of the great family of the mighty British Empire; and finally we are all called
on to possess together the same land of the living, after we shall
have finished our pilgrimage in this land of exile."

Papineau answers by founding the *Democratic Party*, (also called the *Rouges*) which is made up of young radicals. He demands
abrogation of the Union and once more tries to stir up Canayen
nationalism.

Monseigneur, with Lord Elgin's blessing, again launches the
campaign for land colonization to counter emigration to the United
States. Between 1844 and 1849, twenty thousand Canayens left
Quebec. The Clergy, "the most powerful influence in Lower Ca-
nada," according to Elgin, encourages young Canayens to go and
chop down trees in the Lac-St Jean region for the capitalist
William Price and in the St Maurice and Ottawa Valley for the
American capitalist, Philémon Wright.

During this time, Lafontaine, in the *Revue Canadienne* speaks
to the young *Rouges:* "... tell us, at what period of our history
has the French Canadian people been more brilliant, more honoured, more respected, or has occupied a higher position than it
holds today?"

At the same time, the British government is moving toward a
new kind of commercial policy: free trade. Free means the abolition of preferential treatment for the colonies. The metropolis
does not wish to pay higher prices in the colonies for what it can
get more cheaply elsewhere. The Canadian wheat and lumber
industries suffer. The Montreal merchants are discontent. Further, 100,000 destitute immigrants come to Canada in the one
year, 1847.

In January 1849, Parliament reconvenes. Lafontaine and Baldwin
form the government. They propose indemnities for losses suffered in Lower Canada during the Rebellion -- just as was done
for Upper Canada some years earlier. Parliament passes the
Rebellion Losses Bill; but the day Elgin signs it, some 1,500 English come down from Westmount. The *Gazette* urges them on:
"It is the beginning of the End! Anglo Saxons! You must live for
the future, your blood and your race henceforward will be your
supreme law, if you are faithful to yourselves. You will be Eng-

lish, even if you no longer may be British". They loot and set fire to Parliament. English gangs prowl the streets of Montreal and, for a whole week, ransack the houses of the Reformists.

One law destined to aid the habitants whose farms were burned by Colborne is an occasion for the Westmount racists to raze to the ground their most cherished institution, their Parliament. They use this same opportunity to show their opposition to the mother country's commercial policies of free-trade. They create the *British American League* which promotes severing the British connection and annexation to the United States.

The Union Fails

The alliance between the Reformists of Upper and Lower Canada, between Baldwin and Lafontaine, allowed for a parliamentary majority.

But now new tendencies are developing and consequently new parties are forming. No party can now have a majority in Upper as well as in Lower Canada at the same time. Baldwin and Lafontaine, exhausted from their ten-year spin on a political merry-go-round, retire from public life.

In Lower Canada there are now:

- The Tories, largely the English merchants and English colonists of the Eastern Townships
- The Reformists, for the most part Canayens of the collaborating elite
- The Rouges, heirs to the Patriotes, who denounce the Union and demand constitutional reforms; the Patriote programme minus armed struggle. Papineau is a member of this party. The Tories and the Reformists will get together and form the *Bleus*. Morin and Cartier are the leaders of this aligment.

In Upper Canada:

- Tories, in this case administrators and conservative merchants
- Reformists, representing the petit-bourgeoisie of Upper Canada
- The *Clear-Grits,* radical farmers who oppose urban commercial interests.

113

POLITICAL PARTIES UNDER THE UNION

Lower-Canada	Upper-Canada
Tories	Tories
Reformists	Reformists
Rouges	Clear-Grits

Reorganization of the Parties

Tories and Reformists unite to make up the *Bleus* in Lower Canada and the Liberal Conservative Party in Upper Canada. *Bleus* and Conservatives (Liberal Conservative Party) will work together in the conservative party. The *Rouges* will become the liberal party.

Lower-Canada	Upper-Canada
Rouges	Conservatives
Bleus	Clear-Grits

They call for non-denominational schools and elected governors.

These Clear-Grits are violently anti-Canayen. In 1851, when the population of Upper Canada exceeds that of Lower Canada, they'll demand proportional representation of the population. Their leader is newspaper publisher George Brown. Boulton, one of their spokesmen, will state at a banquet, "The negroes are the great difficulty of the States and the French Canadians of Canada".

114

As in Lower Canada, the Tories will get together with the Reformists to form the *Liberal Conservative Party*. Macdonald will be their leader.

We can see that in Upper as well as in Lower Canada the landowning bourgeois class (Tories) and the petit-bourgeoisie (Reformists) are making peace and working together for their common interests. The Tories have understood that certain reforms (like responsible government) and certain alliances with elements of the petit-bourgeoisie must be accepted. And the Reformists, having obtained their desired reforms, find their position very close to that of the Tories and see that it is in their interests to work with them. This is how someone like Cartier, who had been sympathetic to the Patriote cause, became a Bleu, a conservative working in the interests of the pro-British Tories by becoming the lawyer for the Grand Trunk Railway.

The Upper Canadian Conservative alignment (Tories and Reformists) shared the same pro-imperialist interests with the Bleus of Lower Canada. This is the social basis of the Macdonald - Cartier alliance.

The Rouge Party of Lower Canada, however, is violently opposed to the Bleus, Conservatives *and* Clear-Grits. There can be no question of collaboration between the Rouges who oppose the Union and some other party in Upper Canada which supports it.

When the Clear-Grits get a majority of seats in Upper Canada in 1857, the government is completely paralyzed. The Bleus, who have the majority in Lower Canada, cannot form a government because if they did the Grits would be up in arms against 'French Domination'. And if the Grits formed a government, Lower Canada could not be represented in the government. This dilemma will be resolved when the Grits collaborate with Macdonald in 1864 on the condition of changing the constitution or, in other words, adopting the federal system. The Grits will get their confederation, which will mean greater autonomy for Upper Canada. In order to get it, they will have the support of the Bleus and the Conservatives who anticipate economic expansion under confederation. The Rouges, the representatives of radical elements in Lower Canada, can do nothing but withdraw. Confederation will be imposed on the Quebec people.

Confederation

Economic interests Underlying Confederation

With the defeat of the Rebellion, the English became the uncontested masters of Canada. The Montreal English merchants were able to extend their economic domination without opposition and help themselves to Canayen *cheap-labour* to their hearts' content. They had at their beck and call, the clerical and lay puppet rulers. The Clergy played its role and the bourgeoisie including sell-outs like Georges-Etienne Cartier would also play theirs perfectly.

The merchants relied on the wheat and lumber trade. These products entered England duty-free. The merchants exploited this situation to the extent of buying these products in the United States to sell them in England.

The St Lawrence was therefore an important waterway for the shipment of this merchandise. Montreal and Quebec were the two important ports. The rapids and falls that obstructed shipping were diverted by a series of canals: the Welland canal to avoid Niagara Falls, the Rideau Canal to connect Lake Ontario and the Ottawa River, the Lachine Canal to avoid the Lachine Rapids, and the Cornwall and Beauharnais Canal to join Lake Ontario with the mouth of the Ottawa near Montreal.

These English merchants exploited Canayen cheap-labour as lumbermen in the Lac-St Jean region, in the Mauricie and in the Ottawa Valley. They also exploited the cheap-labour of the Irish

116

immigrants -- 30,000 Irish were arriving each year because of the potato famine back home.

They were crowded into ships used for shipping wheat and lumber to England; the typhus and cholera they brought with them reached epidemic proportions here in 1847-48. There would be 800,000 more to come. The English merchants were pleased to have these English-speaking immigrants replace the Canayens who were themselves emigrating to the United States in great numbers. The remaining Canayens worked as wood-cutters and loggers for companies like Price Brothers. Similarly in agriculture: in 1840, the English merchants owned two-thirds of the seigneuries; the habitants were used as their cheap-labour.

In spite of all this, these merchants have their problems too, though not in the area of cheap-labour, but from the British. The metropolis adopts a free-trade policy because the English merchants and bourgeoisie find it less profitable to buy goods at preferential tariff prices when they can buy them cheaper in the U.S. The metropolis cuts preferential tariffs on wheat and lumber coming from Canada. Result: the Americans no longer sell lumber or wheat to the Montreal English merchants but go direct to England; the wheat and lumber merchants of Upper Canada send their products to New York via American canals. The Montreal merchants immediately turn to the United States for a solution. They are tempted to join the U.S. but finally opt for the Reciprocity Treaty of 1854 that abolishes duty on wheat and lumber, fish and coal between the Canadas and the United States for a ten-year period.

Developing a railroad network becomes another solution for the merchants. In 1850, the United States had 9,000 miles of railway, Canada had 66. With a railway line running from the Great Lakes to the Atlantic seaports, they could ship their lumber and wheat to England in winter as well as summer. However, a great deal of capital would be required for such a network. The merchants are not ready to risk their own capital so they turn to the state treasury. But here again the state is too small for this kind of economic expansion. United Canada is limited to the shores of the St. Lawrence in the east and the Great Lakes in the north. Why not join the maritime colonies (Nova Scotia and Newfoundland) to

United Canada to form a country that would take on proportions relative to the grand economic ambitions?

A confederation stretching from the Atlantic to Lake Superior with a strong central government would perfectly serve the interests of the English merchants. What were they waiting for? In a country of this size, the Canayens would be reduced to one third of the population and could not prevent the masters of the country from governing them as they wish. The uneasy relationship with the American neighbour provides another reason for federation. The U.S. is on the verge of the War of Secession (1861-66). The southern states, fed up with domination by the industrial north, want to withdraw from the union. Because England supports the southern states, the north refuses to renew the Reciprocity Treaty. In United Canada there are fears of invasion by U.S. troops and even of annexation by force.

Where is the opposition to this confederation?

The metropolis, at first dubious, backs it to the hilt. A rearrangement of its North American colonies would cut down certain expenses that could be assumed by a larger and stronger colonial state, and provide a more secure base for British investment − especially in view of the expansionist aims of the American neighbour.

The English merchants from Upper and Lower Canada are all in favour of confederation which they, after all, conceived to benefit themselves. This parasite, sell-out bourgeoisie stands to profit from the railways and the increased resource extraction and trade they will bring. Georges-Etienne Cartier, leader of the Bleus, is already working for the Grand Trunk.

The farmers and small businessmen who form the petit-bourgeois backbone of Brown's Clear-Grits promote confederation because it means a larger economic unit in which to operate and more money for public works. The Clear-Grits are an expansionist party with the outlook of the national bourgeoisie, which means that they want to take over political and economic power from the ruling pro-British Tory merchants. They also see confederation as a way to prevent annexation to the U.S. and to further reduce Canayen influence.

As for the workers of Upper Canada, they are not consulted. But their opposition to George Brown, leader of the Clear-Grits, is as one man throughout this period. As publisher of the *Globe* Brown organizes Toronto employers against the workers' movement for a nine-hour day, personally calling the police to arrest trade union leaders in 1872. "Ostracize the union men and drive them from Canada," was the slogan of this great 'reformer' who had been opposing trade unions since 1845. The Nine-Hour Movement succeeded and Brown was assassinated in 1880 by one of his own workers!

The Canayen people are against confederation but are not consulted. The Rouge party tries hard to demonstrate the Canayen opposition to a second union which simply confirms their defeat and reduces them to a still more insignificant minority.

The Red men, the first inhabitants of the country, are not even informed of the White man's political manoeuvres. They will be kept in mind when the *British North America Act* is drawn up to give the central government the power to put them in concentration camps called *reserves*.

In the Maritime provinces, however, the local capitalists organized resistance to confederation. These merchants who reaped great profits from the trade with Britain and the U.S. feared that the scheme, worked out behind closed doors in the United Canadas, would wipe out their monopolies and saddle them with debts. The masses of the people saw their regional identity threatened. The Newfoundland government which supported confederation was defeated at the poles. Prince Edward Island also opposed it.

In Nova Scotia, Joseph Howe's lieutenant Annand said: "We will not willingly allow ourselves to be brought to subjection to Canada or any other country". He demanded "exact equality" and not "the detestable confederation that has been attempted to be forced upon us. . . a union brought about by corrupt and arbitrary means".

No sooner had the Canadian Assembly endorsed confederation than the New Brunswick electorate repudiated it in March, 1865. It was only through the combined efforts of the Colonial Office, the Governor General, the Lieutenant-Governor of New Brunswick, the Canadian government and the Grand Trunk railway that it was passed the following year. Tilley, one of the great 'Fathers of Confederation,' sent Macdonald a telegramme saying , "We'll need 40 or 50,000." The money was sent to Tilley via a Grand Trunk manager Brydges who passed it on through a wealthy New Brunswick shipowner in Portland, Maine.

Macdonald was well aware of the widespread opposition to confederation, for he wrote in a letter to Tilley shortly after this 'victory': "It appears to us to be important that the Bill (i.e. the British North America Act) should not be finally settled until just before the meeting of the British Parliament. The measure must be carried *per saltum* (in one leap) and no echo of it must reverberate through the British provinces until it becomes law... The Act once passed and beyond remedy, the people would soon learn to be reconciled to it."

In short, the merchants can go full speed ahead over all opposition. United Canada already has a debt of $19,000,000 because of the construction of canals benefitting the merchants. Around 1860 the debt will increase to over $54,000,000 all for financing railways which will also benefit the merchants.

Let us stop for a moment to examine the relationship between the merchants and the state. The state is the administration of the country; it is a government that administers and a parliament that approves certain laws made for 'good' administration. This state, this government, is at this time (and still today) in the hands of the class of people who control the means of production -- that is, the bourgeoisie which owns the wealth of the country. This class is elected by the people but is not responsible to the people. The people had to struggle hard for democratic rights. The bourgeoisie conceded the right of election only because it was forced to do so. But, he who owns the wealth can afford to *buy* elections, and no sooner are elections granted than they are perverted by the ruling class. The people are given the choice of which master they want, but whenever the opportunity arises for them to choose to have no master, the rules are changed or elections are suspended. There is nothing to prevent a man of the people from being elected but this most often means that he gets nowhere, or the bourgeoisie unseats him, or the bourgeoisie corrupts him.

120

The merchants ask for state aid when it is a question of far-reaching projects like railroad contruction. The state agrees because it is under their control. The state takes money from the taxpayers and lends it to railway companies (formed by the same merchants) at a very low rate of interest. If the state does not receive enough money from taxes, it borrows. But from whom? From banks, which also belong to the merchants. But here, it often borrows at a very high rate of interest. The state then borrows from the merchants at high rates to lend to the same merchants at low rates, consequently incurring a debt that the taxpayers must repay. The merchants make fantastic profits that allow them to buy the next elections, increase their investments and extend their economic, political and cultural domination over the people.

The English bourgeoisie have systematically played these political tricks on the Canayen people. In order to cover their own tracks, they enlist the aid of certain Canayens, men like Georges-Etienne Cartier.

Georges-Etienne Cartier's father was one of the founders of the Bank of Montreal and the St Lawrence-Lake Champlain railway. His grandfather had made money in the salt, fish and wheat trade and his family owned large properties. We immediately see that his class interests lead him to collaborate with the English bourgeoisie. He received a 'good' education with the Sulpicians and became a lawyer. He briefly joined the Patriote movement, which included members of the non-landowning petit-bourgeoisie, but quickly came back to the fold as a moderate and fought against the young Rouges. He was elected member from Verchères in 1848 and soon after began to ask for state aid to construct the St Lawrence and Atlantic Railway in which his family and English bourgeois friends had interests. Serving the same interests a few years later, he became lawyer for the Grand Trunk Railway Company joining up with Hincks, Galt and Merritt who, like him, play the double role of merchant and politician. In 1871 this is repeated with the creation of the Canadian Pacific. He got along so well with the English bourgeoisie that they adopted him. He became attorney-general, then formed the Macdonald-Cartier government which brought about Confederation.

This sell-out tried to make the Canayens swallow Confederation and had the audacity to call them his compatriots. He spoke of the 'dangerous isolation' of Quebec and about the threat of absorption by the United States if Quebec did not enter Confederation. He said incredible things like: "In confiding their interests to a federal government, the French population give proof of their trust in our English fellow countrymen." As a traitor to the Canayen nation, he could speak of "trust in our English fellow countrymen" because he worked hand in hand with the fellows in the same class as himself. But the people, twice defeated by force of arms, were not able to trust. It is not possible to trust a colonizer who uses every means to maintain his domination.

Under the United Canada regime with two provinces equally represented in Parliament, the Canayens, although they had no say, obstructed by their mere existence, the smooth functioning of the government. That was at least one form of opposition. But with Confederation the English bourgeoisie and Cartier eliminated even this mute opposition. There would be two levels of government, federal (or central) and provincial (or local). At the federal level where all the important powers were centralized, Quebec no longer found itself with half of the membership in Parliament but with less than one third. Less than a third is less than a half but the sell-out Cartier tried to make the Canayens believe that Confederation was for their benefit. Since he could not make figures lie, he said that the Canayens could do whatever they wanted on the second level of government, the provincial. (We will later see the limited powers at this level of government).

The Clergy saw that its interests would be protected in Confederation if it stuck with Cartier who proclaimed: "Those of the Clergy who are high in authority, as well as those in humbler positions, have declared for Confederation, not only because they see in it all possible security for the institutions they cherish, but also because their Protestant fellow countrymen, like themselves, are guaranteed their rights as well. The Clergy in general are opposed to all political dissension, and if they are favourable to the project, it is because they see in Confederation a solution to the difficulties which have so long existed."

What Cartier did was to rally the most conservative, the most anti-democratic elements of Canayen society. He even used the

American War of Secession to sully the principle of democracy and to promote the benefits of monarchy. "While the American union has divided against itself, the Canadians who have had the advantage of seeing republicanism in operation for a period of eighty years, of perceiving its faults and vices, have been convinced that purely democratic institutions cannot assure the peace and prosperity of nations, and that we must unite under a federation so formed as to perpetuate the monarchical element."

Opposition to Confederation was organized in Quebec under the direction of the Rouge party who denounced English capitalist interests behind the project and the adoption of the new constitution without consulting the people. Petitions containing 20,000 signatures were presented to Parliament but to no avail. The English bourgeoisie, Cartier and the Clergy were not afraid of the Canayen people. They had made short work of them in 1837-38 and felt they could now lead them as they saw fit.

The People's Silence

In relating the history of 1837-1867 (Rebellion to Confederation) we are forever talking about responsible government, the Durham Report, elections and government problems. What we are really discussing is the colonizer's testing of new formulas to keep the people in subjugation. During this time, what has been happening among the people?

The Canayen people, who responded to the *Patriote* leaders' call for revolt with thunderous revolutionary enthusiasm, find themselves, after the failure of the Rebellion, in a serious state of collective despondency. In point of fact, *Patriote* leaders had deserted the people. They were not of the people and did not integrate themselves with the people. The people fought, sacrificed themselves, spilled their blood, were beaten down, whereas almost all the leaders emerged unharmed. The people felt that they had been tricked, if not betrayed, by the leaders who dangled such bright prospects of liberation before them. As we have seen, some *habitants* emigrated to the United States. The others, mistrustful, withdrew into themselves. They took refuge in passivity and listened to the voice of the Clergy who now more than ever would exploit the defeat of the Rebellion to boost its leadership and consolidate its domination over the people.

The Rouge party tried hard to keep the Patriote fervor alive but in the eyes of the people, the Rouges presented a sterile opposition after the defeat. Did the Rouges seriously consider continuing the struggle by founding a people's army of liberation? No. The Rouge party carried on the struggle at the level of propaganda only, by publishing newspapers and books. The people would come to see the Rouges as a club of intellectuals becoming less and less radical, more and more reformist and in the long run, an inoffensive Liberal Party.

This Rouge party made up of elements from the radical, petit-bourgeois, Canayen elite published three newspapers, *L'Avenir, le Pays* and *le Défricheur* and carried on a tough verbal struggle against the Durham report, against the Union of the Canadas, against the Reformists and against Confederation. It became the primary force behing the *Institut Canadien de Montréal,* a literary and scientific association founded in 1844 as an intellectual centre for graduates of the classical colleges in the absence of a French lay university. (Remember that the English already had McGill University in 1829). Young men in the Rouge party read, in the Institut Canadien library, works of Voltaire, Lamartine, Pascal, Montesquieu, Montaigne and Lamennais, authors in the Index of forbidden books. They engaged in lively discussions on political freedom of expression and thought. In 1857 the Institut Canadien boasted 700 members.

The Clergy soon counter-attacked with the creation of parallel institutions *l'Oeuvre des bons livres* and the *Cabinet,* a reading-room. Monseigneur Bourget, successor to Lartigue, led the battle. He had pastoral letters circulated condemning the Institut. Members of the Institut attempted to make the authorities understand that the books in their library did not attack religion or Catholic morals. In 1869, Bourget had the Institut's catalogue put in the *Index,* which meant excommunication for those who dared to open it.

That same year, the printer Guibord, member of the Institut, died without receiving the last sacraments. The priest who he called to his bedside refused him the last rites because of Guibord's affiliation with the Institut. The parish priest of Notre

Dame also refused to bury him in the consecrated part of the cemetery. Guibord's friends, of the Institut, confronted with this refusal, showed up with the body the following Sunday at the Côte-des-Neiges cemetery. The care-taker refused to let them in. So, they went instead to a Protestant cemetery to bury the body temporarily and then took action against the parish-priest. The trial soon became a contest between, on the one hand, the staunch supporters of the laws, privileges and authority of the Church, and on the other, supporters of civil liberties, freedom of speech and thought.

This conflict was a good indication of how much Canayen society had regressed in such a short time after the big economic and political conflict of the Rebellion. The colonized, who were now defeated and set aside from the mainstream of history, went backwards a few centuries and found themselves pouring all their energy into medieval quarrels. The colonizer no doubt found it amusing to see the colonized cursing each other while lugging around a corpse from one cemetery to another. The colonized people were caught up in sterile wrangling. The colonizer's tactic of divide and rule had worked: now he just had to watch the show.

The judge, who had liberal leanings, ordered the parish to bury Guibord in the Catholic cemetery. The following year his judgment was repealed by the Court of Appeals which said that the Clergy had been within its rights. Guibord's friends appealed to the Court of the Queen's Bench which confirmed the judgment of the Court of Appeals. So they took the affair to the Privy Council in London. This Council ordered the parish to bury Guibord in the Catholic part of the cemetery by evoking the subordination of canon law to civil law under the French Regime.

On September 2nd, 1875, Guibord's friends exhumed the coffin, covered it with an English flag and carried it to the Catholic cemetery where thousands of enraged Catholics were waiting. They blocked the entrance and chased the liberals out to the Protestant cemetery, pummelling them with stones. On November 16, after more lawsuits and heated debates in the newspapers, the coffin again left the Protestant cemetery for the Catholic one but under guard of 1,235 soldiers. The grave was filled with cement to prevent it from being desecrated and a guard was placed beside it. In a pastoral letter, Monseigneur Bourget said that despite the burial in a Catholic cemetery the grave would always be separated from consecrated ground. As an epitaph he suggested: "There lies a rebel who has been buried by force of arms."

London, by taking sides with the liberals against the Clergy, accentuated the division amongst the Canayens, aggravating the sterile, ridiculous quarrels which prevented the colonized from organizing against the colonizer.

Why did the Rouge party fall into this trap? It seems that those who claimed to be the heirs of the Patriotes were in fact nothing but their pale reflections. Why the desire to give Guibord a Christian burial-place? Why did they not bury him in a non-denominational cemetery that they could have inaugurated for the occasion? How did they think that they could advance the cause of civil liberties by forcing the Church to accept recalcitrants into its bosom? Why the English flag on the coffin? Could they not see that this symbol would identify them with the colonizer? As progressives who wished to win the people over to their cause, they stupidly contradicted themselves and alienated the people, who rightly rejected a group of intellectuals parading around with a coffin covered with the symbol of their oppression. These members of the Rouge party, these liberals, were in brief, moderate Catholics who spent all their energy combatting the extreme Catholics, more Catholic than the Pope.

It was a quarrel between parishioners and not at all between proponents of civil and religious liberties on the one hand and defenders of absolute theocracy on the other. The Rouge party who thought it was progressive, was not. They merely imitated the vocabulary of the progressive forces of the times. They tried to adopt progressive ideas like the separation of Church and State, but in actual combat it was clear that they carried on a rearguard struggle and gathered together conservatives disguised as radicals. Once aware of this deep conservatism behind a progressive mask, we can understand how the so-called radical Rouge party became the Liberal Party we know today.

When we consider the fact that the progressive elite can resort to brawling over a corpse in the middle of a Catholic cemetery, we realize what a fantastic hold the Church had got over the Canayen people since the Rebellion.

Here are a few other examples of this domination.

The historian François-Xavier Garneau wanted to take up Durham's challenge whose report described us as a people "without a literature and without a history." He wrote, *The History of Canada from its Discovery to the Present Day*. As soon as it was published, he had problems with the Clergy who felt that he did not sufficiently emphasize the religious aspect of the colonization of New France. Garneau, who had been sympathetic to the Patriotes, forgot his radical past as quickly as possible and in the following editions stated that the survival of the Canayen people was definitely linked to its Catholic faith. But this was not enough. The 1859 edition underwent the censure of the Clergy who tore out paragraphs and demanded that the author rewrite certain pages. Our first historian submitted to the dictatorship of the Clergy.

After the Rebellion, the Clergy realized what strength there was in nationalism. After all, it had seen habitants lay down their lives for the liberation of Quebec. It understood that Canayen nationalism would be the instrument for keeping the Canayens under its thumb. That is why the Clergy demanded that Garneau write that the Canayen people could not survive without the Catholic faith, in other words, without the Clergy. From then on it spread the idea that "it is thanks to the Clergy that the Canayens still exist". We still hear this utter fabrication today.

But the truth lies elsewhere. If the Canayen people have survived, it is *despite* the Clergy which was prepared to commit the worst kind of national betrayal in order to maintain its domination. Some nationalists like our poet Crémazie were daring enough to say that language played a role in preserving our nationality. He stated that our language was "the second guardian of our nationality, since religion is the first."

Reverend Casgrain set himself up as a literary critic and watched over the literature of that time like a dictator. He said, "If literature is a reflection of the mores, character, capacities and genius of a people as it undoubtedly is, ours will be serious, meditative, spiritual, religious, evangelical like our missionaries, generous like our martyrs, strong and persevering like our pioneers of old. But it will be, above all, religious, imbued with faith. . . That is its sole condition for existence. It has no other *raison d'être.*" He insisted that Philippe-Aubert de Gaspé alter some passages of his *Anciens Canadiens,* a work already so anti-revolutionary, so monarchist, so Catholic that one would think it was written by a medieval monk. The poets of *L'Ecole de Québec* which brought together Crémazie, Garneau, the Reverend Ferland, Gérin-Lajoie and a few others, always submitted their works to the arch-Catholic Casgrain's scissors.

The most appreciated literary works fell into the category of Gérin-Lajoie's *Jean Rivard, the Colonist.* The author preached a return to the land and the necessity of hard work and frugality. The hero of the book decides, after finishing his studies, to serve his country by going to clear virgin lands, building a home for his sweetheart and founding a parish that would attract other young people who may be tempted to emigrate to the United States.

The propaganda of the Clergy turned the revolutionary nationalism of the Rebellion into a conservative, reactionary monarchist nationalism, a nationalism looking to the past, a nationalism which promoted the myth of a chosen people. In 1855, the arrival of the *Capricieuse* the first French boat to arrive at a port on the St. Lawrence since the Conquest, sparked off demonstrations of this kind of nationalism. There was joy and cheering dancing and singing; "France has come back." There were festivities and demonstrations of patriotic fervour.

An attempt was made to awaken among the people an allegiance to a mother country they had rejected a long time ago, an allegiance to a good old mother who had erred, one must admit, by falling into the arms of the Revolution. At the same time the British kept a close eye on the goings-on in case France tried to promote her liberal ideas here. The *Capricieuse* had come to pay a courtesy call after Queen Victoria had made an alliance with Napoleon III, Emperor of the French. France had not come back. She had simply paid a little visit. A sort of longing was whipped up among the Canayens for a mother they would never see again except in a few portraits.

In fact, a cultural colonialism vis-à-vis France was being devised. The Canayens were kept out of contact with reality, in dreams of past grandeur when France dominated Canada. In this way the colonized Canayen was prevented from becoming self-reliant, from identifying himself as a Canayen, as a man from this country, colonized to be sure, but ready to struggle against this colonialism. They tried to keep him in an infantile state. The Clergy made the people into children, kept them in crass ignorance and blind dependence in order to establish its total domination over them.

Another example of this aberrant nationalism, this nationalism steeped in reactionary Catholicism is the raising of the *zouave* army in 1867. The same year that the clerical-bourgeois elite, the Clergy, Cartier and friends locked the people into the prison of Confederation and subjected them to a greater degree of economic, political and cultural colonialism, 135 volunteers were sent to Italy to defend the economic interests of the Pope.

At this time Italy, which was divided up into numerous independent little states among which were the Papal states, was in the process of unification. Garibaldi and his troops had the Italian population of these states and even those of the Papal territories on their side. The Pope who saw his temporal power collapsing cried for help and declared a holy war. Napoleon III, no more Catholic than Garibaldi but no more anxious to see a united Italy which could represent a threat to French power, sent some troops, called the papal *zouaves,* to defend the Pope against Garibaldi. Monseigneur Bourget felt it his duty to do likewise even though the Pope had asked only for financial assistance. He raised a contingent of 135 volunteers, chosen more for their moral conduct than for their military prowess. They left for Paris in 1868 but did not see any action because Garibaldi's movement collapsed and the transfer of the lands of the Papal Estates to a unified Italy was brought about by negotiations. At the same time a propaganda campaign against liberalism was in full force. According to Monseigneur Laflèche, French Canada had a "Providential mission of maintaining and spreading the Kingdom of God in the New World." It was therefore necessary to avoid all contamination from liberalism.

These arch-religionists called *Ultramontains* preached the supremacy of the Church over the State, the absolute control of the Clergy over every activity of the ordinary citizen. Monseigneur Bourget had some religious orders sent over from France. The Jesuits extended their influence even more. Numerous colleges were founded. In 1852, Laval University under absolute control of the Clergy was founded but the Institut Canadien which the liberal intellectuals had wanted to convert into a lay university was crushed. When the Canayen workers began to organize in unions around 1850, the Clergy accused them of forming "dangerous secret societies." The American union, *Knights of Labour* which at that time represented a workers' movement that wanted to change the social structure in favour of the working class, managed to get a toe-hold in Quebec in 1881 but five years later disappeared from the scene because of virulent attacks by Monseigneur Tachereau.

The Clergy began to create Catholic unions which were nothing but company unions, sold out from the start to the bosses.

On the political level, the Clergy as a whole was Bleu. A few Rouges could be found amongst them but they kept silent. Yet the *Ultramontains* were not satisfied with the influence they had in the party and tried to found a *Catholic Party* with a *Catholic programme* inside the Conservative party itself. This would oblige the Conservative members of parliament to legislate on marriage, education and the establishment of parishes "as the Bishops of the Province might request, in order to harmonize with the doctrines of the Roman Catholic Church."

The Clergy installed a theocratic regime that locked the Canayen people into the catacombs of history for a whole century.

The Population Situation

In the 1871 census, the white population of Quebec numbered about one million people. Three-quarters of them were Canayen. The rest were English speaking (English, Scottish, Irish).

The Canayens, the majority in Quebec were a minority in Canada as a whole. They represented only one-third of the white population.

In Quebec, 85 per cent of the population lived in the countryside. Most of this rural population was Canayen. The cities were more English than French. Quebec city was 40 per cent English.

Montreal, on the other hand, becomes the leading city in Canada. The harbour is rebuilt in 1857. Montreal becomes the import and export centre. In 1861 the export of agricultural products is more important than that of lumber products. As Victoria Bridge links up with the Grand Trunk, Montreal becomes a railway centre and a focal point in the in-river network. This is the administrative and financial centre for Canadian business, organized in the interests of the English merchants and a few bourgeois Canayens like Cartier. The Canayen people derive some benefit from this, but indirectly, the young habitants who leave the farms to seek fortune in the city take the poorly-paid jobs offered by the new commercial enterprises. Sherbrooke develops in a way similar to U.S. cities with its paper and textile factories.

The Quebec habitants on their little farms that don't always produce enough to live on cannot compete with the wheat producers of the American Midwest. They try to diversify by developing the dairy industry.

The Economic Situation

As a matter of fact, the economic situation for the Canayen people is deplorable and this is the result, not of their lack of business sense as we have been repeatedly told, but simply of their situation as a colonized people, a people deprived of all political and economic means of development. The greater majority are on the farms, but agricultural development is insignificant compared to that in Ontario and the United States. There are two reasons for this: first, the lands along the river, the only productive lands belonging to the Canayens, are in fact very small compared to the vast extents in the Midwest and secondly, the Canayens have no control of the market. It is in the hands of the English merchants who do not give a damn about the agricultural development of Quebec if they can make more money selling American wheat to England.

It must never be forgotten that the merchant is motivated by profit. The merchant will be a nationalist and promote national development if it makes money for him (remember how the merchants concocted Confederation). And, if he can make profits, selling the nation, he'll do that (think of Cartier and his participation in Confederation).

The young habitant who leaves the farm because his eldest brother will inherit it anyway, can become a lumberjack. He will then be exploited by the English companies in the Lac St. Jean, Mauricie and Ottawa regions. If he comes to the city, he becomes a poorly-paid employee of some English company. Whatever the case, he is trapped; exploited, colonized, a man degraded by British colonialism.

The young habitant who has had his education paid for by the parish priest feels indebted and will more often than not enter a religious order. At the same time becoming a priest means climbing the social ladder. It means in fact becoming a member of the new Canayen aristocracy. This term is not too strong. When the Clergy established the supremacy of the Church in Quebec, its theocracy, every member of the Clergy received a privileged status. It made a privileged class of its priests to whom one owed reverence, respect, obedience and submission, to whom one paid homage. Did not the parish priests demand the same mark of respect, deference and reverence, as did the aristocracy under Louis XV? Did not the Clergy have the same ideology as those nobles in preaching blind obedience and absolute submission to their authority of divine right? Did they not prefer a monarchy as a social order rather than a bourgeois democracy with its liberal tendencies? It is to be noted that even though we use the expression clerical-bourgeois elite to describe the head of Canayen society made up of the Clergy and the collaborating petit-bourgeoisie, we must not think that this elite was imbued with bourgeois ideology. As a matter of fact, it was much more seeped in French pre-revolutionary aristocratic ideology than bourgeois ideology which was then developing in French, English and American liberal circles. This Quebec clerical-bourgeois elite was to preach the values of the "Ancien Regime" (faith in God, respect for religious and civil authority, scorn for business, the cult of honour) and not those of the bourgeois class (faith in God modified by faith in reason and man's creative strength, respect for the people's elected authority, the cult of commercial exploitation and scorn for "honour," social climbing through the individual's own resources). But in fact, all the while the Clergy is preaching aristocratic values, it is practicing bourgeois economics. It quietly invests in North American capitalist enterprises and makes huge profits; it will play along with those "elected by the people" to keep control of bourgeois democracy in Quebec. It will disgrace every Canayen who contests its authority; it will exploit Canayen desire for social advancement in order to enlist them into its ranks. This schizophrenia [1] of the clerical-bourgeois elite will keep generations of Québécois outside reality, outside the real world, outside History and will explain the abortive attempts at intellectual research, the bankruptcy of our political endeavours and the emigration of our most gifted sons.

The young men who do not chose the priesthood on graduation from the classical college become lawyers, notaries and doctors. Those who have undergone eight long years of intensive brainwashing by the Clergy become members of the elite. The lawyers and notaries work for themselves or for English companies or as civil servants. If some of these members of the lay elite manage to accumulate a bit of money, they invest it in small family businesses. In the 1850's and 60's there are already quite a few. This small Canayen capital goes into the manufacture of bricks, of shoes, of finished lumber, a few saw-mills and several tanneries. In 1871, Canayen industry exploited 7,300 Canayen workers while English industry exploited 50,000 to 75,000 in the forests or in the factories. American industry in Maine, Massachusetts and Vermont exploited about another 75,000.

Near the end of the century, the main industry of the province will be pulp and paper. American capital smells the profits, gets huge lumber concessions for next to nothing and hires Québécois *cheap-labour*. American penetration of capital in the primary sector, that is to say in extraction (like wood for paper, asbestos at Thetford) and the gradual subordination of English capital to

---

1. *schizophrenia:* mental illness in which the patient has lost all touch with reality and the external world. He lives in an internal world he has created for himself. Here the word is not used in the strict sense. It is used to indicate the contradiction between what the Clergy preaches and what it actually does.

American capital heralds the new regime under which the Cana-yen people will fall.

Confederation (1867)

The Union of Canada, which had been composed of Upper and Lower Canada, is now altered. The new colony is called 'Canada.' It consists of four provinces: Ontario, Quebec, Nova Scotia and New Brunswick. It is administered by a federal or central government whose capital is Ottawa, and by provincial governments in each province. The federal government keeps all significant power, especially economic power, in its hands. The provincial governments for the most part have only insignificant care-taker powers.

The Division of Power

The federal government arrogates to itself the following powers:

● the means of financial control of the country: the Bank of Canada, the issuing of coins and paper money, the public debt, inspection of savings banks, control of all taxation, public loans and bankruptcies.
● the means of commercial control of the country: shipping (by railway or water), communications, the post-office, navigation, the fishing industry, harbours, external trade, customs and public property.
● control of national defence: the militia, military service, the navy.
● control of 'justice': criminal law and prisons.
● control of civil law: marriage and divorce, copyrights and patents.
● population control: the census, statistics, immigration.
● control of foreign relations, embassies etc.
● control over all matters except those expressly and exclusively attributed to the provinces.

The powers of the provinces are limited to purely local administration.

● the right of direct taxation for provincial purposes, and the right of borrowing only on the credit of the province.

● the administration and sale of public lands belonging to the province, including forests.

● municipal administration.

● the administration of schools and regulation of education (though subject to federal disavowal).

● administration of hospitals and asylums.

● administration of public jails.

● administration of provincial courts of civil and criminal law.

● issuance of sales permits and liquor licences, issuance of company charters.

● local road construction.

● marriage ceremonies.

● regulation of private property.

The two languages, English and French, are official at the federal level, but strictly in parliamentary debates, reports and bills. In everything else pertaining to the federal government, the language is English.

At the provincial level the offical language is English, except in Quebec where both are official.

The Canadian Parliament comprises two houses: the Senate (the former Legislative Council), whose members are appointed by the party in power; and the House of Commons (the former Assembly), which is elected.

A governor-general represents the Queen.

The provincial governments consist of a lieutenant-governor and a legislative assembly, except that the Province of Quebec, in addition to these, has a Legislative Council nominated by the party in power.

Right from 1867 the federal government takes the lion's share. Direct taxation at this time is unpopular and almost non-existent. Indirect taxation is the main source of government revenue. This is why the federal government appropriates customs duties, which represent 80% of all revenues, while income from other indirect taxes (permits for cutting wood, sales permits), amounting to only 20%, is given to the provinces. From the very first years of this confederation, provinces like New Brunswick and Nova Scotia have to beg for subsidies from Ottawa in order to make both ends meet. The provinces' dependence on Ottawa is assured from the beginning and can only intensify with time, especially during periods of crisis such as world wars or economic depressions.

The provinces in fact are colonies of the federal government, just as on the international level the federal government itself is a colony of Great Britain, "All Canadian law is nil, insofar as it contradicts Imperial law as applied in Canada," reads the British North America Act. Canadian international affairs are in fact administered by the British Colonial Office. A declaration of war by England automatically implicates Canada in that war. Nor can Canada sign any international treaty for itself.

The first federal and provincial elections are held in the summer of 1867. At the federal level, Macdonald's and Cartier's Conservatives get two-thirds of the seats and form a government which is to stay in office until 1874.

The first measure taken by the Ottawa government is the purchase of the western plains. The Hudson's Bay Company had now been exploiting these vast territories for a very long time. Cartier and a certain Mr. McDougall go to London to negotiate the deal. The Company cedes the territory for $1,500,000, but reserves the lands around the trading posts. The territory covers 2,500,000 square miles. Obviously no one thinks of consulting the population of 75,000 inhabitants, consisting of thousands of Red men, 10,000 Canayen Metis, and a few thousand other Canayens, Scotsmen and Eskimos.

Riel and Manitoba

Confederation was only a few years old when the Manitoba crisis revealed that its main purpose was really to make Quebec into a kind of 'reserve' for the Canayens. The English would fight to the death before they would allow the Canayens and the Canayen Métis on the Red River to create a French-speaking province west of Ontario. One province of Quebec was already too much for the English-Canadians. They had to nip in the bud any Métis coalition on the Plains. They had to massacre them if necessary, and bring in the English to make Manitoba at all costs an English-speaking province.

Ottawa organized and carried out this project, efficiently, right through to the murder of Louis Riel in 1885.

In the West, the Hudson's Bay Company had been exploiting the fur-trade. The Red men, the Canayen Métis and the Canayen trappers are the *cheap-labour* of this trade. The 10,000 Métis and the few thousand Canayens are evenly settled along the Red River and its tributaries, according to the Quebec system of settlement - strips of narrow lands stretching from the river deep into the hinterland. They also concentrated at St Boniface, where Bishop Plessis sent missionaries as early as 1818. On the other side of the Red River a few thousand Scottish settlers, who had come over with Lord Selkirk in 1812, are cultivating the fertile lands of the region. The majority of the population is Canayen Métis and very conscious of its identity.

The Hudson's Bay Company, like all the monopoly companies at this time, has fantastic privileges. It has established a virtual political administration in the region. It nominates a governor and a Council, which has dictatorial powers over the population. The Company gets along well with the Scottish settlers who restrict themselves to agriculture; but it shamefully exploits the Métis. Already in 1826-27 the Metis had revolted against its tyranny.

In 1849 the Company prosecuted, before its own 'court of justice', a Métis accused of illegal fur-trading. What this Métis had done in fact was to sell his furs to some Americans who offered him more than he would normally have received from the Company. During his 'trial' before an agent of the Company, a group of Métis invaded the court-room and forced the acquittal of their comrade. Jean-Louis *Riel,* a miller from St Boniface and father of Louis Riel, was the leading figure in this insurrection.

During the 1850s and '60s a few thousand Canayens who are forced to leave Quebec but do not care to emigrate to the United States, go to settle along the Red River and devote themselves to clearing the lands, engaging in agriculture, and founding parishes.

Meanwhile the Americans, who are expanding to the Pacific, have their own designs on these rich plains. And the English from Ontario are reading anti-Canayen articles by George Brown and William McDougall, who want to make the Prairies an extension of Ontario. They see clearly that they must put a stop to the Canayens organizing a society there, and at the same time prevent the Americans from annexing the region to the United States.

In 1864, the promoters of Confederation meet in Quebec, and discuss the admission of that region then called the North-West Territories (present-day Manitoba, Saskatchewan, Alberta, the Yukon and Keewatin). When the Métis learn that their fate is being decided without consulting them, their resentment increases.

In 1868, Ottawa illegally sends a road construction team into the Red River district, ostensibly to give work to the Métis, whose economic situation is desperate due to grass-hoppers ruining the harvest. The following summer Canadian land-surveyors begin to mark out the roads without regard to the Métis' strips of farms along the river. They contemptuously ridicule the Métis protests. And when Prime Minister Macdonald hears of these protests,

LOUIS RIEL and HIS COUNCIL 1870

John Thomas
Bruce Bunn

Louis Riel

all he does is utter injurious remarks about the Métis. He treats them as 'half-castes,' as degenerates.

Negotiations between Ottawa and the Hudson's Bay Company are concluded. On December 1, the territory is officially handed over to Canada for a sum of £300,000 sterling. The Canadian government nominates a governor and a council for the region. William McDougall is named governor to take up his post as of December 1st. All the members of the Council, except for one sellout Canayen, are militant anti-Canayen Protestants.

The Métis, however, have been organizing their resistance since October.

On October 11, the young Louis Riel at the head of a group of Métis disperses a team of surveyors.

On October 20, the Métis meet and elect a Provisional Government modelled on their organization for buffalo hunting. John Bruce, a Scottish Métis, is elected president, and Riel, secretary. Their goal is to gain recognition of their rights from Canada before December 1, the day on which the territory is to be handed over to Canada by the Company.

The Council of Assiniboia, the local Company council, summons Riel to appear before it and explain himself. Riel appears, and defends the rights of the Métis by protesting against any government over them originating in Canada without their consent.

Meanwhile McDougall and his Council make their way to the Red River via the United States. At Pembina, in American territory, a Métis representative warns them not to cross the border. On October 30, McDougall tries to cross, but a Métis commando group under the command of Ambroise Lépine stops him. On the same day, Riel seizes Fort Garry, the main Company trading post, in the name of the Provisional Government.

Meanwhile Colonel Dennis, leader of the surveying team, tries to organize a *coup d'état* to get McDougall in by force. On November 6, Riel invites the Scottish parishes to choose representatives to meet with the Canayen Métis on November 16.

But on that day MacTavish, governor of the Company, issues a proclamation protesting the decision of the Provisional Government and demanding a return to 'legality.' In order words, he would like to get rid of the Provisional Government, but does not dare say so for fear of the people's reaction. One of his English colleagues proposes a solution: both English and Métis should get together to form a new Council to negotiate with Ottawa.

Riel considers accepting, but smells the rat in time. On the 23rd of November, he and his troops seize the provisions and funds of Fort Garry, and take command of all its entrances and exits.

At the end of November, McDougall, who is still waiting at the border, receives a letter from Prime Minister Macdonald, telling him not to try to move in to this 'foreign country' by force. But at the same time, Colonel Dennis, with 20 Canadians and 70 Red-men, tries to attack Fort Garry and overthrow the Provisional Government. They fail miserably.

On December 5, Louis Riel publishes his *List of Rights*, in which he proclaims the necessity of consulting the Métis people as to whether or not they wish to join Canada. On December 9th, he arrests the leaders of the pro-Canadian Party and locks them up in Fort Garry. He hoists the Provisional Government's flag, a shamrock and a fleur-de-lis. The supporters of the pro-Canadian Party hardly dare to show their flag, which is nothing but the Union Jack with *Canada* embroidered on it.

The Canadian government is really vexed: the coveted territory is not falling into its hands like an apple from a tree. Macdonald decides to send two well-chosen emissaries -- a priest, Father Thibault, who has spent 27 years in the region, and Charles de Salaberry, son of the hero of Chateauguay. A third character, Donald Smith, the Hudson Bay Company manager, carries with him a little bag -- and in it the money needed to buy off the rebel leaders. The plan is to offer the Métis two seats on a Council, two-thirds of which will be elected by the population of the colony; to promise to respect property titles; and to offer Riel a post in the territory's police force.

All these promises are to be accompanied by hard cash, "to construct," as Macdonald puts it, "a bridge of gold over which McDougall can cross into the territory."

On December 6, a royal proclamation urges the Métis to lay down their arms and promises an amnesty.[1]

1. *amnesty: a special law granting pardon.*

Riel assumes the presidency of the Provisional Government. When the representatives of the expansionist Canadian government arrive, he prevents them from speaking to the people, but agrees to engage in discussion with them. The Métis leaders do not allow themselves to be bought off. Riel demands that Ottawa recognize his Provisional Government as the only constituted body that could negotiate the entrance of the Red River region as a full-fledged province into Confederation.

The Ottawa emissaries are obliged to recognize the Provisional Government officially on the 20th of February, so that Ottawa also recognizes it *de facto*. The Provisional Government at this point agrees to send in return a delegation of three men to Ottawa: Father Ritchot for the Canayen Métis; Judge John Black for the English-speaking Métis, and Alfred H. Scott for the American and English colonists.

During these discussions between the representatives of Ottawa and the Métis leaders, the supporters of the pro-Canadian Party resolve to raid the fort and slaughter all the Métis in it. They are utterly unable to accept that the Métis, whom they so despise, are carrying out the negotiations with the federal government.

Among this gang of blood-thirsty colonizers is Thomas Scott who managed to escape from Fort Garry where he had been imprisoned by Riel on December 7 along with other leaders of the pro-Canadian party.

During the night of February 14, this group under the command of a Major Boulton descends on Fort Garry, but soon withdraws when Riel promises to do them no harm if they disperse. Upon leaving, these cowards cannot restrain themselves from attacking a Métis named Parisien and taking him prisoner. Parisien escapes and the next day shoots an English colonist, who he believes is following him. The Métis leader Lépine surrounds the Boulton gang and locks them up in the fort. Boulton goes before the Provisional Government's War Council, and is condemned to be shot. The emissary Smith intercedes on his behalf and manages to get him a suspended sentence.

Thomas Scott is brought to trial, and he too is condemned to be shot. Again Smith tries to intercede, but this time it is wasted effort. Scott had tried to murder the chief surveyor Snow when he worked under him, and was one of the leaders agitating against the Métis. During his earlier imprisonment, he had not for a moment ceased to insult Riel and his Provisional Government. He had escaped in January, and was now the instigator of this new attack against the Provisional Government, recognized even in Ottawa. The War Council cannot go back on its decision. Thomas Scott is executed on March 4th.

His execution further inflames the conflict. The Ontario aggressors are fuming with rage. Bishop Taché, immediately recalled from Rome by Macdonald, uses all his influence to persuade the Métis leaders to give in to the pressures from Ottawa. Riel regards him as an agent of the Canadian government; but nevertheless frees the rest of the prisoners on March 16th, proclaims peace on April 9th, and on April 23rd replaces the Provisional Government's flag on the Fort with the Union Jack. The Provisional Government remains in control, with Ottawa's consent, until the arrival of the new governor.

The three representatives of the Provisional Government, on their way to Ottawa to negotiate their country's entry into Confederation, are arrested in Toronto on the instigation of Thomas Scott's brother. They have to be released, however, when the Ontario government is unable to prosecute them.

After a month of negotiation between Ottawa and the Provisional Government, the Province of Manitoba is created. The federal government holds on to public lands in exchange for small concessions to the Métis. Denominational schools, Protestant and Catholic, are guaranteed. French and English are both to be official languages. The Métis get what they fought for, but fall into a trap anyway. They have won their cause only on paper: Manitoba becomes a province, and not merely an extension of Ontario. But in reality the Métis will not gain much from the rights they acquire with the creation of the new province, because the English will chase them out, modify the school laws and take control in order to make Manitoba a white Anglo-Saxon Protestant province like Ontario.

On July 15, 1870, Manitoba officially becomes a Canadian province. Under the orders of Colonel Wolseley, Lieutenant-Governor Archibald arrives with an armed force. The Métis do not understand the need for this display of military might. They think the question is settled: Manitoba is a province, with laws guaranteeing their rights. Besides, Riel and his troops have already withdrawn from the Fort when Wolseley arrives.

The repression begins. Smith sends out a warrant for the arrest of Riel and other Métis leaders. Immigrants arriving by the thousand from Ontario begin a Métis-hunt. The Métis are persecuted and murdered. Even governor Archibald is forced to admit this. In a letter to his boss, Macdonald, he writes: "Many of the French half-breeds have been so beaten and outraged by a small but noisy section of the people that they feel as if they were living in a state of slavery." He adds that the newcomers from Ontario "seem to feel as if the French half-breeds should be wiped off the face of the globe."

The new colonists from Ontario are allowed to chase the Metis off their ancestral lands, burn their houses and take over their farms. Killing Metis becomes a sport, as killing Blacks is for the Southern Whites in the United States. Two soldiers from the "Ontario Rifles" shoot down Elzéar Goulet like an animal. Instead of being arrested they are encouraged and commended for their bravery.

The Métis reaction to this persecution is to emigrate further west and north. Riel and Lépine are now somewhat isolated. Governor MacTavish calls on them to combat the Fenians - Irish refugees in the United States who were attacking Canada in order to weaken England and thus help to liberate their homeland from English domination. And Riel and Lépine actually recruit about 300 Métis for this purpose in October, 1871. Bishop Taché has indeed managed to convince Riel that collaboration with and submission to Canadian authority is the only answer for every Manitoban Christian.

In the Federal elections of 1871, Riel is elected for the district of St Boniface. Cartier, who has lost in a Montreal east-end riding because the Canayens there find him a disgusting sell-out, manages to convince Riel to give up his seat so that he, Cartier, can become Member of Parliament for St Boniface instead. Bishop Taché and Cartier both shamefully manipulate Riel. He is a believer whose religious sentiments can easily be exploited by these two characters for their own ends.

In 1873 Lépine is arrested, judged and condemned to death. Bishop Taché protests against a government that breaks its promise of amnesty. Lépine's sentence is commuted to two years in prison, but he loses his civil rights. This same bishop Taché hands over some money from Macdonald and Cartier to Louis Riel to encourage him to get lost in the United States.

The death of Cartier in that same year however, leaves the riding of St Boniface vacant. Riel is re-elected in 1874. But how can he sit in Ottawa, when the entire population of Ontario is out to get him? A price is put on his head: $5,000 to the person who arrests him and places him in the hands of the Ontario authorities.

Despite this danger, Riel presents himself in Ottawa and takes the oath as a Member of Parliament. Such hysteria ensues, however, that he is expelled from the House of Commons. We can see that the laws of democracy work only for the masters, the English gentlemen. According to their own tradition a duly elected Member of Parliament is supposed to be protected from arrest when exercising his functions. This is what is called parliamentary immunity. But Louis Riel has no right to it. The masters make their laws for their own benefit, and prevent their colonized subjects from taking advantage of them. Riel is chased from the House of Commons like a bum. And in order to justify this action the members from Ontario officially declare him a fugitive from justice.

The British democratic circus is not yet over: in 1875 a Royal Commission of Inquiry is created to find out if the rebels had indeed been granted amnesty. This Royal Commission concludes that Scott had been judged and executed by a legal government, the Provisional Government recognized by Ottawa; that an amnesty had in fact been granted according to the promises of Macdonald, Cartier and Co., as proved by the fact that Governor Archibald had called on Riel and Lépine to help fight the Fenians. This Commission of Inquiry mildly chastises the government, in order to clear its conscience. To say that things should have been otherwise is but a petty 'mea culpa' after the crime.

Now that the Métis are subdued, the Federal government has nothing to lose by saying that it should have been nicer to their leaders.

Acting on the report of the commission, the government decrees a general amnesty for all the rebels except Riel, Lépine and a certain O'Donaghue. These are all exiled for 5 years.

Lépine freed from prison in 1876, goes to Batoche on the Saskatchewan River, where many Métis sought refuge from persecution by the English who had stolen their lands on the Red River.

Riel seeks refuge in Quebec with the fanatic Catholic Alphonse Desjardins. In this period he has mystical visions. Desjardins has him confined to asylums in Longue Pointe and Beauport from 1875 to 1878. Riel emerges from time to time, to speak for the Métis cause. He leaves Beauport in 1878, and makes his way toward the American west. He settles at the Jesuit mission of St Pierre in Montana, marries a Métis and teaches at the local school. He becomes a U.S. citizen in 1883, but still does not renounce the Métis cause.

The creation of the province of Manitoba does not solve all the problems on the prairies. The Métis have taken refuge west of Manitoba along the Saskatchewan River. As for the English who have grabbed Manitoba, they are still not satisfied. They need the entire territory, all the way to the Pacific. Colonialism has no limits.

The Métis, who hunt buffalo for food, witness the disappearance of their food supply. The Americans slaughter entire herds for skins or simply for sport; in addition, the Canadian Pacific Railway and more colonists penetrate into their hunting territory. The Métis repeatedly complain to Ottawa about the slaughter of the buffalo and about the speculators who are stealing their property, but Ottawa turns a deaf ear. In fact, Ottawa encourages speculation, hoping for higher property taxes to help defray the enormous costs of railway construction. The fate of the Métis has no importance in Ottawa.

So once again the surveyors begin to subdivide the Métis lands and chase them out. The Métis send petition after petition to Ottawa. Nothing happens. There is finally nothing left but self-defence.

In the spring of 1884, a delegation composed of Gabriel Dumont, Moïse Ouellet, James Isbister and Michel Dumas make their way to Montana, to urge Riel to come back and organize the struggle. Riel accepts. He even hopes to establish a new Métis nation west of Manitoba.

He arrives in the region in July, and immediately has the support of the Métis, the Red men and some of the Whites. He demands recognition of the Métis, property rights on all Métis lands, and proposes the creation of the provinces of Alberta and Saskatchewan.

Sometimes he has fantastic visions: the creation of a society in the west free from exploitation where poverty and misery would disappear, where men would love each other, work together and create an ideal society together. Some of these ideas come close to Che Guevara's concept of the "new man." These visions frighten the missionaries, for whom man is necessarily an evil being who must live in misery, guilt and fear in order to earn his place in heaven. A man who speaks of a better society in this world is to be dreaded. Father André refuses Riel the sacraments, considers him crazy and thinks about trying to get him to leave the country.

Father André is present at the negotiations between the Federal government and Riel at the end of 1885. Riel agrees to return to the United States if the government gives him $35,000 for the lands he would be abandoning. The government refuses all compensation, and instead reinforces the Royal North-West Mounted Police [1], a force created expressly for the repression of the Métis. It tries to buy off the Métis leaders by offering them jobs. Isbister and Dumas are offered posts as agricultural instructors for the Red men, while Gabriel Dumont is offered a ferry license.

Riel understands that the federal government once again is seeking to buy him off. So he asks for sums the government cannot pay.

In February, 1885, he organizes secret meetings in which he prepares his men for guerrilla warfare. When the priests hear of these preparations, they quickly oppose and condemn all action that is not legal or constitutional. Riel replies, "The spirit of God is in me" and "Rome has fallen".

The priests take these words as proof that Riel must be crazy. How could God be in the heart of a man who takes up arms to defend the rights of his compatriots, and dares to claim that

1. This special army of repression in the name of the Federal government is later to be called 'the RCMP.'

Rome has fallen when it is well-known that Rome and the Catholic Church, like the British Empire, extends its grasp over a large part of the earth?

But Riel is right. He speaks the language of simple and brutal truth. If we agree that the word 'God' is a synonym for love, for life, for fulfillment, then Riel really has God in him. He is a leader who wants to take his people through a liberation struggle and create a better society, where love, justice and a free and full life will prevail. And he is right in saying that "Rome has fallen" because the Catholic Church, founded by a revolutionary who wanted to establish a kingdom of love, has become an exploitative capitalist institution, power-hungry and permeated with the spirit of oppression, domination and colonialism. The Church gets along well with the bourgeois class, the imperialist British government and the aspiring imperialists in Ottawa. Is not Father André himself in favour of Canadian expansion in the west as long as he can keep his job as evangelist among the Métis?

If his words are given their true meaning, Riel's religious - political declarations show us a man fired by a revolutionary vision of the world. He is among that category of men who, realizing the misery that comes with the exploitation of man by man whether in its pharisaic or capitalist form, engage in a struggle to the death against this repression and do not back down, even if they are forced to pay the supreme sacrifice.

On March 17, 1885, Riel establishes the Provisional Government of Saskatchewan at St Laurent. Riel is president, Dumont adjutant.

On March 18, Riel seizes the church at Batoche. Father Moulin protests. Riel gently pushes him aside, referring to him as a 'Protestant' comrade, and takes a few prisoners.

On the 21st of March Riel draws up an ultimatum to be sent to Major Crozier, commander of the Mounted Police at Carleton and Battleford. He threatens a war of extermination, and demands that Crozier hand over the police stations and withdraw from the country.

On March 6, about 30 Métis had prevented soldiers from entering Carleton. The police counter-attacked but had to abandon the fight and leave twelve dead, after an assault by Gabriel Dumont and his buffalo hunters. The armed struggle has begun.

Riel tries to win over the English colonists, at least to neutrality if not to the cause, by promising to prevent the Red men from entering the conflict. But the colonists remember George Custer's defeat at the hands of the Sioux in the American West.

This fear of seeing the Red men join their brothers, the Métis, to demand their rights brings out a military expedition from the Ottawa government to crush both the Red men and the Métis. This will be easier than in 1870, because the Canadian Pacific now links Winnipeg to Edmonton and Calgary, and the telegraph links Ottawa to the smallest station in the West.

To bolster the hundreds of Mounties, Ottawa sends 5,000 militia from Ontario, Quebec, Nova Scotia and Manitoba. The militia from Ontario think they are engaged in a holy war against 'the French and Indian rebels,' and the Québécois who participate in this expedition believe that they are going to fight a crazy heretic and his 'savage' allies.

The Crees and the Stoneys join with Riel. Big Bear's Crees execute 2 Catholic missionaries and 5 traders. Poundmaker and his Stoneys lay siege to Battleford.

The rebels, Métis and Red men, number about 700 in all. Several times, they ambush advancing army columns of 5,000. Gabriel Dumont's guerrilla warfare spreads terror among the Canadian ranks.

In spite of everything, the Métis stronghold, Batoche, falls on May 12. Riel surrenders to two scouts. The generals telegraph to Ottawa to say that they have 'captured' him.

Ten days later, Poundmaker gives himself up. The Rebellion is crushed. Canadian oppression is victorious.

The expedition and the repression cost $4,500,000. The Hudson's Bay Company, which supplied the provisions and land transportation, claims $1,737,032.00; the Canadian Pacific $852,231.32.

We see that the Canadian propaganda managed to raise troops in Quebec by making Canayens believe that the Métis and their allies, the Red men, are all vicious savages. But with Riel's surrender this same propaganda shows its real face: this war of repression is directed against the Canayens settled in Manitoba and against their Métis cousins. A Toronto newspaper writes, "Riel should be strangled with a French flag." The federal government prosecutes Riel on July 20 in Regina, on a charge of high treason.

The Canayens, deceived not only by Canadian propaganda but also by their own clerical-bourgeois elite about the war of repression against the Métis, are now becoming aware of the reality of the situation. The Canadians want Riel's head because he dared to conceive the idea of making the West a French-speaking province of Canayen Métis. Riel is now seen as the symbol of the Canayen people.

A campaign to save Riel is organized. Even though journalists like L.O. David consider Riel the spiritual heir of the Patriotes of 1837, the campaign becomes a mere political football when the Liberals grab it to attack Macdonald's Conservative government.

Riel's trial is a monumental judicial farce. From the beginning the dice are loaded against him. He is judged by an English magistrate assisted by a French Justice of the Peace before a jury of six men, all English colonists and English merchants.

Riel's English secretary, William Henry Jackson, who insists that he shares responsibility with Riel, is tried during one of Riel's own trial adjournments. Jackson is declared insane in half an hour and locked up in an asylum, from which he easily escapes to the United States. From this incident we can see clearly that Canadian justice had no intention of prosecuting an English person, even when he declared his solidarity with an individual accused of high treason.

Riel himself asks for the Deputy Minister of the Interior, who has his official documents and the Métis petitions. The judge rejects the request.

Riel demands that his personal papers seized at Batoche be returned to him. The judge denies this request too, since the Crown Attorneys are busy using the papers to prepare their case against Riel.

The lawyers for the accused, intimidated in advance or already sold out for some time, try to prove that Riel is a mental case whose wild conduct should be excused. Dr Roy from the Beauport asylum is a witness for this plea, but he loses all credibility under cross-examination when he cannot express himself in English. Dr Jukes of the Mounted Police declares Riel sane.

With remarkable eloquence, Riel repudiates all his own lawyers' arguments, assuring the court that he is sane. He explains how as *founder of Manitoba and prophet of the New World* he wanted to make the West a free country for all the oppressed nations, not only for the Métis and Red men but also for the oppressed peoples of Europe.

He recalls the schemings of Macdonald and Cartier to try to buy him off, the provocations of the Mounted Police, the promises to the Métis that the government never kept. He attacks the Clergy for its complicity with the government, and ends with a call for a trial before a complete jury, and an examination before a medical commission.

Seven days later, the jury returns a verdict of guilty with a recommendation for clemency. But on August 1, the judge condemns Riel to be hanged on September 18 in Regina. Riel appeals to the Manitoba Court of the Queen's Bench, which confirms the verdict, and then to the Privy Council, which refuses to hear the case.

During all this time a great campaign is in full swing in Ontario for the execution of the sentence. In Quebec, on the other hand, a campaign is organized to obtain a pardon for Riel. Despite the Clergy's warnings, the Canayens recognize that Riel is one of them, and that he is valiantly struggling againt Ottawa for all the oppressed people of the West.

In Ottawa, the question is settled. Has not Macdonald proclaimed, "Riel must swing".

As a matter of procedure, the government grants three stays of execution to give the condemned man time to make his various appeals. In addition, a medical commission is set up. It finds that Riel is not insane, in the eyes of the law, and is therefore fit to hang.

In the end the government refuses to commute the sentence on November 12, and Riel is executed in Regina on November 16th. The justice of the masters, the colonizers, has run its course; again the agents of imperialism have put down the indigenous people by perpetrating the necessary murders, though at the same time clearing their own consciences with a mock-show of justice, judges, law-court, lawyers and legal parlance, the whole masquerade needed to cover up the most shameful political crime of the era.

The murder of Riel occasions a considerable political backlash in Quebec. The majority of the population rise up in protest against Macdonald. His Canayen ministers are burned in effigy. On November 22, a huge popular assembly (50,000 strong) is held on the Champs de Mars in Montreal. The fever is at its pitch. Not since 1837 has the indignation of the Canayen people risen so high.

Unhappily, the spokesmen at this rally are not up to the situation. They cannot provide the leadership necessary to mobilize the people, arm them and begin again the struggle for liberation. They are not even worthy of addressing the people, for they are in fact mere petty politicians anxious to exploit the situation for their own personal ambitions.

Wilfrid Laurier, the Liberal, claims "If I had been on the banks of the Saskatchewan I too would have shouldered my musket." But why then did he not go and join Riel on the shores of the Saskatchewan? Couldn't he afford a ticket to get there? Didn't he have a gun? Riel could have supplied him with everything--ticket, gun, bullets, buffalo coat and pemmican[1]... But no such thing happened. Laurier really was one of that race of weak little men who exploit the gestures and even the death of others, to make political capital. This high-sounding rhetoric is nothing but bad literature, well-turned phrases to pass himself off as a different kind of man. He steals Riel's heroism, and conceals his own underhandedness. Behind these lovely words is written large, "Vote Liberal, Vote for Me, I want to be Prime Minister of Canada." And we will see, when he does become Prime Minister, how his handling of the Manitoba school question confirms his utter baseness.

The second speaker is the arch-Catholic leader of the *Ultramontains,* F.-X. Trudel. According to this fanatic, Riel died defending a Catholicism that was threatened in the West by Protestants of all kinds. According to Trudel the Canayens must launch a crusade, like the medieval knights, with a sword in one hand and a cross in the other.

---

1. *pemmican: dried meat, pulverized and mixed with melted fat.*

The third speaker, the Liberal Honoré Mercier, had prepared in advance the Resolutions of the *Champs-de-Mars* as the basis of a new national political party with him as leader. He too exploits Riel's murder to his own ends. He claims that Riel was "a victim of fanaticism and treason!" This reference to fanaticism and treason, only proves that Mercier does not at all understand the nature of imperialism and its Canadian agents. Ottawa wanted to take the West, to exploit it economically. The fanaticism of the Ontario English was only the outward trapping of this exploitation. As for treason, where was it if not in Mercier's foggy mind and literary expressions?

The English Canadian bourgeois were not betraying anyone in conquering the West. They were being most faithful to their colonialist mentality. They could hardly be said to have betrayed the Canayens, since they never promised them anything other than oppression and subjugation.

The Canayens, ready for action, are greatly disappointed in their so-called leaders. Yet they continue to hold meetings all over Quebec; they sing the *Marseillaise,* and proclaim Riel a national hero.

The Clergy is really running scared, and gathers all its strength to combat this national movement that is taking a revolutionary turn. Bishop Taché of St Boniface, Riel's advisor until he took up arms, now calls Riel a "miserable fool and a sectarian."

The *Ultramontain* movement is torn between two factions. The bishops are all against Riel and consequently for the Conservative Macdonald. But opposing them is the zealot Trudel who supports the rebel, Riel.

Laurier loses no time in dissociating himself from Mercier and the movement. The movement has served its purpose for him, helping to fill the ranks of the Liberal Party with his supporters. This goal accomplished, he puts the brakes on.

When Parliament opens again in Ottawa in 1886, the Riel question is first on the agenda. A Canayen Conservative, the sell-out Philippe Landry, makes a motion of deepest regret for Riel's execution. That is to say, the murderers wish to apologize for having killed Riel. But in fact they regret nothing. They simply have to prevent the Liberals from exploiting the affair any further.

Bishop Taché, who follows the debate in the public gallery, advises all the Canayen Conservative members to vote for Landry's motion. This indicates that some Canayen Conservatives still had a few principles, but also that the dictatorship of the Church was for them stronger than their convictions.

On the 16th of March it is Laurier himself who alleviates the tension in the House. This sell-out par excellence declares in a speech (entirely in English), that Riel "at his worst was a subject fit for an asylum; at his best he was a religious and political maniac." He adds a prediction that Mercier will commit political suicide in trying to form a national party. He chastizes the government for not heeding the "Métis complaints." He suggests that the government should have shown clemency and not vengeance in Riel's case.

Immediately the English see in Laurier the successor to Cartier, the lay Negro-King indispensable for the continued domination of the Canayens. He has only 10 years to wait to become Prime Minister.

As for Honoré Mercier, he continues to promote the national movement, so well in fact that in 1887 his *Parti National* comes to power in Quebec. He becomes Prime Minister of Quebec.

In 1867, Pierre Chauveau and his Conservatives had formed the provincial government. All the laws they passed had no other purpose than to help the Church and private enterprise take over new lands. By 1887, 60 per cent of the province's budget ($1,535,536) is derived from federal subsidies.

In 1873, Ouimet's Conservative government had resigned following the Tanneries Scandal: speculators had slipped hush-money to some cabinet ministers to get the government to buy lands in the Montreal region at prices twenty-five times the market value. The Conservatives, however, were brought back to power with Boucherville as Prime Minister, thanks to the Clergy who went so far as to threaten to refuse the sacraments to those who dared vote Liberal.

In 1875, Boucherville, obedient to the same bishops who had supported him, abolished the Ministry of Public Instruction (ministry of education).

Education was henceforward to be entirely in the hands of the Council of Public Instruction, founded in 1869 and divided into two committees, Catholic and Protestant. The Protestant Committee was to be responsible for the English Protestant schools, and was at liberty to set up its school system as it pleased. The Catholic Committee was composed of all the bishops of Quebec and an equal number of laymen nominated by the government. So this new law put virtually all of Canayen education into the hands of the Clergy.

In 1878 Chapleau, another Conservative, became Prime Minister of Quebec. His major accomplishment was to sell the Quebec-Montreal-Ottawa and Western Railway for 7 million dollars. It had cost the province 12 million. He also got involved in a few other frauds with a speculator named Senecal, and was succeeded in 1882 by the moderate conservative Mousseau, who is turn was replaced in 1884 by an *Ultramontain* conservative John Ross.

So much for the activities of the Quebec government until the arrival of Mercier. In short, until then, the government had been clearly an instrument in the interests of the Church and the speculators.

Is anything to change with Mercier, the man who had the audacity to call himself Riel's brother in his speech of November 22nd? Will this former provincial Liberal, now leader of the *Parti National,* really do something different? As a matter of fact, nothing is going to change. The corruption continues and the Church extends its power.

In 1854, the seigneurial system had been modified. Two-thirds of the seigneuries were by then in the hands of the English merchants, who pressured the government into buying them at a high price and then selling the lands back to the *habitants* at prices higher still. But even though some of the *habitants* could now claim to be owners of the means of production in this one economic sector, production remained entirely at the mercy of a market completely controlled by the Canadian bourgeoisie. Western grains, for example, could be brought in to flood the Quebec market.

In this way the Canayen farmer was forced to orient himself towards the dairy industry. But here again he had no important outlets; very often he simply withdrew from the market, content to produce enough merely for subsistence. Some small mixed farming, a little grain cultivation, a little cattle-raising, some vegetable, eggs and milk production are all that is necessary to feed his family, with a little surplus to be able to buy those necessities he cannot produce.

In the other economic sectors the Canayen is a worker -- in the forests, in factories, on the docks and in shipyards. The workers' conditions are so bad and the workers so discontented that in 1884 Macdonald establishes a Royal Commission of Enquiry into the relations between capital and labour. Among other things the report reveals: fines imposed on workers that are often higher than their weekly salary; the unbelievably high number of workers who can neither read nor write; the exploitation of children 8 years of age; a working day 14 hours long; children sent to the factory prison known as the "black hole" as a disciplinary measure; instant dismissal without previous notice; total lack of job security; unsanitary and over-crowded housing.

Macdonald of course hides the report in the back of a drawer, since the employers would hardly welcome having to change these conditions of the working class. Macdonald and the government are in the service of the employers, and if they dared pass laws favouring the working class they would soon be thrown out by their bosses.

What does Mercier do about all this? He creates the Ministry of Agriculture and Colonization. He leads it himself, with the parish-priest Labelle as Deputy Minister.

He builds a railway to Lac St Jean, lengthens the Montreal line from St Felix-de-Valois to St Gabriel-de-Brandon, and gives parents of twelve children or more 100 acres of land. He speaks a lot about the autonomy of the provinces and about the necessity for Quebec to assert itself as a province of the French and Catholic nation.

In short he does precious little, except to persuade the people to clear land that won't yield, to perpetuate the myth of the Canayen vocation of farming, and to exploit the national sentiment of the people in order to stay in power.

What does he do with the Manitoba school question? The same thing, nothing.

In any case, he is to be defeated before the question is resolved. After a triumphant tour of Europe, where he is decorated by the

President of the French Republic, by the Belgian king and by Pope Leo XIII who makes him a papal count, he comes home to a scandal in his administration. Contractors for the construction of the Baie-des-Chaleurs railways, it seems, had paid no less than $100,000 to the Liberal treasurer, Ernest Pacaud.

So in the 1892 elections, the *Parti National,* built on Riel's scaffold, falls into the most abject political corruption. Pacaud and Mercier stand trial soon after. Arthur Buies, one of the more honest journalists of the time, writes in *La Patrie:* "Mercier had in his hands the most brilliant opportunity that has ever been given to a Canadian statesman; he had a whole people behind him and a glorious role to play; his vanity, his egotism, and his absolute lack of moral sense has lost him everything."

The Conservatives come back to power in Quebec. Taillon is Prime Minister, then Flynn.

But what has been happening meanwhile in Manitoba in 1890?

The Manitoba Constitution, established in 1870, provided for a denominational school system, a Catholic section for the Canayens, and a Protestant section for the others. In 1870 the Canayens made up one half of the population. By 1890 they are only one-third. In this position of strength, Greenway's Liberal Manitoba government is able to move to abolish the Catholic section. Hereafter only English schools are to receive state subsidies. If the Canayens and the Canayen Métis want French schools so much, let them pay for them out of their own pockets. We can see that the same Anglo-Saxon imperialism that assassinated Riel continues its work of annihilation of all traces of Canayen or Métis culture in the West.

The Manitoba Canayens appeal to Macdonald to disallow this provincial act under Article 93 in the Constitution, which is supposed to protect minority groups' school rights. Macdonald of course refuses, and advises them to appeal to the courts. The Supreme Court passes the buck to the Privy Council in London, which declares that the province has the right to adopt such an act but that the federal government can pass a remedial act if it wants to.

It is therefore up to the federal government to defend the rights of the Canayens of Manitoba. Macdonald's death in 1891 results in a government shake-up that gives the Liberal Party, with Laurier now at the helm, the opportunity to exploit the Manitoba Schools Question in order to win elections. In the English provinces Laurier wins support with the line that he has no intention of meddling in the affairs of provincial governments. But in Quebec he promises to do something to settle the question.

In 1896, the Liberals win the majority of seats in the federal elections. Laurier becomes Prime Minister, thanks to the Québécois who vote three to one in his favour. In the other provinces the Liberals make a fairly good showing.

Why this Liberal support in Quebec? What other choice did the Québécois have? If they do not vote Liberal, they must vote Conservative. Conservative means Macdonald's party, the party that forced them to swallow Confederation, that assassinated Riel, that had hardly come out in support of the Manitoba Canayens. In addition 'Conservative' means the Church and its continuing domination. The Canayen, instructed by the bishops that to vote Liberal is a 'mortal sin,' nevertheless voted against the Church and against the party in power. He voted for Laurier who was Canayen in origin, and who was at least opposed to Riel's hanging.

As soon as Laurier takes over, he moves to settle the Manitoba School Question. He negotiates with Greenway, the Liberal Prime Minister of Manitoba. And here is the Greenway-Laurier Compromise: the Manitoba school system is to remain neutral--that is, English Protestant.

However, in some cases, a teacher can teach the religion of his choice and teach in either French or English in a school where there is a high percentage of Canayens. With a bit of patience the English will soon see the Canayens disappear from Manitoba. The Canayens of Manitoba know full well that Laurier sold them out.

Nor are the Canayens in Quebec satisfied. Still, Laurier can afford to lose a few supporters in Quebec, in view of his widespread popularity in that province. What interests him is not to protect the Canayens against English domination, but to govern a country 'from sea to sea' in the name of Her British Majesty Queen Victoria. And another event, this time on the international scene, is soon to confirm Laurier's treachery.

British Expansionism

The Boer War

By the end of the nineteenth century, the British bourgeoisie rules a huge empire and has come to believe that they are a chosen people, a superior race. With all their 'possessions,' (Canada, Australia, New Zealand, India, half of Africa, Malta, Gibraltar) they can claim, as does secretary of the colonies Joseph Chamberlain, that the Anglo-Saxon race "is the greatest ruling race the world has ever known." Dilke, another senior British civil servant, takes a tour of the Empire and concludes that "the Saxon Empire will rise triumphant from its long-drawn-out struggle with inferior races."

This Anglo-Saxon superiority complex is churned up by the bourgeoisie into an hysterical, fanatical racism, due to the threat of competition from a newly united Italy and a newly united Germany, and from a United States of America newly risen to the ranks of a world power. England had been well out in front of all the other colonial powers, including France. But now she feels the others are catching up. Her commercial supremacy is challenged by Germany and the United States. Her policy of free-trade, profitable as long as it went unchallenged, is now modified to a system of reciprocal trade.

England also tightens the bonds with the colonies – economic, political and sentimental. As a matter of fact, the ties are to be so close that the colonies might become simply parts of a

"Greater Britain" with a single administration, a single economy and a single army. John Robert Seely holds: "We must cease altogether to say that England is an island off the northwestern coast of Europe, that it has an area of 120,000 square miles and a population of thirty-odd millions... When we have accustomed ourselves to contemplate the Empire in its entirety and to call it all England, we shall see that here too is a United States. Here too is a great homogeneous people, one in blood, language, religion and laws, but dispersed over a boundless space." He writes as if there are no Canayens nor Red men in Canada, no Indians in India, no Blacks in Africa.

In this vein, England must not only consolidate her empire but enlarge it, and must lay claim to all that is left of that part of the world still not subjected to colonialism, before Germany or France grab their share. The Empire must be extended in Africa to effect "the necessary work of colonization and civilization." In the campaign to conquer the Sudan in 1884, English officers even have 367 Canayens and about a dozen Red men from Caughnawaga under their command. They recruit them mostly from among the loggers. These Canayens and Red men in English uniforms are used as English cannon fodder in the *Gordon Relief Expedition*.

In 1889, when England decided to grab South Africa, despite the fact that it had already been colonized by Dutch settlers called Boers, she calls up her colonial troops. The English-Canadian chauvinists, racist nationalists, boast about invincible England's capacity to crush these 'dirty' Boers.

Wilfrid Laurier is now called *Sir*. He earned the title at Queen Victoria's Jubilee in 1897, when he said things like: "It would be the most glorious moment of my life if I could see a Canadian of French descent affirming the principles of freedom in the Parliament of a Greater Britain," and "I am British to the core."

On October 13, 1899, Sir Laurier adopts an order-in-council [1] that provides for equipping and sending 1000 volunteers to fight in the English army against the Boers. The English-Canadians are delighted.

1. *order-in-council:* a law decreed by the Prime Minister and his Cabinet without going through the House of Commons.

The only Canayen Member of Parliament to oppose this participation in the colonial wars of imperialist England is Henri Bourassa. He resigns. And when he asks Laurier if Quebec opinion has been taken into consideration, *Sir* Wilfrid replies: "My dear Henri, the Province of Quebec has no opinions, it has only sentiments." In this characteristic response we can see the disdain this sell-out has for the people whose origin he shares. In sugar-coated words he says that the Canayens are too stupid to have any ideas about the desirability of participating in British imperialist adventures.

The English officers recruit throughout the country. But they run into a bit of trouble in Quebec (we can guess why). They manage to recruit one company there (100 men). On their departure for Africa, Sir Laurier tells them that they are going to fight for the cause of justice, of humanity, of civil rights and religious liberty. The fact is that they are going off to get themselves killed so that the English merchants can grab the South African diamond and gold mines, the richest in the world.

A week later, Sir Laurier offers to recruit a second contingent. In all, 7,500 men are recruited in Canada, and this British colonial war costs the Canadian treasury $2,800,000. Canayens are enrolled alongside English-Canadians in the British army, and are slaughtered so that England can do to the Boers what she has already done to the Canayens themselves: subject them to colonialism.

Not many, however, enlist. Most Canayens are opposed to the war. In March, 1900, street fights break out in Montreal between McGill University students, fanatic supporters of the war waving the Union Jack, and students from the Université de Laval waving the tricolour.

Bourassa, re-elected by acclamation, continues to criticise Laurier on the question of Canada's participation in the war. He thinks Canada should exercise more independence from England. He is a nationalist – but a *Canadian* nationalist, not a Canayen nationalist. He is not for an independent Quebec. He wants an independent Canada. He is opposed to British colonialism, but *for* a Canada from sea to sea.

These distinctions are important, because Bourassa's nationalism has often been confused with a desire for Quebec independence.

160

If anyone claims that Bourassa was a great 'nationalist,' it must always be understood in the context of *Canadian* nationalism, not *Québécois*. He was in favour of a Canada made up of two nations living in harmony. It would be more precise to qualify him as an anti-imperialist pro-Canadian.

In March, 1901, when England at last succeeds in crushing the Boers, Bourassa proposes a resolution in the House, urging that Britain grant South Africa its independence. Laurier ridicules the proposal, observing it is too late for independence by virtue of "the terrible logic of war," and that "when the British flag flies over South Africa, they shall have that which has been found everywhere else during the last sixty years under the British flag -- liberty for all, and justice and civil rights for English and Dutch alike..." Bourassa's resolution is soundly defeated, and the House sings *God Save the King*.

Bourassa's *anti-imperialism*, now beginning to spread in Quebec, cools down Laurier's imperialist enthusiasms. After all, he has to depend on Liberal votes in Quebec to stay in power. At Edward VII's coronation he refuses the title of 'Lord', but nevertheless continues to promote the expansion of the Empire.

In Quebec, however, the broad anti-imperialist movement grows still stronger. Among Bourassa's supporters we find young people willing to go farther: they begin to speak of the independence of Quebec.

Then there is the reactionary nationalism of Bishop Paquet, who makes much of "the vocation of the French race in North America." He boasts: "... We are not only a civilized race, we are the pioneers of civilization; we are not only a religious people, we are the messengers of the very idea of religion; we are not only submissive sons of the Church, we are, or ought to be, numbered among its zealots, its defenders, and its apostles. Our mission is less to manipulate capital than to exchange ideas; it consists less in fighting the fire of factories than in maintaining and making shine far and wide the luminous fire of religion and thought."

The young nationalists form the *Ligue Nationaliste* with a programme drawn up by Olivar Asselin, who asks for maximum autonomy for Canada inside the Empire and maximum autonomy for Quebec inside Canada. On the other hand, some priests including the Reverend Lionel Groulx found the A.C.J.C. (Catholic Associa-

161

tion of French-Canadian Youth) with the watchword "piety, study, action." The classical colleges propagate a nationalism mixed with religion; they preach a nationalism that believes in Canada as a homeland where the Canayens can spread their so-called French culture and 'their' Catholic religion.

The Québécois nationalism of today sees Quebec itself as the homeland of the Canayens, who must take back the economy that has been stolen from them. To do this they must exercise sovereignty as a free people amongst other peoples of the world. But this kind of Québécois nationalism was inconceivable at that time. It was to take another fifty years before it began to appear.

The A.C.J.C. brings together all the young French-Canadians "who believe in Catholicism and in its universal efficacy for the good of individuals and societies, in the French-Canadian race and its providential mission; of all who are aware of the dangers which beset our Catholic faith and our French-Canadian race." This nationalism shows keen opposition to the policies of the federal government concerning the entry of Saskatchewan and Alberta into Confederation in 1905.

Laurier, as always, yields to English-Canadian demands that the public schools in these new provinces be English and Protestant. Separate schools are allowed, but at the expense of the parents. French instruction is allowed, one hour each day from 3:00 to 4:00 p.m. in districts where the Canayens are numerous. Catechism is to be taught after class.

Bourassa delivers several speeches in Montreal deploring the fate of the western Canayens, but it is a lost cause. His colleague, Lavergne, presents a bill for the issuance of bilingual bank-notes and stamps, but the government rejects it. Faced with this continued opposition from the federal government, Bourassa and Lavergne turn to the provincial government to promote the Canayen cause in Confederation. They abandon the federal level and run as Nationalists allied to the Conservatives against the Liberals of Sir Lomer Gouin in the provincial elections of 1908.

Bourassa and two other Nationalists are elected, but Gouin's Liberal government retains a strong majority. The Nationalist movement is bogged down in party politics, with no precise goal or clear idea of what it stands for. Does Bourassa speak of the liberation of the Quebec people? No. Does he speak of overthrowing Anglo-Saxon colonialism? No. He speaks of the French language as protector of the Catholic faith, and of a great Canada where the French-Canadian and English-Canadian can get along like brothers.

This reactionary nationalism is simply too far from reality for the Quebec people to identify with. The people vote Liberal at the federal and provincial levels hoping to undermine the power of the Church, whose political tool is the Conservative Party. Yet Bourassa, the man who appears to take over the leadership of the liberation movement, allies himself with the Conservatives and the Church. The people refuse to support the reactionary path he has taken. They maintain their own passive resistance to Anglo-Saxon colonialism, and are skeptical of all these 'leaders,' both those who practice patronage like the Conservatives or Liberals, and those who practice religious austerity and talk in intellectual abstractions like the Nationalists.

While Bourassa prates of "our language as the guardian of our faith," American capital flows into the province and gobbles up our natural resources. The American Regime is upon us. U.S.-owned companies take over our hydro-electric resources, the pulp and paper industry, the textile industry, the mining industry and railways.

By greasing the palms of the politicians in power these companies receive almost unlimited concessions that allow them to rob us of our resources and to exploit our man-power.

What in fact did the provincial Liberals accomplish after their rise to power in 1897?

Under Premier Marchand, American capitalists were invited to come and exploit us. The benefits? A few dollars added to the provincial treasury from payments made for the right to cut timber and sell lands, (money that wound up in the Liberal Party treasury), and a few more jobs for the *habitants* as lumberjacks or unskilled labourers.

One in five Québécois could neither read nor write. This was a result of the bill that had handed over education to the Clergy. When the Marchand government tried to remedy this situation by re-establishing a ministry of education, Bishop Bruchési of Montreal successfully opposed it and the bill was eventually rejected.

In 1900, Parent replaced Marchand as Premier. By this time the province's debt was eating up a third of its revenue. But the provincial government continued to play the domestic servant, keeping house for foreign capitalists and the Church. They put the province into more debt by constructing roads that principally served the exploiters. Lomer Gouin, who replaced Parent in 1905, spent $20 million for this purpose.

This same Gouin passed a law prohibiting children under 14 from working in factories, but industry refused to comply with it. Another law set the work-week at 58 hours in the textile industry. There was still no law guaranteeing a minimum wage rate, and provision for unemployment insurance. A little consolation : Ottawa gave back Ungava (New Quebec) to the province of Quebec. However, this law also fixed the boundary between Quebec and Newfoundland in Labrador, three miles from the coast.

The Naval Question

Around 1909, England begins to see its naval supremacy threatened by Germany which is in the process of building a powerful fleet. England hurries to enlarge hers and calls on her colonies for help.

Laurier obediently proposes a bill creating a Canadian Navy at England's disposal. The Conservatives oppose it, favouring instead a direct contribution in millions of dollars. The Nationalists oppose both proposals, seeing in them only more British imperialism.

Bourassa founds *Le Devoir* in 1910; he invites as collaborators Olivar Asselin, Jules Fournier, Omer Héroux and Georges Pelletier, the latter two representing the religious nationalism of the A.C.J.C. The newspaper systematically attacks the Naval Bill, but Laurier still manages to get it passed.

In the federal elections of 1911, the Liberals are defeated. The Conservatives now have the majority, and Borden becomes Prime Minister. The Nationalists, who helped the Conservatives get elected in Quebec, now see these same Conservatives turn against them and support Borden on policies even more imperialistic than those of Laurier. The Nationalist strategy of allying with the Conservatives proves disastrous. Borden goes so far as to offer England a gift of $35,000,000 to build three warships but his bill is blocked in the Senate by the Liberal majority. Then the first World War (1914-18) gives him the opportunity to show England just how generous he can be – at the expense, of course, of the Canayens.

World War I (1914-1918)

German capitalism developed quickly after the unification of the country and Bismarck's efficient administration. Germany tried hard to catch up with the other advanced capitalist countries, England, France, and the United States. The nation rapidly industrialized, launched out into world trade and colonized the few African territories not yet grabbed by the other imperialist countries.

France and England are not pleased to see the rise of this rival. France stands to lose her predominance in Europe, England hers on the seas. So both powers form an alliance with Russia against Germany and her ally Austria-Hungary.

The armies are all ready. Germany invades Belgium. France and England counter-attack. Trench warfare drags on for four years in north-east France. The United States enters the war against Germany in 1917, and sends more troops. Germany is eventually to be defeated.

In Canada, right from the beginning of hostilities, Parliament votes 50 million dollars to recruit a Canadian army. The call goes out for a voluntary enlistment. English-Canadians, their pro-British chauvinism stirred up by bourgeois propagandists, quickly enlist.

	1901	1911
White population of Quebec	1,648,898	2,005,776

The Canayens do not see much sense in enlisting. Why should they? Canada is not threatened. Why go and fight to defend British and French imperialist interests? Moreover, how can they be expected to enlist in an army that anglicizes all Canayens, and in which there is no place for Canayen officers? How can they enlist in a foreign army alongside English-Canadians who are willing to see the French language suppressed in Ontario? For it is just at this time that the question of French schools in Ontario comes to the fore.

French Schools in Ontario

Already by this time thousands of Canayens are living in Ontario, especially around Ottawa, Sudbury and Windsor. The Orangemen [1] of Ontario, who can't stand Quebec and who earlier played a major role in repressing the Riel rebellion, don't like the looks of these Catholic Canayens in Ontario. The Irish Catholic Church in Ontario is also against the Canayens, and especially against instruction in French.

In 1912-13 the Ontario Ministry of Education proclaims English the only language of instruction in all the Ontario schools, public or separate. The study of French is to be limited to one hour per day. The Catholic separate schools must submit to the authority of English Protestant inspectors. Subsidies from Ottawa for separate schools are discontinued.

Bourassa, Lavergne, Olivar Asselin, Jules Fournier, the A.C.J.C., the Church and all other nationalist and Catholic elements combined launch a campaign to resist this discrimination against their Ontario compatriots. They pressure Borden's federal government and the Ontario provincial government. Fiery speeches are delivered. The newspaper *Le Droit* is established in Ottawa. When war is declared and the English-Canadians try to promote enlistment in the Canadian army in Quebec, the nationalist elements reply that the Canayens have no business

1. *Orangemen:* English Protestant fanatics and reactionaries utterly opposed to the persistence of the French and Catholicism in Canada.

fighting for the British Empire when they don't even have the right to learn French in Ontario.

The Church declines to go that far in opposing the government. Instead, it organizes a campaign against Bourassa. Bishop Bruchési, speaking in favour of the Patriotic Fund, says, "England is engaged in a terrible war, which she sought to avoid at all costs. Loyal subjects, recognizing in her the protectress of our rights and our liberties, we owe her our most generous cooperation."

The Conscription Crisis

While our clerical-bourgeois elite was unanimous in its desire to safeguard the Ontario Canayens' religious and linguistic rights, it was still divided on the question of participation in the war. On the one hand, nationalists like Bourassa and Lavergne continued their fight against British imperialism in favour of greater Canadian autonomy, while on the other, the Clergy and elements from the sell-out Canayen bourgeoisie still sympathized with British imperialism.

The Borden government appealed to the Church to propagate the notion of a Holy War. This it eagerly did by having a statement read in all Quebec churches, giving the Church's blessing to the British war policy and to the sending of troops.

To further entice Canayens to enlist, the Borden government creates the 22nd Royal Battalion in 1914. But the Canayens are all privates, plus a few non-commissioned officers.

Despite this ruse, the Canayens don't rush to enlist. They agree with Bourassa, who writes in *Le Devoir*: "In the name of religion, liberty, and loyalty to the British flag, French-Canadians are enjoined to go fight the Prussians of Europe. But are we to let the Prussians of Ontario impose their domination as masters in the very heart of the Canadian Confederation, under the shelter of the British flag and British institutions?" Bourassa also attacks the Borden government for the profits that some MP's and their friends are accumulating on war contracts.

In 1916 the Ontario government abolishes the Ottawa Commission of Separate Schools and replaces it with another commission that includes only one Canayen. But the Canayen teachers continue to teach French in the schools, without a contract and without pay. The school itself is guarded by mothers armed with hat-pins. The Orangemen accuse Bourassa of being the instigator of this movement and demand his arrest. The Québécois decide to boycott Ontario manufacturers.

By 1916 eleven battalions of Canayens have already been drawn up. There are 12,000 Canayens in the Canadian army, 4.5% of the total. Despite Laurier's speeches, the encouragement of the bishops and of all the newspapers except *Le Devoir*, enlistment is minimal.

The authorities now begin to insist that it will never come to compulsory military service — that is, conscription. Which is just a way of preparing people for the worst. The Borden government supported by Bishop Bégin and Bishop Bruchési begins registration for national service.

In May, Borden announces conscription. Mass demonstrations break out all over Quebec. In Montreal an angry crowd smashes the windows of *La Patrie* and *La Presse*, two newspapers that had sold out to Ottawa for quite some time now. In Quebec the crowd does the same to the offices of the *Chronicle* and *L'Evénement*.

Confronted with a people in revolt, the clerical-bourgeois elite, the editors of *Le Devoir* and even Bourassa himself immediately start preaching restraint and discipline. The lower Clergy breaks from the hierarchy and joins the people in their opposition to this compulsory military service.

All summer at rallies in communities throughout Quebec, the cry: "Vive la Révolution!" can be heard on all sides. Another popular slogan is "Down with Borden!" The people charge through government buildings, break windows and fire blank cartridges. At one of these demonstrations, the speakers urge the people to take up arms. The police charge into the crowd. One demonstrator is killed. On the 9th of August, property in Cartierville belonging to Lord Atholstan is blown up. Bourassa bemoans sterile violence that only serves to arm the enemy, the English.

Borden kicks off his election campaign with a proposal to unite the parties during this war period. He gets some Liberals to join his 'Union' government, though Laurier refuses to take part. This Union government (really a union of the Conservatives and Liberals from the English-speaking provinces) wins by a strong majority. All of Quebec, except of course the wards in English Westmount, votes against the government. The House of Commons is clearly divided between Canayens and English-Canadians. Not a single Canayen is in Borden's new cabinet.

The Canayen people clearly indicate to the clerical-bourgeois elite that they've had enough of Confederation, this constitutional prison. They have been made to submit to English-Canadian domination, but they will not be used as cannon fodder in an imperialist war. The clerical-bourgeois elite, accustomed as it is to servility, responds very timidly to the popular reaction. In the Quebec Legislative Assembly, Liberal member Francoeur mildly proposes Quebec's secession from the rest of Canada.

Sir Lomer Gouin tries hard to prevent the debate, but it takes place anyway. It drags on for weeks, each member presenting his little speech *for* and *against* separation, when, in fact, this is a vital decision for the Québécois people. Francoeur withdraws his motion, declaring his satisfaction with the effects it has produced.

Without waiting for the outcome of these debates, the people go into action. In the spring of 1918 hundreds of Canayens take refuge in the woods from the hunt for conscripts that's now in full swing.

On the evening of March 29 in Quebec, the federal police (the R.C.M.P.), arrest a Canayen who cannot produce his military service exemption papers. Thousands of Canayens quickly get together and burn down the R.C.M.P. station. Singing "O Canada" and the "Marseillaise," they go on to the *Chronicle* and *L'Evénement* to do the same. The next day, they attack enlistment bureaus and burn their files.

The municipal police allow them to do this. The R.C.M.P., outflanked, has to call on the army. A batallion from Toronto arrives and charges into the crowd with fixed bayonets. But the demonstrators come back the next day. This time the cavalry pushes them away with axe handles.

169

On April 1, despite all the threats from the civil and military authorities and the appeals for calm from the religious authorities, the people, armed with makeshift guns, fire on the occupation troops. The soldiers bring out their machine-guns. The cavalry attack with swords. Four demonstrators are killed, several are wounded and 58 are arrested. The armed struggle comes to an end on April 2nd. The Church and the press condemn these new *Patriotes,* and the federal government suspends *habeas corpus* and decrees immediate enlistment of all the rebels. Borden agrees to the formation of an entirely Canayen brigade.

Laval University actively participated in the new effort at recruitment. Some 19,500 Canayens were persuaded or coerced into joining the service, while 18,827 others managed to evade the draft call. By the war's end in November 1918, 15,000 Canayens had fought at the front, 5,000 others in the Navy, and 15,000 more were still in training.

The Aftermath of War

Despite their victory over Germany, England and France come out of the war weakened and in debt. The country that really emerges victorious is the United States. Although the U.S. participated militarily only in the last two years of the war, the American bourgeoisie knew very well how to exploit the situation, how to profit from the production of armaments, munitions and war supplies.

In short, the bloody war stimulated the American economy and allowed the U.S. financial and industrial institutions to tighten their hold on Canada and to penetrate into war-weary Europe. In fact, as soon as the war ended, England lost its predominance in Canada and was gradually replaced by the new metropolis, the United States.

This period represents the end of the English Regime and the beginning of the American Regime.

PART 3 THE AMERICAN REGIME (1920-?)

The Growth of American Control

American capitalists come here to invest their capital in the exploitation of our natural resources. What does this mean? Flourishing American companies, rich in capital, look for resources that can be extracted at a low cost and sold for huge profits. Quebec is rich in forests and minerals. Its hydro-electric potential is fantastic. There are markets for lumber products, minerals and electricity.

Why do the Canayens not develop their resources themselves? At the beginning of the century, Errol Bouchette rightly told them : "We must take charge of industry." But to do so one must have the means. Under capitalism the means is capital, sums of money to equip an enterprise to get it going until it brings in returns.

The Quebec government could have developed Quebec resources for the benefit of the Canayen people. It could have borrowed money to launch our economy. But it was prevented from doing so because it was dominated, through the Clergy and through petty Canayen politicians like Sir Lomer Gouin, by the Anglo-Saxon bourgeoisie. The provincial government was at the service of Anglo-Saxon capital. The petty politicians came to power and stayed there because of Anglo-Saxon money. Once in office they had to answer to those who had financed their campaign, and not to the people. In 1931, as one example among many, it was discovered that the company that had obtained the contract for the construction of the hydro-electric works at Beauharnois had coughed up $864,000 for the Liberal party's treasury.

A few small Canayen capitalists like Dubuc in Chicoutimi, Rodolphe Forget in Montreal or Amyot in Quebec did start some industries. But their investments were insignificant beside those of the English-Canadians, and especially those of the Americans.

With no trouble at all, the United States capitalists took hold of the primary sector of direct extraction – the entire pulp and paper industry, hydro-electric works, asbestos, gold and silver mines. The provincial government was clearly no more than a caretaker for Anglo-Saxon capitalists.

The *Duke-Price* and *Aluminium* companies invested $100,000,000 in the Lake St John region for the installation of pulp and paper mills and an aluminum factory.[1] The construction of the necessary hydro-electric plants caused widespread flooding of arable lands. The Canayens who worked in pain and misery to clear their lands now see them disappear with the coming of capitalist industrialization. The *habitant* becomes the employee of the big companies, who come to rob him of his land and resources.

In 1926, the pulp and paper industry grossed 107 million dollars. A very impressive sum. How much of it went to Canayens?

The U.S. pulp and paper companies sold paper worth $107-million to other Canadian or American companies.

Where were the profits for the Canayens? And it was our forests that were being destroyed.

The habitants did all the work, but for the total 1926 pulp and paper production, less than one million dollars was paid out in salaries for the thousands of work-hours supplied by thousands of Canayens. The provincial government collected a few thousand dollars in tax returns that went into road construction for the benefit of these same companies. In short, of the $107 million of that year's production, a mere 2 or 3% went to the Canayens who were the real producers – just as they are the real owners – of the wealth of Quebec.

1. The location of this factory is not due to the presence of any bauxite necessary to the production of aluminum in that region. It is because of the large quantities of electricity needed for the production of aluminum, power that is supplied by the Saguenay River.

This is the way the Americans and the English-Canadians systematically rob our resources, exploit Canayen cheap-labour, make huge profits and leave us the crumbs. This legalized, institutionalized robbery makes us slaves in the lumber yards and factories of our own country.

Our politicians collaborate with these international crooks. The Church collaborates too, and invests money in these companies that exploit the Canayens.

The Canayen workers who are aware of their exploitation organize and affiliate, as we have seen, with American unions. In order to combat radical unionism, the Church creates the Confederation of Catholic Workers of Canada (CTCC) in 1921, organising 26,000 workers into company unions. These unions recognize the 'authority' and the 'rights' of the owners to exploit the workers, and try to get the workers to accept their inferior position "because this is the way God wants it." They encourage the workers to collaborate with the owners, their supposed superiors, "because one must respect established order and authority."

When Quebec farmers try to organize a radical movement, the Church tries the same thing. It founds the Catholic Union of Farmers.

Faced with this U.S. seizure of our natural resources, one segment of the clerical-bourgeois elite who supported Bourassa's Canadian nationalism now re-orients itself towards a Quebec nationalism. The Reverend Lionel Groulx is the leader. His newspaper *L'Action Française* founded in 1917 (which becomes *L'Action Canadienne-Française* in 1929) is the organ for the defense of *French-Canadian* rights. It preaches *la revanche des berceaux* – 'the revenge of the cradle' – a high Canayen birth-rate so that Canayens may become the majority in Canada and thus get their rights respected.

This type of nationalism amounts to a kind of religious cult of the homeland and the French language. It considers fervent Catholicism the driving force for national unity. It approves a corporate capitalist form of government like that of Salazar in Portugal: dictatorship by an ardent Catholic who defines the roles of the professions, the trades and the working class in such a way that each class knows its place and stays in it.

173

The Higher Clergy, the general staff of the armed forces and the industrial elite rank just below the dictator; below them are the liberal professions, the civil servants, the Lower Clergy, and at the bottom the workers and peasants.

This kind of nationalism is tantamount to restoring a feudal system in Quebec. It really requires a dictator who, with his army, can chase the English out of Quebec and institute the Catholic religion as the only religion, the French language as the only language. He would sustain the rise of an industrial bourgeoisie to develop the nation's resources and keep the working class in the lumber yards and factories. In short, this miracle-dictator would install an absolute order, "the will of God," according to which the dictator would rule, the army maintain order, the Church spread blessings from heaven, the bourgeoisie exploit, the doctors practice medicine, and the workers go on working. After a while this dictator might get himself crowned by the Bishop of Quebec, and all would be for the best in this best of all possible worlds.

The enemies of this nationalism of the *Action Française* are: atheism and all systems of thought that do not recognize the Church as the only source of truth; bourgeois liberalism and bourgeois democracy with their lack of respect for religious authorities; and especially socialism that calls for a working class struggle by all means necessary to overthrow dictatorships and ruling classes in order to build a classless society.

Reverend Groulx wrote a book with a very significant title – *Notre Maître le passé,* 'Our Master, the Past.' In it he glorified the past, our ancestors and the French regime, in which, according to him, the Catholic religion and French culture magnificently illuminated North America. He made heroes of those famous exploiters of the Red man – Dollard des Ormeaux, Jeanne-Mance, Maisonneuve, Marguerite Bourgeoys and the rest.

The ideas propagated by the publications and speeches of the *Action Française* actually only attracted those elements of the clerical-bourgeoisie who were conscious of the real danger of the extinction of the Québécois people. The other half of the clerical-bourgeois elite, already committed to federalism and English interests, tried to resist this nationalism that could threaten its position.

At the University of Montreal this federalist elite insists that Reverend Groulx sign a document promising not to attack federalism any more. Groulx refuses to sign, but later consents to an arrangement by which he is to devote himself exclusively to historical research.

The Clergy itself is divided between Groulx's nationalism and a comfortable federalism. Father Villeneuve and several professors from some of the classical colleges go along with Groulx. But the majority of bishops remain loyal to the federal government.

The people are not much interested in the nationalism of *L'Action Française*. To them it's just more of the theories of intellectuals, with nothing to offer workers and farmers. They see in it a system in which they would find themselves no better off than they are now. French culture is foreign to them and always will be. Catholicism may be alright, but there are already enough priests and bishops who have been telling them what to do for long enough. And as for a dictator, they could never go for that. In short, there is nothing good in it for them, so they remain aloof.

Politics :
More of the Same

While Groulx, Father Villeneuve, Edouard Montpetit, Olivar Asselin, Louis Durand and Anatole Vanier dream of a French state that they might perhaps call *Laurentie*, those in power continue to keep the people in the dark, confuse them and sell out the country.

On the federal level, Meighen replaces Borden as Conservative Prime Minister. The Liberals hold a convention American-style and elect a new leader, Mackenzie King, who spent the war years not at the front but as 'industrial relations' advisor to one of the biggest American exploiters, the notorious Rockefeller. Mackenzie King needs a Canayen lieutenant. He first selects

175

the Premier of Quebec, Lomer Gouin, who is delighted to serve as Negro-King to the federal government. But King soon realizes that Gouin has too close ties to the Montreal English financiers. This could cause him to lose votes in the West, where the farmers are struggling against the domination of Montreal financiers over the federal government. Gouin is administrator of the *Bank of Montreal*, the *Royal Trust* and several other financial institutions. King forgets about Gouin and calls on Ernest Lapointe, who comes running like a loyal dog.

In the federal elections of 1921, no party can obtain a majority because the prairie farmers upset the comfortable two-party system with their *Progressive Party*. The Liberals get 117 seats, the Conservatives 50, the Progressives 65 and Independents 4. Horse-trading begins. The Liberals woo the Progressives. But the result is a minority government.

Again in 1925 there is a minority government, with the same behind-the-scenes horse-trading. But the Liberals get caught in a customs scandal. Some Liberals have been making tidy profits for themselves by smuggling Canadian liquor into the United States where prohibition [1] is now in force.

In 1926, new elections. Another minority government. Bennett replaces Meighen as Conservative leader. Mackenzie King tries to form a government by making alliances with the Progressives. During these years of prosperity, the government does almost nothing. It enjoys the "prosperity" brought by the invasion of American capital. In 1926, the value of U.S. investments in Canada as a whole surpasses that of the British. The country passes into the hands of foreign capitalists, and the federal government becomes a caretaker government for the American exploiters.

---

1. *prohibition:* From 1919 to 1933, the act of prohibition of alcohol forbids the consumption of all alcoholic beverages in the U.S. This law, aimed at eradicating evil at its roots, provoked instead the creation of a contraband network and the burgeoning of speak-easies. It did not stop the consumption of alcohol, but instead allowed certain 'free enterprisers' to make a fortune in a few years. Think of the owners of Canadian distilleries in particular, who overnight became suppliers of contraband liquor to the entire northern United States. It is an open secret that the owner of Seagram's made his first millions during prohibition.

In 1926, at the London Imperial Conference, the English colonies become full-time members of a Commonwealth in which England is only one country among others. In other words, British imperialism is dying. Canadian politicians shout from the rooftops that Canada is independent. Bourassa himself sees his ideas of Canadian nationalism being realized. The joke is that American imperialism is quietly on its way to making Canada its most exploitable colony.

1927 marks the Diamond Jubilee of Confederation. The elites deliver their nice little speeches. The Canayens stay home. To win them over to a collective Canadian joy, bilingual stamps are issued, and "O Canada" is sung in French and English. The Canayens continue their passive resistance.

Quebec in Depression

In 1920 Taschereau replaces Gouin as Liberal premier of Quebec. He acts exactly like his predecessor. The English-speaking financiers grease his palms, and he becomes their caretaker.

In 1926 the federal government takes the question of Labrador to the Privy Council in London. That authority decides to give Labrador back to Newfoundland -- without, of course, consulting Quebec. One hundred and ten thousand square miles are stolen from Quebec, but Taschereau's caretaker government says not a word.

Taschereau gives $1,000,000 to McGill, already well-endowed and also well on its way to supplying trained personnel for the companies that exploit us. The University of Montreal, which has just become autonomous from Laval University and which has to serve a population ten times larger than that of McGill, gets no more than the English-language university.

Besides financial aid for universities and hospitals -- aid that is non-accountable -- this caretaker government builds roads for the exploiting companies. In 1930, Quebec has an insignificant debt. The caretakers keep the door-steps clean for the international exploiters. Beautiful roads, beautiful resources, an infinite amount of cheap labour. A typical Taschereau comment of the times is, "Yes, there is American money in the province and it is welcome. As long as I and my colleagues are here we will invite foreign capital to come in and help us develop our province."

But this false-bottomed prosperity is not to last. To inflate this prosperity the big financial institutions have lent money far beyond their capacity. Credit has its limits. The speculators grow suspicious and uncertain. Suddenly everyone wants to sell his shares at once before they lose their value. Panic sets in on the New York stock exchange, then in every other exchange around the world.

The companies slow down production, first for lack of investment capital, then for lack of markets. The buyers have lost their credit as well. The factories grind to a standstill; unemployment spreads. No more work: no more production. No more production: no more consumption. Capitalism has known recessions before, but never anything as serious as this. It is called the Great Depression, and lasts all through the thirties. In fact, it really does not begin to subside until the Second World War. War stimulates the economy -- this is one of the laws of capitalism.

In Canada, prairie wheat no longer sells. Mining companies can no longer sell their minerals. In the 1930 elections, the Conservatives come to power with Bennett as leader and vote $20,000,000 for public works projects designed to give jobs to the unemployed. They also approve a rise in customs tariffs to protect Canadian industry.

One result of this economic crisis is the creation of new political parties. In 1932, together with western workers and farmers, Woodsworth founds the *C.C.F.* (Cooperative Commonwealth Federation), which calls for nationalization of health services, socialization of financial institutions, the adoption of a work code and a new tax assessment.

William Aberhart founds the *Social Credit Party,* whose principal theory is the distribution of dividends to the population to start the economy going again.

In 1935, King and the Liberals come back to power. The C.C.F. and Social Credit win a few seats. The federal government gives itself the exclusive right to handle social problems like unemployment, and takes over the administration of succession and corporation taxes from the provinces.

The depression has left its marks on Quebec. The pulp and paper mills are almost at a standstill. In the cities, the shoe, textile, and clothing factories are paralyzed. The 394 American companies that exploit the Québécois have to lay them off. The religious communities lose a lot too.

Thousands of unemployed workers are forced to fight one another for jobs in public works, or to get relief from the state. In 1932, 100,000 persons receive direct help.

In 1931, when unemployment reaches gigantic proportions (27% of unionized workers alone), the Taschereau government passes an act to promote a return to the farms. Workers are invited to leave the cities, the industrial world, to go and till lands in no way suited for farming. This infamous back-to-the-farm reaction is the historically typical response of the colonialized Québécois to hard times. The first such movement came after the Conquest, a general withdrawal to agriculture. After the defeat of the Rebellion, again there were sermons of return to the soil. This third time was during the crisis of the thirties.

Camilien Houde, leader of the provincial Conservatives, had dared to speak out against American investment. He is elected mayor of Montreal in 1930, and gives up his place as Conservative leader to Maurice Duplessis, a young lawyer from Trois-Rivières.

In 1934 Paul Gouin, disgusted with the corruption of Taschereau's Liberals, founds *L'Action libérale nationale*, which stresses the necessity for the economic and social liberation of Quebec. Gouin's honesty and integrity brings him supporters. He speaks of the abolition of party treasuries, of the corruption of politicians, of the need for state intervention in industry and social problems. He wants to change the existing political mores. He manages to hold 119 meetings in one year, and the people believe something new is happening.

But Duplessis, the Conservative leader, makes an alliance with Gouin to defeat the Liberals in the elections of 1935. If the Liberals are defeated, Duplessis will become Premier, and Gouin can name the other cabinet ministers. In the elections, however, Taschereau returns to power with a weak majority.

The Liberals get 48 seats, the A.L.N. 26 and the Conservatives 16.

A scandal then reveals that Taschereau and his friends have had their palms greased. Taschereau resigns, and Adélard Godbout who succeeds him has to call another general election.

The holy alliance of Gouin and Duplessis´is now broken. Duplessis exploits the situation to attract most of Gouin's supporters, and leaves Gouin in the lurch.

In the 1936 elections, Duplessis' party, now called the *Union Nationale,* wins 76 seats. The Liberals keep 14. Duplessis has profited from all of Gouin's work and from his bold programme of reforms. Once in office, however, he does nothing. He has no intention of nationalizing the electric power companies. Like Taschereau he believes in private enterprise, and in the freedom of American capitalism as long as it fills up the Union Nationale's treasury. The people have been taken in again. And an honest but naive man like Gouin finds himself nowhere.

What does Duplessis and his Union Nationale do, besides get rich by handing over our natural wealth to the Americans? He has an old-age pension bill passed, and one for needy mothers. Another bill recognizing unions is passed, but it gives the government the right to change collective bargaining as it pleases -- that is, in favour of the employers. Another statute establishing fair wages sets them so low that certain employers actually lower the wages of their workers to conform to the law.

Another famous Duplessis achievement is the Padlock Law (1937), which allows the government to close down the business of anyone it suspects of wanting to overthrow the government. A communist newspaper is obliged to stop publishing under this law. Yet in the same year Duplessis allows Adrien Arcand and his Nazi Party, called the *Christian National Socialist Party,* to hold meetings and organize a convention in Kingston to extend their fascist association from coast to coast.

In the crisis of the thirties Groulx's *Action Canadienne-Française* is revitalized. In 1933, it is called *L'Action Nationale* and has as collaborators Esdras Minville, Arthur Laurendeau and René Chaloult. Again there are articles published on the Catholic mission, French culture, the return to the soil, corporate capitalism.

L'Action Nationale and *Les Jeunes-Canada* work closely together. Together they organize talks on 'corporatist organization', and 'Canada in the commonwealth.' There are vague allusions to separatism. They speak of the French state of America, of *Laurentie,* independent but a member of the Commonwealth. They urge the adoption of the *Carillon* flag, the present *fleur-de-lys.*

World War II (1939-1945)

Germany's defeat in 1918 left her in a disastrous position. The imperialist powers that had defeated her -- England, France and the United States really took revenge in order to satisfy their own international ambitions. The military defeat was followed by French occupation of a part of Germany rich in resources and industry. Moreover, Germany had to pay war reparations that were impossible for her to meet.

The Social Democrats[1] who came to power in Germany were unable to stabilize the economy. The German Communist Party, which had hundreds of thousands of members, tried to provoke the overthrow of the capitalist system; but its setbacks and the weakness of the Social Democrats paved the way for Adolf Hitler and allowed him to play on the humiliation of the German people, to build himself a small personal army and -- most important -- to forge an alliance with the German capitalists. He became chancellor and granted himself dictatorial powers, beginning by killing off the Communists who were his chief opposition.

Hitler makes a pact with the German capitalists to get the economy off the ground. In this New Order the German people have work, and Germany gets back on her feet. But in order to continue to develop according to the laws of this imperialist

1. *social democracy:* the political philosophy that has as its objective the improvement of the conditions of the working class and the underprivileged in general, without, however, altering the capitalist basis of the structure. This vain hope to 'civilize' capitalism -- that is, the desire to see the rich a little less rich and the poor a little less poor -- is the mark of all Social Democrats. In Canada, the N.D.P. today plays this role of serving capitalism by trying to reform a few of its worst effects.

system, other countries must be conquered, other peoples must be enslaved.

Hitler concentrates on war production. According to his imperialist ideology, the German people are a superior race, other nationalities like the English and French are slightly inferior, the Slavs are sub-human and the Jews are a race that must be exterminated.

Having consolidated his power at home by massacring the Communists, collaborating with the capitalists and cultivating illusions of grandeur in the German masses, Hitler's army marches into the Rhineland. He provokes a *coup d'état* in Austria and annexes it to Germany. He makes a pact with Mussolini, the Italian fascist dictator who wants to become the great power in the Mediterranean.

All the while the British with Chamberlain and French with Daladier are appeasing Hitler. They hope that he will attack the Soviet Union.

They 'give' him half of Czechoslovakia at Munich and wink when his army takes the other half.

Stalin, seeing the danger, understands better than the British or French that German imperialism *must* try to conquer the world, and especially the juicy plums of the British and French Empires.

After being rebuffed in attempts to sign an alliance with Britain or France, the Soviet Union signs a non-aggression pact with Germany to buy time.

In Asia, Japan follows Germany's path. It grabs Manchuria and begins a systematic invasion of all southeast Asia. Japan signs a pact with Hitler. Capitalist powers, England, France and the United States see their interests threatened by the expansionist policies of Germany, Italy and Japan.

When Hitler invades Poland, England and France declare war. It is September 3, 1939. The Canadian government declares war on Germany on September 10, and Parliament votes $100 million for war operations. A Canadian expeditionary force is quickly organized. Enlistment is voluntary.

Hitler invades Denmark and Norway. On May 10, 1940, his forces enter Holland and Belgium and then France. The French are unable to withstand the assaults of German planes and armoured tanks. Marshal Pétain capitulates and begins to collaborate with the Germans, while General de Gaulle takes refuge in London to assemble the Free French Forces.

England prepares to resist the expected German invasion. Hitler takes Hungary, Rumania, Bulgaria, Yugoslavia and Greece. In 1941, he advances into the Soviet Union, but is stopped definitively at Stalingrad.

The Americans enter the war on December 7, 1941, when Japan attacks Pearl Harbour, the U.S. Hawaiian naval base. The Germans and Italians invade North Africa.

In Canada, King's Liberal government proclaims compulsory military service in June 1941, *but for the defense of the country only*. The Québécois do not oppose this law. The Québécois people are ready to defend their country. This reaction contradicts all the accusations of cowardice thrust at the Québécois by English-Canadians. The Québécois are ready to fight when it is a question of defending Quebec, but they have no desire to get killed defending the interests of imperialist powers.

When the federal government jails Adrien Arcand in May 1940, due to his Nazi sympathies, no Québécois demonstrates against his internment. This clearly demonstrates that Naziism, fascism and Hitler had no real support in Quebec. Even though a certain elite may have played with the corporatist idea, even though Groulx had praise for Mussolini, the people were against Hitler right from the beginning.

The surrender of France has a profound effect on Quebec. The Québécois do not want to go defend England, not any more than in 1914. But they are ready to fight to the death against an eventual German invasion of Quebec. They are even the first to fill the voluntary ranks for overseas service: as early as January, 1941, 50,000 Québécois have enlisted. Of course, a good many did not enlist by choice, but took up a soldier's life as the only way of escaping unemployment and earning pay that would enable them to house and feed their families.[1]

However, when the United States enters the war [2], King decides

---

1. Gabrielle Roy's *The Tin Flute* describes this very well.
2. The decision to impose conscription in Canada during World War I was also made just after the United States entered the war.

to ask for overseas service. The Conservative opposition and most English-speaking Canadians demand full conscription.

King holds a plebiscite on April 27, 1942. He asks the population to reply *yes* or *no* to the following question: "Do you agree to free the government from all obligations resulting from previous promises restricting the methods of mobilization for military service?" Which is a round-about way of saying "Are you for or against full conscription?"

In Quebec, 71.2 per cent answer NO. The Québécois (the population of Quebec minus the English in Westmount and the Eastern Townships) in fact vote 85 per cent NO. The other provinces vote 80 per cent yes. The Québécois are opposed to fascism but refuse to have a uniform put on their backs to be sent overseas and used as cannon fodder for the English.

This sentiment is confirmed on the 18th of August by the disaster at Dieppe. The British general staff wants to know how well the Germans are defending the French coast. They send out 6,100 soldiers, of whom four-fifths are Canadians, in 253 boats to the French coast to test the German defenses. These poor guys run into a German convoy three miles from the coast, and the massacre begins. When they manage to land on the French coast near Dieppe, German machine guns shoot them down like ducks. After two hours of this butchery, the general staff decides that the Germans can really defend the coast pretty well. The order goes out to evacuate. Of the 4,963 Canadians, 2,752 perish under German fire. The remaining 2,211 men, of whom 617 are wounded, manage to get back to England. The colonized always serve as cannon fodder for the imperialist, even in a war against fascism.

In the Quebec elections of 1939, the Québécois reject Duplessis and his shady dealings and vote for Godbout's Liberals. Godbout collaborates closely with King's federal Liberals.

At the time of the plebiscite André Laurendeau, Jean Drapeau, Gerard Filion and Georges Pelletier, editor of *Le Devoir,* found the *Ligue pour la défense du Canada,* which urges the Québécois to resist conscription. In September, Maxime Raymond founds the *Bloc Populaire* with André Laurendeau, Paul Gouin and Jean Drapeau. This party is against conscription but does not yet know what it is for -- corporatism, liberal capitalism or socialism.

In Ottawa during this time, King presents his bill in favour of full conscription (compulsory overseas service). This same King, who is Prime Minister thanks to Quebec Liberal votes, has the audacity to insist on conscription even though the vast majority of Québécois reject it. This behaviour is typical of a colonialist government that goes out to get votes with splendid promises but then does the opposite of what the people want.

The Québécois again are duped by the Federal government. Nothing is to be gained in Ottawa. And all the more so when this same government uses the war as an excuse to secure for itself formerly provincial powers such as the collection of personal income tax and corporation taxes.

The War Economy

Thanks to the war, Canada, like the United States, is experiencing a prosperity never known before. Thanks to the killing of 50 million men, women and children as the result of rival capitalists' greed, North America is able to pull out of the crisis and rebuild its economy.

It is also thanks to the war between European countries that the U.S. and Canadian governments can find the necessary capital to lend to those industrialists who manufacture arms and munitions for sale back to the governments. The governments in turn sell them to an allied country at war or use them for their own forces.

Thanks to the war too, American capitalism regains confidence and is ready to invest in Canada's war industries. The U.S. soon emerges as the principal supplier of war material to the Allies. After the war, the U.S. easily gains control of the economies of most of western Europe and much of Asia just as it already has control of Canada and Latin America.

The Canadian government sells millions of dollars of Victory Bonds to Canadians. Ottawa also lends huge amounts at low interest (if it does not give the cash outright) to capitalists eager to make fantastic profits. In a few years, Canadian industry is producing tanks, warships, synthetic rubber and radar equipment.

War demands production; production demands workers. So unemployment disappears. It is working class men, of course, who are called up to get themselves killed on the battlefield. But many sons of the bourgeoisie manage to find important positions that render them 'indispensable,' as they say, to war production.

Thanks to the war economy, the Simard brothers of Sorel develop into industrialists of some importance in Quebec. Manufacturing heavy guns and ships, they employ as many as 6,000 workers. Meanwhile, U.S. capitalists continue to infiltrate the Quebec economy, using the English Montreal businessmen as their chief allies. Quebec industrialists like Simard are not numerous enough to offer any real competition; instead they are invaluable collaborators in the exploitation of Quebec's wealth and people.

While capitalist industry increasingly subjects the Quebec people to a war economy, and the federal government trains our youth to shoulder guns like the English, our clerical-bourgeois elite continue their rear-guard debates.

Many *Bloc Populaire* supporters, seeing the capitalist expansion with its trusts and monopolies, turn to corporatism as a solution. At the same time, they allow a millionaire, Edouard Lacroix, to join them. Lacroix has no desire to see capitalism restrained by the imposition of a corporate system of government; on the contrary, he feels that capitalism can be developed most satisfactorily with the institutions already at its disposal.

On the national question, the *Bloc* does not know whether to be separatist or federalist. Some *Bloc* supporters see socialism as an international conspiracy against the people of Quebec. Others say that the Jews of Montreal are our worst enemy.

At the beginning of the twentieth century, Jewish immigrants from Russia, Poland, almost everywhere in Europe, found themselves like most other immigrants at the bottom of the social ladder. However, by playing the capitalist game, a few of them managed to escape from the exploited class to become the owners of small businesses, factories, shops and grocery stores -- copying the life style of the Montreal English bourgeoisie. They adopted the exploiter's language, English, using French only to give orders to their employees in their shops and to their maids at home.

So to some people, the exploiters of the Québécois no longer seem to be the English who are pulling the hidden strings of high finance and big business, but the Jews of St Lawrence and Craig

Streets and the Jewish shoe and clothing manufacturers who operate more openly.

But anti-semitism in Quebec existed largely in the minds of the English who were only too happy to stir it up on occasion and bring it forward as more 'evidence' that the Québécois are inescapably fascist and reactionary, and not to be trusted to govern themselves. The English rejoiced all the more when the Québécois could be persuaded to blame the Jew as his chief exploiter. Hiding behind the big enterprises and institutions of high finance, the English and American capitalists cynically played off Jews against Québécois. In fact, the real anti-semite was the English imperialist colonizer, who kept the Jewish bourgeois out of his social clubs and shuddered to see Jews buying property in Westmount.

The renowned *Bloc Populaire* merely gathered together various disgruntled elements of the clerical-bourgeois elite, but it had no coherent political philosophy of its own: it was against the big trusts but favoured small ones; it was against Hitler but for Salazar and Franco; it was for nationalization of electricity but against socialism. Despite this complete absence of structured political thinking, the *Bloc,* according to a 1943 poll, could claim 33 per cent of the Québécois vote. This means that a considerable section of the Québécois were ready to vote for the *Bloc* simply to get things going on the road to decolonization.

The C.C.F. party, modelled on the British Labour Party, managed to get its existence sanctioned by the Quebec bishops. But since it understood little about the position of the colonized Québécois and remained federalist, it had no real chance here.

Meanwhile that clever petty politician and leader of the opposition, Maurice Duplessis, was organizing his electoral machine and picking out the promises of the other parties that seemed to appeal to the Québécois. By talking bravely about provincial autonomy, he exploited Quebec nationalism, not to liberate the Québécois people but simply in order to get into power. He made sure that he got along well with the U.S. industrialists who filled his treasury for his election campaigns. Once in power he would open the field for them to exploit the people more fully.

While the *Bloc* supporters are squabbling amongst themselves in the newspapers, on the air and at their convention over issues concerning trusts and the return to an agricultural economy, and while Paul Gouin, Philippe Hamel and René Chaloult are resisting André Laurendeau's leadership, Duplessis quietly and carefully plots his return to office. He attacks Godbout's Liberal government for having nationalized the Montreal Light, Heat and Power Company, thus winning over the industrialists who have long been terrified of government economic intervention. He concentrates on the rural districts favoured on the electoral map. Although two-thirds of the population is in the cities, only one-third of the candidates can be elected from urban areas.

Duplessis promises the clergy that he will enforce the Padlock Law, the famous law that allows him to seize all so-called subversive literature. And of course he speaks out against conscription. The *Bloc* meanwhile drags Bourassa out of retirement to get all the nationalist votes; but Bourassa in his speech advises his audience to vote C.C.F.

In the provincial elections of August 8, 1944, the *Bloc* gets 15% of the votes, but only four seats. The Liberals win 37% of the votes and 37 seats; the Union Nationale receives 36% of the votes, but wins 48 seats. The C.C.F. has one candidate elected, and René Chaloult is re-elected as an independent. The farmers have voted almost unanimously for the Union Nationale. The other parties divide up the vote in the cities.

We can see that the electoral system allows a party that knows the game to gather only 36% of the vote, little more than a third, and yet obtain a majority of seats to gain power.

On the Federal Scene

During all this time the English-speaking Canadians in Ottawa are pressuring King to enforce conscription. The war is drawing to a close, but reinforcements are needed. Despite Bracken's Conservatives' persistent fight for conscription for overseas duty, King refuses. He knows full well that if he enforces it, Quebec will revolt more violently than in 1917.

The pressure, however, is too strong for King. He has to ask Parliament's approval to send 16,000 men overseas. This is called 'limited conscription.' Thirty-two Quebec members of Parliament, mostly Liberals, vote against it. Nevertheless the bill passes, with the support of the C.C.F. and Social Credit.

In Montreal the *Bloc* organizes a rally. André Laurendeau accuses "the dictatorship of the majority of being as tyrannical as any kind of fascism." Two thousand demonstrators race through the financial district, smashing the windows of the Bank of Montreal, the Montreal Trust Co. and the National Selective Service. In Chicoutimi and Rimouski demonstrators burn the Union Jack. Some English-Canadians advise the government to use machine-guns to put Quebec in its place. Instead, the popular resentment is channelled into Camilien Houde's re-election to the mayoralty of Montreal after Houde had been interned for 'subversion' -- that is, for having fought against conscription.

The provincial Liberals break away from their Federal party and launch a newspaper, *Le Canadien*. At the same time they concentrate their efforts on the working-class sections of Montreal, where the C.C.F. and the Labour Progressive Party (the Communist party) have been gaining ground. Fred Rose, a Communist candidate, is elected to the federal House from the working-class riding of Cartier.

As for the soldiers themselves, of the 10,000 due to leave for Europe on January 3rd, 1945, 7,800 go AWOL. Of a total of 18,943 deserters, Quebec contributes close to 10,000. These Québécois, all in uniform and ready to defend their country to the death if attacked, refuse to get butchered in Europe for the benefit of England, France and the United States. These patriots whom the English treat as cowards and traitors are opposed to fascism, but also have the courage to fight the colonialism of Ottawa, London and Washington by this individual action, and to face the consequences. They have even more reason to do so as the war is almost over and reinforcements are not as necessary. The Conservative Party has built up this conscription crisis as an issue on which they can attack the Liberals and take office.

In the June 1945 elections, the Québécois have a choice between the Conservatives, who want to keep them in line, the C.C.F. that works with American unions, and the *Bloc Populaire* that still doesn't know where it is going. They prefer to vote Liberal once more.

The elections do not change the composition of the House of Commons. The Liberals retain the majority and continue to govern. The Conservatives get 67 seats, the C.C.F. 28, the *Bloc*

Populaire two, and a few go to Social Credit. Fred Rose, the Communist member from Cartier, is re-elected.

Thus at the end of the war the Liberals are in power in Ottawa, the Union Nationale in Quebec. These two ruling bodies are to stay in power for quite some time.

After the War

The war cost Canada 21 billion dollars. In addition, the former colony gave England 4 billion in financial and material aid, loaned her 2 billion and sold her food supplies at reduced prices.

This money, which came from the Québécois as much as the Canadians, was used in this way without Québécois consent. The Federal Government, in the service of British and U.S. capitalism, used its right of taxation to squeeze out money from the people and put it at England's disposal. Instead of allowing the Québécois the freedom to decide for themselves how they might help the allied powers fight Hitler's fascism, Ottawa imposed its way of participating in the war without taking into account the will of the Québécois.

This is the way Ottawa has always governed, keeping Quebec as a reservoir for exploitation. At the end of the war, when the time comes to convert the economy of destruction (the war economy) to an economy of consumption, the federal government invites American capitalists to come and exploit us more. The federal government remains a caretaker government for American exploiters. And the provincial government does the same. Both the federal and provincial governments are caretakers elected by the people to serve the industrial and financial monopolies that plunder the people's natural resources.

Having exhausted the supply of their own resources at a fantastic rate, U.S. capitalists now look beyond their boundaries for the raw materials indispensable to their industry. American ca-

pital flows into Quebec to be invested in mines and forests. Along with English-Canadian capitalists, they now control the entire primary sector, the extraction of raw materials. Gradually they take hold of the secondary sector as well, the transformation of raw materials into finished or semi-finished products.

In all this the Québécois is the guy at the bottom of the mine, the one who saws wood, the water-carrier, the labourer who works like a dog while the U.S. capitalists and their English-Canadian agents rob him of his resources with his own hands. The caretaker governments of St.Laurent (King's successor in the federal government) and Duplessis keep reminding him that American capital creates jobs, and gives the worker the chance to 'prosper.'

It is true of course that foreign capital creates *jobs*, but at what price? When Duplessis lets iron ore go at one cent a ton, what does this mean? It means that 10,000,000 tons of our ore go directly to the United States and bring in $100,000 to the provincial government. The mining of these 10,000,000 tons gives work to a few hundred Québécois for a few years. But this is insignificant when we realize that the company that obtained these 10,000,000 tons for $100,000 will employ thousands outside Quebec in converting this ore into semi-finished products and make from 75 to 100 million dollars profit.

We can agree that this is good for us if we also believe that we were born to be poor, that we are and always will be water-carriers. But when we understand that the resources of the Quebec soil are the inalienable property of the Québécois people, that they should be extracted by the Québécois people and converted by them for their own consumption and for an external market, we can only conclude that the Americans are international crooks and that our caretaker governments are traitors and sell-outs, lackeys and parasites of American capitalism.

What does a caretaker government do? First of all, it accepts 'gifts' for its party treasury from the companies. These pay-offs enable the government to stay in power and continue its policy of servility to the U.S. companies.

Secondly, the caretaker government 'concedes' our resources at ridiculous prices, as we have just seen in the case of iron ore.

Thirdly, the government builds bridges and roads, making it easier for the companies to get at the resources.

Fourthly, such a government passes laws to keep the workers in their place. If the workers should get restless, it sends the police to crack down on strikers in the name of 'private property and free enterprise.' Example: the 1949 Asbestos Strike. The 'Canadian' Johns-Manville Co. Ltd. (which despite its name represents nothing Canadian, far less Québécois) is the company that exploits the mining of our asbestos. This company pays almost nothing to the provincial government for the right to steal our asbestos, which it ships to the United States for the manufacture of finished products.

Of course, Johns-Manville hires Québécois workers to mine the asbestos. It pays them miserable salaries and forces them to work in impossible conditions (asbestos dust in particular attacks the lungs). The Québécois labour at starvation wages, mining the ore as if it did not belong to them. Many of them really believe that the asbestos belongs to the company and that they are lucky to have a job. It is as though the company were generous, a kind of Saviour who gives them their daily bread. This is what Duplessis and the parish priests preach. "Bless our exploiters for they give us some crumbs when they steal our natural resources."

The Asbestos Strike

But the workers aren't fools. They are disgusted by the working conditions and the exploitation to which they are subjected. They strike. The law says they must first go to arbitration before they go out on strike. They don't give a damn about "labour legislation," so they strike anyway.

The company appeals to the Negro-King Duplessis who has to obey if he wants to stay in power. Johns-Manville has decided to lay off the recalcitrant workers and hire scabs. So Duplessis is ordered to send in the Quebec Provincial Police to beat up the strikers and usher in the scabs.

Caretaker Duplessis obeys. On February 19, he sends 150 provincial police to "maintain law and order." The police arrest the

Asbestos strike (1949).
Truckloads of food and clothes for the strikers arriving in Asbestos from different parts of Quebec.

strikers, threaten and beat them. But the workers are not intimidated. The strike continues.

On May 5, a convoy of 25 Provincial Police cars head for Asbestos. One hundred and eighty workers are arrested. They are punched whipped and kicked in the testicles. So Québécois cops fight Québécois who are wage-earners like themselves. These provincial police, ordinary guys who have joined the force because it was a job 'like any other,' find themselves working for Duplessis who in turn works for Johns-Manville, who exploits the Québécois workers. The ones who should be whipped are the directors and owners of Johns-Manville. No-one else, not even Duplessis the caretaker. The responsibility rests with the imperialist exploiter.

Johns-Manville, the big U.S. capitalist company, exploits the Quebec workers. To continue this exploitation, the company has to use the government it controls by means of the party treasury. It orders the government to put down the workers. Caretaker Duplessis orders the Provincial Police to beat up the workers. And the cops do their 'job' as they are told.

Here we can plainly see how the bourgeois possessor class also possesses the state. This is the essence of bourgeois democracy.

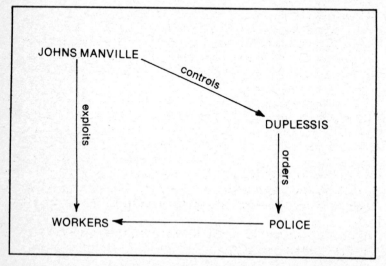

The people elect their Members of Parliament, but democracy stops right there. The Members are tied to a party that is tied to financial interests through the party treasury. We elect members whose real responsibility is not to the voters but to the possessor class, the wealthy class, the class that own the means of production -- The U.S. imperialist bourgeoisie.

One single member of the Clergy dared to protest against the police brutality, and took the side of the workers. He was Bishop Charbonneau of Montreal. Despite everything, this man remained sensitive to the oppression of the working class and had the courage to give voice to his indignation. But it took only a few months before strings could be pulled to have him exiled to British Columbia.

Johns-Manville made it perfectly clear to caretaker Duplessis that they didn't want any bishop on the side of the dirty workers. Duplessis obediently called on the other bishops to make them understand that Johns-Manville did not want any bishop on the side of the dirty workers and neither did he. So, if they wanted to keep their privileges (no taxes, absolute control of education etc.) they too had to be on the side of the capitalist exploiters and therefore Charbonneau had to leave. The bishops understood immediately: Authority comes from God by way of Johns-Manville. Bishop Charbonneau ends up in exile in British Columbia, speaking broken English but shutting up in French.

To repair the damage done by Bishop Charbonneau, Camille Roy Archbishop of Quebec mediates the dispute; which is really to say that the Church does everything it can to convince the miners to get back on the job. This time it works.

The Clergy, servile as ever to the colonizer, takes up its role as Negro-King with great vigour. The parish priests make the strikers understand that they must respect authority (God and Johns-Manville), that the lot of the worker is to labour in misery (hoping to get to Heaven) and that the world is this way because God has willed it (that is, Johns-Manville). On July 1, the miners go back to their jobs without a contract, without a guarantee of collective bargaining, without anything settled. The workers have lost.

With this conflict in mind, we can define the composition of post-war Québécois society.

Apparent Political Structure

This applies as much to the federal as to the provincial.

The people elect the Members of Parliament.

The M.P's of the majority party form the government. The leader of the majority party becomes Prime Minister and finds among his colleagues the various cabinet ministers he needs to govern the country.

The M.P's of the minority party form the opposition. Their work consists of criticizing the government so that it will pass better laws for the people.

Real Political Structure

The people elect Members of Parliament, who are attached to parties. The parties 'win' their elections with electoral campaigns financed by big business.

The party in power first of all must pass laws to favour the companies, then other laws to appease the people (such as family allowance, labour laws, welfare, etc.)

The government is in the service of the companies. It is a care-taker government.

This kind of democracy is called bourgeois democracy.

This bourgeois democracy is really a dictatorship by the pos-sessor class.

Apparent Social Structure
(what they want us to accept)

They tell us that:

● The rich are richer than the others because they have worked harder. So that they deserve the grand life they lead.

● Everybody can become rich like them.

● The middle class means everybody, or almost; it includes the labourer, the judge, the doctor, the janitor, the Prime Min-ister, the farmer, you and me. If we worked a little harder and saved a little more we could become very rich, but we stay where we are because we do not have the *will*, the *courage* or the *ability*. However we really shouldn't complain because there are those who are poorer than we are.

● The poor are stupid and don't have the courage to work. Look at them: when you give them money they waste it in the tavern. They deserve their fate.

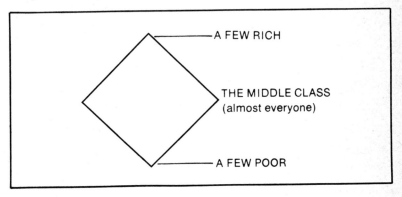

The Real Structure of Quebec Society

There are two main groups involved — the workers and the bourgeoisie. The worker is the producer par excellence. He converts material into a product which is used for the subsistence and development of society.

The bourgeois owns the means of production. He has under his control:
● the materials
● the equipment
Then he buys the labour-power of the worker and appropriates all of his production in return for a wage.

The materials can be natural wealth (forests, mines, etc.) or semi-finished products which undergo a transformation. The equipment includes the buildings, machines, tools, everything needed to convert the materials. Labour-power is the energy the worker uses to convert the material with the aid of equipment.

The bourgeois controls the entire productive process but he does no productive work himself.

THE BOURGEOIS

The bourgeois wants to make profits.

To do this:

- he looks for real or imagined human needs to satisfy
- he looks for raw materials to process to satisfy these needs and the equipment to manufacture them
- he accumulates money, capital, either from his own business or from other bourgeois through a financial institution
- he buys the labour-power needed to produce his commodity

The wheels of industry can now be set in motion. The bourgeois sells his commodity at a price that allows him to pay for his materials and equipment, to repay the capital he has borrowed, and to pay his workers' wages. At the same time, he keeps enough to satisfy his own needs and to expand his industry.

THE WORKER

His only property is his labour-power and a few personal belongings. In a society of exploitation like ours, his labour-power is considered a commodity – and to survive he must sell it to the bourgeois, his employer. In return he receives a wage, just enough to keep him and his family alive to continue their lives as slaves.

He tries in vain to work harder to escape; it is almost always impossible. His wages will disappear in the purchase of necessities and some indispensable entertainment to escape momentarily from the conditions of his life.

The bourgeois takes *all* of the goods that the worker produces in his working day. Now, the special quality of the commodity 'labour-power' is that it can produce more than it costs the

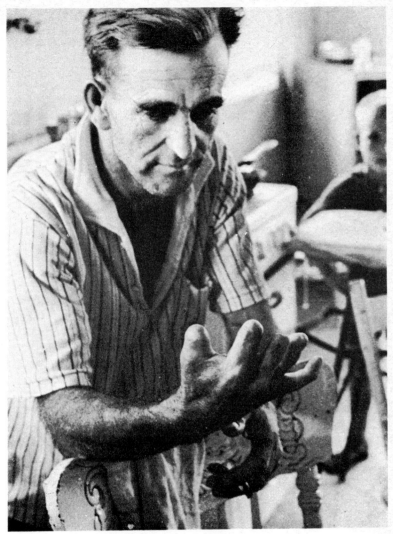

Dominion Ayers strike at Lachute (1966).

Worker showing why Ayers plywood plant was called the 'finger-chopping factory'.

capitalist. A worker may produce enough commodities in the first two or three hours to cover the wage he is paid for the whole day. The rest of the day he works for the bourgeois for free.

In taking everything the worker produces, the capitalist is taking a surplus value,[1] some of which goes to pay back his loans and taxes, and the rest he keeps for personal consumption and for re-investment. Also out of this surplus value comes the money to pay a large number of working persons whom we will call non-productive workers.

Productive and Non-Productive Workers

A *productive worker* produces a commodity[2] which will realize surplus value for the bourgeois. The class of productive workers is known as the proletariat. It is because the whole capitalist system is based on the fact that workers produce the surplus value which is the source of capital, that the proletariat – along with the bourgeoisie which appropriates that capital – is the most important class in that social system.

Productive workers include:

1. Those who extract raw materials: *lumberjacks, miners, wage-earning fishermen, wage-earning agricultural workers*

2. Those who convert raw materials into goods for sale (commodities): *manual workers and technicians in the factories, construction workers*

3. Those who bring the commodities to market: *stevedores, truck drivers, warehouse workers, railway workers*.

A *non-productive worker* is one whom the bourgeois, or the state apparatus, hires as his servant, either personally or professionally and who is paid by him out of the surplus value created by the worker; for example, a textile worker works in the mill for twelve long hours and the factory owner uses part of her

---

1. Workers produce *value*. Some of this value they get back in their wages. The rest is surplus value that is appropriated by the capitalist.

2. A *commodity* is a product used as exchange value.

unpaid labour (surplus value) to hire her sister as a maid, her brother as a teacher and her cousin as a policeman or soldier.

This does not mean that only productive workers are dominated by the bourgeoisie. All those who work for wages or salaries, without ownership of means of production and without power of decision, are oppressed like the workers. This includes the secretary, the civil servant, the school teacher, the professor, the artist, the writer.

One might object by saying that the announcer at the CBC sees nothing in common between himself and the doorman who opens the door for him. Here we must distinguish between subjective outlook and objective reality.

The announcer subjectively sees himself in a white shirt, admires himself on the television screen, receives admiration from many viewers because of his deep voice and charm. The doorman sees himself in the doorman's uniform opening the door to these important ladies and gentlemen.

These two subjective outlooks are radically different and correspond to two different objective realities. But these different objective realities (talking on TV and opening a door) are determined by one common fundamental reality. Both men own no means of production and have no real power of decision. Both submit to a system of oppression that makes them sell their ability to work and prevents them from participating in the decisions that affect every aspect of their lives.

Blue collar workers or white collar workers, the difference in their standard of living may not be too great. Blue collar workers work mostly with their hands whereas white collar workers work more with their head and fingers. The point is, they are all oppressed, all without the power of decision. The bourgeoisie uses the difference in the colour of their shirts to keep working people divided, to prevent them from uniting and becoming a force that could threaten their privileged position.

bourgeois:	● owner of the means of production	● decision-maker
white and blue collar workers:	● wage or salary workers	● without powers of decision

The semi-proletariat

The *semi-proletariat* consists of those non-productive workers who both in the kind of work they do and in their standard of living are very close to the productive workers. They are often paid less than productive workers, they may work harder under worse conditions, but *they do not produce surplus value*.

The semi-proletariat includes:

1. those who do the maintenance work of society: *garbagemen, janitors, dry-cleaning workers*

2. those who tend to the personal needs of the bourgeoisie: *domestic servants, gardeners*

3. those whose functions exist only in a money economy: *store clerks, certain clerical workers*

Socially useful and socially useless work

Another distinction that must be made is that between socially useful work and socially useless work. Socially useful work is work that contributes to the well-being of society as a whole. Socially useless work is that which is detrimental to society.

Policemen in our society do socially useful work when they direct traffic or look for lost persons. But when they beat up workers on strike or students demonstrating against the bourgeois regime, they are nothing but instruments in the hands of the class which is trying to prevent the oppressed from bettering their conditions.

Office workers, salesmen and retail clerks are socially useful but non-productive workers. They do not produce commodities; rather, they carry out certain functions which are absolutely essential to the capitalist system, to a system which distributes goods not according to need but according to ability to pay. In a society which is not divided into exploiting and exploited classes, a society where no one needs to steal to eat or to prove his self-worth through his possessions, it is not necessary to have a huge army of people who produce nothing, but simply guard merchandise, bookkeep it, sell it, and collect bills.

A few people are necessary in any system to allocate and dispatch goods. But, we don't really need to put all this effort into selling the goods of the bourgeoisie and keeping track of their money.

THE PETIT-BOURGEOISIE

The petit-bourgeoisie consists of three categories:

1. The small capitalist who must work himself in his own enterprise in order to live; that is, part of his income is gained from the labour of others and part from his own labour: *shop keepers, small manufacturers, family farmers*

2. those whose specific function is to maintain the system of exploitation by ideological means: *teachers, artists, clergy, members of parliament, judges, civil servants, lawyers, military and police brass, salesmen, office workers.*

3. professionals who market their expertise (as distinguished from workers who sell their ability to produce commodities): *doctors, dentists, architects, engineers, scientists, computer programmers.*

Small capitalists

Small manufacturers own small means of production incidental to the main functioning of the economy and they hire few workers. While they exploit their workers by appropriating the surplus

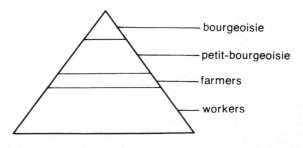

value they create, most often they are personally involved in the productive process. Such small businessmen are the first to go out of business when times get tough and are continually being taken over by the middle and big bourgeoisie.

Businessmen, shop keepers and salesmen derive their income from selling goods. Their power of decision is exercized in selecting and sticking price tags on merchandise and selling it. To the extent that they make goods available to the population, they do useful work. But their work is harmful when they buy up all the goods and sell them at a price few can afford. By such profiteering they work, not for the sake of improving the conditions of humanity, but to accumulate money for selfish use.

Farmers

Quebec farmers, owners of a few acres of land, produce goods like the worker. But can they be considered workers, strictly speaking?

They are not wage-workers.

They are owners of small means of production – their farms.

They have some power of decision.

These are characteristics of the petit-bourgeoisie. Unlike the bourgeois, their holdings are small and they generally employ few if any workers.

However, it must be noted that agriculture in Quebec today is feeling the effects of industrial society and now accounts for only 6 per cent of the working population. Because of this, the small farmer has to change his life.

He might leave the farm to become a worker in the city, or he might manage to buy some land, hire some employees and set himself up as a real country bourgeois farmer. Or, as a third alternative, he might get together with other farmers to form co-operative farms. In the first case he becomes a worker. In the second case he becomes a bourgeois. In both of these cases he is either exploited or exploiter. But, in the third case, he directs himself toward a society where neither exploited nor exploiter exists.

Ideological Workers

The ideological sector employs workers to convey the ideology – the attitudes and way of thinking which enables the dominating class to stay in power and keep the working class and other oppressed classes down.

Teachers perform two functions. They convey knowledge necessary to train workers: auto mechanics, chemistry, typing, mathematics. But their main function is to convey to students the ideology of the dominating class and the values that will make them useful members of the society: neatness, narrowness of vision, unquestioning obedience etc. At great risk, teachers can choose to make their students conscious that the system we live in is a system of exploiters and exploited.

Commercial artists most often participate in the sale of consumer goods which promotes individualism without contributing to a generalized betterment. They can help the people when they use their skills to depict and encourage the struggle of the people against their exploiters.

Parish priests spread bourgeois ideology to the extent that they defend the interests of the bourgeois class by preaching submission to and respect for authority. However, they help the people if they break their ties with the bourgeoisie and integrate into the working class and struggle with it against the exploiters.

Artists, journalists, authors and radio and TV producers are in the same position as teachers. They transmit messages: they have the same responsibility. Those who choose the side of the people will play an important role.

The "professionnals"

There are those who work at trades considered as "professions:" doctors, dentists, lawyers, notaries, architects, consulting engineers. They do not work for a salary or a wage and because of their specialized knowledge they can demand high fees for their services. They can charge what they like – up to a point.

The instruments of exploitation are in their hands. This establishes a distinction between themselves and the workers and so they tend to identify with the exploiters. In their respective fields they have the power to make some decisions but they employ few. The "means of production" which they own are generally their own skills. Their work cannot be considered 'labour' in the strict sense because, unlike the productive workers, they are not hired *to produce commodities*.

The functionaries of the state apparatus

This stratum of the petit-bourgeoisie – members of parliament, judges, policemen, soldiers, civil servants – are employed by the bourgeoisie to run their state in their own interests. They work indirectly for the owners of the means of production and have little, if any, power of decision.

The Member of Parliament in Canada or Quebec today may think he has nothing in common with a kindergarten teacher. He may think he is superior to teachers, that he has decision-making powers and a salary that places him in the bourgeois class. But, in fact, he owns no means of production: he is salaried and for his fat salary he has sold his power of decision. He accepts the decisions dictated to him by the party. And, in Canada, political parties, whatever their class base, accept decisions dictated to them by the big bourgeoisie that is dominated by the bourgeoisie of another country, the United States. There are no parties in Canada or Quebec today which represent the working class.

As for the judge, he too may think himself a big bourgeois with a huge salary and sweeping powers of decision. He can send men to the scaffold. In fact, he receives a salary to make decisions already made for him in the law books by the exploiter class. The lawyer is handsomely paid as well, for helping the judge.

Physical arm of the repressive apparatus

Those whose function is to maintain the system of exploitation (or extend it) by directly repressive means: *policemen, jail guards, soldiers*.

The unemployed are workers. They are paid to do nothing until they are needed. These reserve workers are part of the labour bank of the capitalist system. As such they have no power of decision.

What distinguishes the unemployed from other workers is that they do not do any productive work. They are workers who are not workers.

They are forced to live with this contradiction.

Welfare recipients

This large group of people is rejected by bourgeois society. They are considered unable to produce in a capitalist system because of physical, emotional or intellectual handicaps or because of police records. Nevertheless, society supports them, by dishing out a mere pittance, in order to keep its conscience clear by being 'generous to the disinherited.'

Although welfare recipients are at the mercy of others and have no power of decision over anything at all, they are not workers. They do no productive work and their allowance cannot be considered to be a salary. It is, rather, a pension for the demobilized.

Students

Students form a complex group. To begin with, as students they are neither bourgeois nor workers. They have neither ownership of means of production nor a wage or salary. They have no power of decision. As for productive work, this depends on the future career they choose. The training of a student can make him into a bourgeois or a petit-bourgeois or a specialized worker.

Since students do not participate in production, either as exploited or exploiter, they are really marginal to society.

209

They can be sympathetic or offer moral support to either the exploited or the exploiter, but as long as they are students and not involved in the relations of production as definite bourgeoisie, petit-bourgeoisie, or workers, they are demobilized just like welfare recipients. They are kept outside of the exploiter/exploited realtionship at the level of production because they are financially supported outside of the relations of production. Therefore they have no real involvement in the struggle between the exploited and the exploiters.

The student revolt is predominantly the result of this demobilization, of this state of waiting on the margin of the relations of production, of this state of privileged welfare recipients being prepared for a specific role in the system of exploitation.

THE BOURGEOISIE

The bourgeois in the real sense of the word owns the means of production.

His income comes not from wages but from profits derived from the unpaid labour of his workers at the point of production.

He buys the workers' labour-power at a price well below the value of the product of this same worker's work. The difference between the two is surplus value and from it comes the bourgeois' profit.

The bourgeois has the power to make decisions not only concerning his own life but his workers' lives as well. He spends his time giving orders to those who do the productive work. The money he has accumulated gives him control of production but he produces nothing at all. He is the perfect parasite.

The bourgeois system of production is the world upside down. The real producers, those who produce goods, have no power of decision over their lives and end up with only enough to survive. The non-producers enjoy the power of decision and goods produced by others.

Upper and Middle Bourgeoisie

The bourgeoisie per se consists of two groups, the upper and the middle. What is the difference between the two groups?

Both exploit their workers on a large scale; both have significant powers of decision over our daily lives. However the 'big' bourgeoisie is in all respects bigger and this difference in degree leads to a difference in kind.

The upper bourgeoisie is made up of capitalists whose investments and economic power of decision dominates wide sectors of the country and in a good many cases extends to other countries. It is the ruling class both in its home country and in the countries it dominates.

The middle bourgeoisie is made up of capitalists whose investments and economic power of decision are more modest. It is greatly dependent on decisions made by the upper bourgeoisie and in most cases limits itself to national territory.

The owners of American companies, who exploit not only in the United States but also in other countries in Latin America and Europe and Canada and Quebec, are members of the upper bourgeoisie, and constitute the ruling class in these countries. However, the owners of a company like Vachon Biscuits, in Quebec, are part of the Quebec middle bourgeoisie and have no such power.

This difference between the members of the bourgeois class causes conflicts between them. The upper bourgeoisie tends to become increasingly powerful because it has more capital and so it is always on the look-out to absorb the enterprises of the middle bourgeoisie. There are numerous examples of this phenomenon of absorption of small companies by large ones. Canadair, a middle bourgeois enterprise, was bought out by General Dynamics, a huge company belonging to some upper bourgeois Americans.

The middle bourgeoisie which is often called the national bourgeoisie, identifies with its national territory and may try to rally other classes to help it rid the country of these foreigners so that it may rule in their place. It is, however, quite incapable of this task at this stage of capitalist development.

Members of the upper echelons of the underworld are part of the middle bourgeoisie to the extent that they own means of production and exchange. Until recently most of the bosses of organized crime were local criminals. But, just like other businessmen, they have been brought under the control of New York.

It is known that in some places the underworld controls the distribution of cigarettes, just as it controls prostitution, the drug market, fraudulent bankruptcies and part of show business as well as many 'legitimate' businesses. By so dominating the market for the exploitation of human passions, the underworld is an integral part of bourgeois society where exploitation is the rule.

This is why in private clubs (where important decisions are made) we find members of parliament and leaders of the underworld rubbing shoulders. Everyone remembers the visit of Cotroni, boss of the Montreal underworld, during the Union Nationale leadership convention in June 1969 in Quebec City. M. Cotroni came to "softly pressure" for *his* candidate for leadership of the Union Nationale in exactly the same way as industrialists concerned about government contracts.

The capitalist owners of Dupont of Canada or Canada Packers are more exploitative, more base, more grasping than the underworld bigshots, but they can pass as do-gooders because their kind of exploitation is accepted by official ethics. Members of the underworld are considered bad guys because their kind of oppression is forbidden (in theory only) by the same ethics.

Respectable capitalists and notorious underworld characters are merely two sides of the same coin: exploitation of man by man in every possible way.

Nationalities and Social Classes in Quebec

THE BOURGEOISIE

Both strata of the bourgeoisie which exploit our manpower and resources in Quebec are for the most part foreign.

The upper bourgeoisie are foreigners. The big companies and financial institutions which exploit and govern Quebec belong to Americans and English-Canadians. The companies that extract our natural resources (lumber and minerals) are in the hands of American capitalists. American or English-Canadian capital dominates the secondary sector — conversion of raw materials, pulp and paper mills, textiles etc.

SOME EXAMPLES

Noranda Mines	American and English-Canadian
Iron Ore Co.	American and English-Canadian
General Motors	American
Canadair	American
General Electric	American
Canadian International Paper	American
Dupont of Canada	American
Canada Packers	English-Canadian
Domtar	American and English-Canadian
Seagram's	Jewish-Canadian and American *
Dominion Textile	American and English-Canadian
C.P.R.	American and English-Canadian
Bell Telephone	American and English-Canadian
Alcan	American and English-Canadian

* *Its head office is in New York*

The Québécois upper bourgeoisie is practically non-existent. The middle bourgeoisie is dominated by English-Canadians. Those who own small factories, loan companies, small transport or construction companies, stores, radio or TV stations and newspapers are predominantly English-Canadian, many of whom are Jewish [1] and a few are Québécois.

Jewish-Canadian capitalists have important holdings in food stores, footwear, fur and clothing businesses. French-Canadian capitalists and religious orders are trying to catch up with the English in banking, transport, construction (buildings, houses,

---

1. Persons of Jewish origin form the third largest national group in Montreal. Almost all have become English-speaking rather than French-speaking and now comprise nearly 25 per cent of the English population of Montreal. Thus they must be considered by-and-large part of the English-Canadian nation rather than part of the Québécois.

roads) in mass media (radio, newspapers, TV) and in food stores. And there are now new immigrants from Italy, Germany and France who have managed to get a foothold in some sectors of the economy.

Every Québécois can rhyme off the list: Eaton's, Simpson's, Ogilvy's are English-Canadian; Steinberg's is Jewish-Canadian; Dupuis, Sicotte Construction, Poupart are French-Canadian. But a systematic examination of Quebec business is yet to be done.

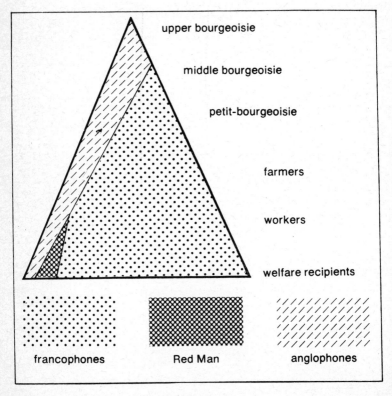

THE PETIT-BOURGEOISIE

Virtually absent from the upper bourgeoisie and in the minority in the middle bourgeoisie, the Québécois make up the majority in the other classes: petit-bourgeoisie, workers and farmers, students, unemployed and welfare recipients.

They represent a bare majority in the upper ranks of the petit bourgeoisie. English-Canadians and especially Jewish-Canadians are well established in the liberal professions and small businesses.

THE WORKERS

Most Québécois are workers. Again, among white collar workers we find English-Canadians and recent immigrants. With the Québécois majority, we find Italian and Portuguese immigrants and some English-Canadian blue collar workers.

Welfare recipients

Most of the welfare recipients are Québécois. There is also a large proportion of Red men on welfare, kept on "reserves."

If we place the whole of the Quebec population in a pyramid we find that the Québécois, who make up 82 per cent of the population, are at the bottom of the ladder. Of the other 18 per cent, two-thirds are of British origin, the rest of Jewish or German or other national origin.

Recent Events

The Fifties and Sixties

Boosted by the Second World War, American capitalism resumed its expansionism throughout the world, constantly increasing its hold on the Canadian economy and, consequently on the Quebec economy. Industrialization in Quebec continued to displace traditional Québécois society. The rate of migration from the country to the city continued to grow, along with the rate of integration of farmers into the working class. Soon the majority of Québécois became cheap labour in industrial centres for American, English-Canadian, French-Canadian and Jewish capitalists.

The habitants brought a rural mentality with them from the farms, but this had to go. A worker does not think like a habitant who owns 30 acres of land. The Québécois in the backcountry and little industrial centres had been kept in ignorance by Duplessis and the Clergy, so that they could be properly exploited by American and English-Canadian capitalists. However the new 'city guys' could not be kept from asking questions and wanting to change the old ways of behaviour and thought.

At the same time the Québécois small and middle bourgeoisie, who had benefitted from the post-war economic boom, began to feel strong enough to establish themselves as a national bourgeoisie – a new elite with the power to dominate Québécois society. American capitalists and the English-Canadian bourgeoisie were willing to collaborate with this Québécois bourgeoisie because they recognized in them an ally that would 'modernize' Quebec and train the Québécois masses to qualify as workers for their factories, and buy their products obsessively, just like the American masses.

The role played by the former Negro-Kings, Duplessis and the Clergy, was not useful enough to our colonizers, American and English-Canadian capitalists, in the modern system of exploitation. The requirement was no longer a Negro-king preaching hard work and an austere existence, but a Negro-king who could make the Québécois people believe that they had to work hard and live extravagantly. That is, that they had to consume, and consume. Therefore, a new elite was needed, a liberal lay elite who would adopt and preach the *American way of life,* gradually Anglicizing the Québécois to make them into 'real' Canadians -- in other words, second-rate Americans who are submissive producers and servile consumers for American imperialism.

So our colonizers supported our small and middle bourgeoisie morally and financially, concentrating on the provincial Liberals. The Party came to power in 1960, led by Jean Lesage's crack team that proceeded to launch the 'Quiet Revolution.'

Our colonizers were happy. The Negro-king, Lesage, was going to modernize the education system as we have seen by creating a Ministry of Education and by applying the Parent report. Every Québécois would have a minimum American education, an American professional and technical education to become good American producers and consumers. This would integrate the entire population into modern capitalism.

The Negro-king, Lesage, was going to nationalize electricity to permit the planned distribution of this source of energy to industry and all important centres. Nothing very revolutionary about this: Ontario had done the same thing at the beginning of the century. Electricity is another service the state offers to industry, just like the roads it builds.

Negro-king Lesage was going to create Soquem (*Société Québécoise d'Exploration Minière),* which would help capitalists find our minerals in the Quebec subsoil.

Negro-king Lesage would create a pension fund, offer hospital insurance, increase aid to the under-privileged, and modernize the Labour Code; all the so-called social measures to appease popular discontent, and to help the whole Québécois population cope with

Demonstration in Montreal (1964).

the capitalist system of exploitation. Each person could find his own secure pigeon-hole – workers at work, welfare people at home, bourgeois in their beautiful clean districts, students at their studies – and everybody would be consuming way over their means with a well-oiled credit system, the golden chain of modern slavery.

As Lesage began to play his new role of Negro-king, a belief was growing among certain elements of the petit-bourgeoisie and certain white collar workers that the Québécois bourgeoisie would have to go further than the Negro-king role and become the national bourgeoisie of an independent country. So, the struggle for Quebec's independence was launched in 1960 with the formation of the R.I.N. *(Rassemblement pour l'Indépendence Nationale)*. It believed that the Québécois had to fight against domination by the English-Canadian bourgeoisie whose political centre of control is in Ottawa, and that the Québécois bourgeoisie was to assume its role as a ruling class in a nation independent of any other bourgeoisie.

But these new Patriotes were not at first mindful of the fact that the English-Canadian bourgeoisie, along with our middle bourgeoisie, are just the means by which we are dominated by the American capitalists.

Soon, a group of young people formed who were enthusiastic about the changes taking place in Quebec and wanted to see them happen faster. The F.L.Q.-63 planted some bombs. These young men thought that the Québécois people would spontaneously rise up as a single man to the noise of the bombs and quickly make Quebec independent. Since the national reflex of the colonized is fear of change, the Quebec people were scared. "The Québécois violent? Impossible." But underneath this fear, complicity and some deep hope lay hidden.

Bombs are a formal protest – they challenged the whole system. The obedient Lesage responded according to his role and quickly jailed the young people who were upsetting the 'Quiet Revolution,' the evolution toward a comfortable consumer society.

When the Queen of England came to see her subjects on the road to Americanization in 1964, Lesage unleashed Minister Claude Wagner, who in turn unleashed the Quebec municipal police on the students who were mournfully chanting "We are joyful, we are overflowing with joy." Wagner's qualities as a defender of law and order were exposed by this "Saturday of the bludgeons."

The same year, the radical monthly *Parti Pris,* which had been publishing concrete analyses of Québécois society since October 1963, rallied together some young people who wanted to change things. In 1965 they created the M.L.P. *(Mouvement de Libération Populaire),* whose manifesto proclaimed the necessity to politicize the workers, demonstrate in the streets, and arouse the masses to overthrow the bourgeois system of exploitation.

In 1966, Pierre Vallières and Charles Gagnon left the M.L.P. to join the F.L.Q.-66, while the other members of the M.L.P. joined the P.S.Q. *(Parti Socialiste du Québec)* where some senior members like Michel Chartrand were trying to rally unionized workers with a programme similar to that of the N.D.P. (New Democratic Party). During the summer of 1966, the F.L.Q. planted a bomb at La Grenade Shoe Company.

Vallières and Gagnon went to the United Nations to plead the cause of the Quebec liberation struggle. They were arrested, brought back to Quebec, and accused of murder, robbery, conspiracy and in fact everything that would keep them behind bars for an indefinite time.

Meanwhile, more adherents were being won to the *Québec Libre* cause. In the elections of June, 1966, surprise! – Lesage's Liberals were defeated. The Union Nationale came back to power with Daniel Johnson as leader. The R.I.N. led by Pierre Bourgault won 10 percent of the votes but did not get any seats. The Union Nationale, however, got more seats than the Liberals with fewer votes.

The number of seats obtained is no real indication of support because the electoral map is unbalanced. The Union Nationale took almost all the country-side, where the counties are over-represented in the Assembly, whereas the Liberals kept the large urban centres where the population per county is larger and consequently under-represented in the Assembly.

What is significant in this election is that during its six years in power the Liberal Party was not able to make the rural population believe that the Liberals represented their interests. The habitants identified Lesage with the Americanization of Quebec, and refused to go along. At this point the Union Nationale could exploit the situation by promising a return to a former 'security.'

The colonizer was not too happy about the Union Nationale's return to power, but soon got over it when Daniel Johnson showed that he was ready to take his turn as Negro-King. With the nationalists he spoke of independence; with American financiers, of internal stability good for investment; with farmers, of better agriculture; with the Clergy, of modernization of rites and rituals; with English-Canadians, of a new federalism; with the city dwellers, of a revival of the 'Quiet Revolution.' Subtle and calculating, Daniel Johnson knew how to give the impression of governing without ever doing so.

Meanwhile in the R.I.N. there was tension between the left and right wings. The left wanted to relate to the workers, support strikes, and institute a radical programme; the right preferred to look for favours from the petit-bourgeoisie.

One member of Lesage's crack team of Liberals, which represented the new lay elite at the service of American and English-Canadian interests, was René Lévesque. Lévesque was becoming ill at ease. He was aware that the crack team was playing the role of Negro-King, and he did not like it. Having some respect for himself as an individual and as a Québécois, he could no longer see himself as a puppet like his Liberal or Union Nationale colleagues. As a Québécois he felt he had to fight for the Québécois. Within the framework of a capitalist economy, this meant fighting for the rise of a Québécois national bourgeoisie which would take charge of the future of the whole Québécois people. Having conceived this kind of alternative, he was now thinking along the same line as the R.I.N. Patriotes.

René Lévesque did not consider getting rid of capitalism and American imperialism in Quebec. His kind of independence means severing the ties of Confederation in order to keep revenues, that are now handed over to the federal government, in Quebec so that the Québécois people can benefit from them in a more equitable system of social security. It means 'civilizing' foreign capitalists by asking them to re-invest their profits in Quebec and give more consideration to the population they exploit. It means that the state will aid Québécois enterprises (the bourgeoisie) with credit so that they can be dominant in Quebec and no longer at the mercy of Americans and English-Canadians.

We have seen that our Patriotes of 1837 wanted the same thing: to establish the bourgeoisie as the leadership of the Québécois people; in other words, a national bourgeois revolution.

221

Farmers' Union members demonstrating in Chicoutimi (1966).

So, René Lévesque quit the Liberal Party to form the M.S.A. *(Mouvement Souveraineté-Association)* in November, 1967. In the spring of 1968, the left in the R.I.N. quit, and a few months later, those who remained dissolved the R.I.N. with the promise to join Lévesque's M.S.A. In October 1968, the M.S.A. became the *Parti Québécois*. After 130 years of repression, the movement was reborn.

These new Patriotes wanted to make a national bourgeois revolution in Quebec. They wanted the Québécois middle bourgeoisie to replace the English-Canadian bourgeoisie, to a certain extent, and to negotiate new relations of exploitation with the American capitalists. In order to reach its goal, this Québécois bourgeoisie must take control of the state by way of elections, declare Quebec independence, and negotiate diplomatic, financial and commercial agreements with Ottawa and use all of the state's powers to finance a Québécois capitalist economy.

René Lévesque had rallied a good part of the petit-bourgeoisie and a number of white collar workers to his side. He was now trying to convince the class he was serving, the Québécois middle bourgeoisie, to support him and join his party. Lévesque invited workers of all types to join, but on certain conditions. They could not demand large social changes; they had to accept the capitalist system of exploitation and the leadership of the Québécois bourgeoisie as well as its growing power over the fate of the Québécois people.

While the P.Q. was slowly but surely consolidating its base and preparing for the electoral contest, other movements were channeling the widespread popular discontent. The Québécois people were beginning to realize how they were being exploited as producers and consumers, and how they have been manipulated by the American capitalists, the English-Canadian bourgeoisie, and by their own elite who play the role of Negro-King. Every day, Québécois were becoming more conscious of their right to sovereignty as a nation and of their dignity as productive workers.

Students were rebelling, striking, and occupying schools and universities. They do not want to be brainwashed into being good, obedient workers or professionals in a system of exploitation which considers them mere instruments of production.

The citizens of the so-called disadvantaged areas were getting together to form committees and engage in a direct struggle against municipal power. Such committees develop workers' solidarity, the consciousness of being exploited and struggling against all those who keep them in that situation. The L.I.S. *(Ligue pour l'Intégration Scolaire)*, led by Raymond Lemieux, entered the struggle for unilingualism, starting at St Léonard. The L.I.S. wanted to extend the fight for the Québécois language into every area where it was threatened.

The C.S.N. (Confederation of National Trade Unions or C.N.T.U.) was moving farther away from the trade-union mentality, that is the striving for little salary hikes. It was becoming radical and spoke of a 'second front,' a workers' political struggle against the exploiters. Michel Chartrand, elected president of the Montreal Central Council of the C.S.N., was increasing his attacks against the capitalist system and all those who support it in Quebec – the Americans, English-Canadians and our sell-out elite.

The Left was organizing demonstrations to 'awaken the population.' The St-Jean-Baptiste parade of 1968 turned into a bitter fight between demonstrators and the Montreal police in front of the honoured guests in the reviewing stand at Parc Lafontaine. Following this, the municipal authorities created an anti-riot squad -- in other words, a little army specialized in repressing demonstrations.

In February, *Opération McGill français* brought out 15,000 demonstrators in front of McGill. The purpose of this demonstration was to expose this university as one the fortresses of English-Canadian and American capitalism, which is keeping the Québécois in a state of economic, political and cultural servitude. Several bombs exploded in Montreal – a few at Eaton's, another at the Montreal Stock Exchange. Three hundred special police hunted for members of the new F.L.Q.-69. Pierre-Paul Geoffroy was arrested, judged and condemned to life imprisonment.

The F.L.P. *(Front de Libération Populaire)* organized a demonstration following the St-Jean-Baptiste '69 parade. There were a few scuffles and the float carrying St-Jean-Baptiste was knocked over. The symbol of the Quebec people's servitude lay on the ground. Québécois youth had knocked down the traditional image that the elite had imposed on the people after the defeat of the Rebellion.

In June, 1969, *Opération Anti-Congrès* brought thousands of workers to the gates of the Quebec Coliseum to ridicule the Union

Nationale leadership convention which was actually a circus. The police attacked from helicopters with tear gas.

On October 7th, the day of the Montreal policemen's strike, the M.L.T. *(Mouvement de Libération du Taxi)* and sympathizers attacked the Murray-Hill garage. Murray-Hill is the company which enjoys the monopoly for passenger service between the airport and downtown. The demonstrators burned several buses. The son of the owner, Hershorn, ordered his employees to guard the garage and fire into the crowd if necessary. The employees, guarding from the roof and the windows, did exactly that. Several demonstrators were wounded and one was killed. The fatality turned out to be a certain Dumas of the Provincial Police, an *agent provocateur* disguised as a demonstrator. The inquest into his death concluded that it was impossible to determine who had killed him. This protection of Hershorn and his hired killers is a striking example of justice – Mr. Hershorn belongs to the class that makes the laws, and makes them for its members. 'Justice' accepts the fact that a bourgeois defends his property by shooting people. Bourgeois property has priority over human life. Hershorn's property was more sacred than a man's life.

In that same month of October, the Bertrand government was trying to pass a bill (Bill 63) that would give parents the right to choose the language of instruction in school. This meant that all anglophones and immigrants who chose English would have the right to English schools. The French language, already badly battered, was now to see its inferiority couched in articles of law.

Bill 63 was the legal confirmation of the domination of the colonizer's language. Bertrand, the Negro-King, was forced by the colonizer to run this bill through parliament 'full steam ahead,' even though every Québécois was against it. The colonizer wanted his privileges written into the law, in order to have a legal weapon against any movement favouring French unilingualism. All he had to do was play around with the Union Nationale's campaign funds to get caretaker Bertrand to make the necessary arrangements.

The opposition of the Québécois people was clear. For two weeks they demonstrated on the streets all over Quebec, and there were teach-ins and general walk-outs in the universities, Cégeps (community colleges), and secondary schools. One of these demonstrations in Montreal numbered 45,000 people. In front of the

Quebec Parliament a gathering of 30,000 people declared their opposition. Officially, this fight against Bill 63 was led by the F.Q.F. *(Front du Québec Français)* which included hundreds of organizations of all kinds, among others, the St-Jean-Baptiste Society, the C.S.N., the C.E.Q. *(Corporation des Enseignants du Québec), l'Alliance des Professeurs de Montréal,* and the L.I.S. But, for most of the demonstrations, the population was mobilized by the *Front Commun Contre le Bill 63,* which rallied more radical groups together, such as the F.L.P., M.S.P. *(Mouvement Syndical Politique),* L.S.O. *(Ligue Socialiste Ouvrière),* and workers' committees.

Bill 63 passed with the support of the Liberals, despite opposition from René Lévesque and a few recalcitrant Union Nationale MPs.

On November 7th, the *Comité de Défense de Vallières et Gagnon* organized a demonstration of several thousand people in front of the Montreal Law Courts. Following the demonstration, some demonstrators broke windows at banks and financial institutions on St James Street to show the population that the capitalists are the ones who oppress the Québécois people.

There was a climate of insecurity in the bourgeois districts in the province. Anglophones were leaving for Ontario. Some companies were moving to Toronto. American imperialists were keeping a close watch on the evolution of the province. The Québécois people felt the need for great changes.

The Québécois people were once subjected to the old kind of colonialism that kept them in the mines, forests and factories as cheap-labour. Now they are subjected to a new colonialism that still exploits them but, in addition, asks them to disown themselves and become average American robot-consumers, narrow limited individualists. Like rats in a cage, the Québécois are to be conditioned in work, family life and recreation to think only of little possessions, of gadgets to be accumulated, of the security which is like that of a worm in its cocoon.

The Québécois people, those who were the undesirables, who were driven back into the wilderness and then drawn to the cities to be made slaves of the capitalist production system, those who were brutally crushed every time they tried to revolt, are making their entance into history.

1970 Before October

The Bertrand government had come to the end of its term of office, and to the end of its rope. The American and English-Canadian colonialists, who had never really been confident in the Union Nationale although they had tolerated its return in 1966, were more than ever anxious to see the Liberals in power.

The sloppy caretaker. Bertrand called elections for April 29th. The Parti Québécois entered the campaign actively in the country-side with a programme of political reform (Quebec independence) and of social reform (better distribution of wealth within the capitalist system).

The Liberal Party with its new puppet leader, Robert Bourassa, tried to regain power by playing on the Québécois' ingrained fears. He spoke of the flight of capital, the collapse of the Quebec economy and the possibility of a bloody revolution if the P.Q. ever came to power.

The Union Nationale, following its tactic of trying to please everybody at once, displeased more and more people.

The Social Credit, which is the reactionary federalist party regrouping the rural petit-bourgeoisie and Quebec farmers who are afraid of the great capitalist monopolies, joined the province's contest against the P.Q. and its 'dirty bearded commie revolution-aries.'

But the enthusiasm for the P.Q. began to shake Westmount. "Are the people going to elect those dirty separatists who want to eat us all up?" the Anglo-Saxophones asked themselves.

The fear of a Parti Québécois landslide was felt throughout the entire province. Some English had already packed their bags.

But there was nothing to fear. Order was restored, thanks to an electoral system rigged to favor the bourgeois, who are already in power, and block the petit-nationalist bourgeois who try to replace them. The Liberals, along with 'Bourassa-the-ideal-caretaker,' came back to power with 44% of the vote and the dis-proportionate number of 72 seats.

The P.Q. obtained 24% of the votes but only 7 seats.

The Union Nationale obtained only 20% of the votes, but never-theless won 17 seats to become the official opposition.

The Créditistes got 11% of the votes and 12 seats.

The Lapalme drivers demonstrating in Ottawa (1970).

The disillusionment was great. The Québécois were slowly learning that bourgeois democracy is bourgeois dictatorship; and that any contest for power that follows the rules of those who will not relinquish it is as predictable as a stacked deck of cards.

The Québécois were also learning that those ridings which elect P.Q. members are the workers' ridings in Montreal. In other words, the Québécois workers are the ones who vote for what seems to be a change, whereas the bourgeois ridings and the francophone petit-bourgeois areas of the metropolis hide behind their dearly-bought Liberal security. The P.Q. thus found itself in the dilemma of working for the cause of the small and middle bourgeoisie while being supported by the working class. This contradiction, and many others, shook the party.

Proud of their overwhelming majority, fraudulent as it was, the Liberals made a grand gesture. They freed Vallières on bail, Gagnon having been released several months earlier by the Bertrand government.

Some young Québécois, angered by the outcome of the elections, resumed bombing. No week could pass without a few downtown businesses and some private homes in Westmount shaking with an explosion. It became part of the 'normal' way of life in Montreal.

Despite the noise of the intermittent bombings, a heavy silence permeated Québécois society. We were in the trough of a huge wave preparing to crash.

October 1970

On Monday, October 5, James Richard Cross, British Trade Commissioner in Montreal, receives an unscheduled visit in his comfortable mansion on the slopes of Mount Royal. The armed visitors identify themselves as members of the F.L.Q. and ask him to follow them.

Mrs Cross phones the police. The news spreads like wild-fire. An earthquake could not have caused a greater shock.

An F.L.Q. cell called *Libération* tries to get communiqués to certain journalists, but the police intercept them. At a press conference, Minister of Maintenance of Quebec, Jérôme Choquette, spells out the F.L.Q. demands for the release of Mr Cross:

1. an immediate stop to the police hunt.
2. broadcast of the F.L.Q. Manifesto.
3. liberation of certain political prisoners.
4. their free passage to Cuba or Algeria.
5. the rehiring of the Lapalme drivers.
6. $500,000 in gold ingots.
7. identification of the informer on the last F.L.Q. cell.

Through this action, the F.L.Q.-70 seeks to polarize the social forces at play: on the one hand, the bourgeois class and the state apparatus it has at its disposal; on the other, the working class, the exploited class of Quebec. The F.L.Q.-70 believes that in directly attacking the state apparatus by kidnapping a foreign diplomat, it can help the working class become conscious of its exploitation as well as the strength it can develop through unity to overthrow the bourgeois state.

But since this action does not spring from the very concrete struggle of the workers, since this action seems to be done more *for* the workers than *with* them, it awakens some support but can hardly lead to mobilization of any kind.

Yet this action shakes up the structure of Québécois and Canadian society. The existing social order is threatened. The caretakers have some work cut out for them. In this case, the Great Caretaker himself will take over. The federal government is to take all the decisions in this affair, and the sub-caretaker government of Bourassa simply has the job of carrying them out.

Arrests are made.

Ottawa indicates it is willing to negotiate through a mediator. The *Libération* cell replies that it rejects all mediation.

Ottawa, then, broadcasts the F.L.Q.-70 Manifesto. Following this, the *Libération* cell reduces its demands to two, an immediate stop to the police hunt and the liberation of the political prisoners.

On Friday, October 10, Jérôme Choquette whose Montreal office is in constant contact with Ottawa offers the kidnappers safe conduct to a foreign country in exchange for Cross' release.

Jérôme Choquette has barely finished speaking when Pierre Laporte, Minister of Labour and Immigration in the Bourassa cabinet is kidnapped in front of his St Lambert home. The Chénier cell that claims to be the author of this second kidnapping re-issues the seven original demands for Laporte's release.

These kidnappings relegate to the background the negotiations under way between the provincial government and the specialists on medicare, as well as the municipal election campaign in Montreal where mayor Jean Drapeau is facing the rise of a real opposition in F.R.A.P. *(Front d'action politique),* a coalition of citizens' committees of Montreal.

The government talks of possible negotiations to kill time and give the police a chance to discover the kidnappers' hideouts, but on Thursday, October 15, it rejects the F.L.Q. demands. That same evening, 3,000 people rally in Paul-Sauvé arena to show their support for the F.L.Q.

Students are starting to move. Classes are boycotted in high schools, *Cegeps* (community colleges) and universities. The F.L.Q. manifesto is discussed everywhere, and everybody is following the match between the government and the F.L.Q. with the greatest interest. Support for the F.L.Q. is mounting in the masses of Quebec. Thousands of Québécois support the goals of the F.L.Q. although they may not endorse the means taken to achieve them. F.R.A.P. and the Central Council of the C.N.T.U. of Montreal come out with statements to this effect.

In the face of this mounting support, the government panics and imposes the War Measures Act on Quebec. On Friday, October 16, Quebec again witnesses the military occupation of its territory. The *habeas corpus* is again suspended and the police have the right to arrest and search without warrant as well as to detain 'suspects' for three weeks without charging them. More than 12,000 police and soldiers are at work. Over 340 Québécois will be thrown in jail in the coming days. The forces of repression behave like Hitler's SS troops. In the middle of the night, they knock doors, down, wake up 'suspects' with machine guns in the ribs, brutalize them, cart them off like criminals and leave behind them terrified women and terrorized children.

Among those arrested are Michel Chartrand, chairman of the Central Council of the C.N.T.U. of Montreal, Robert Lemieux, counsel for many political prisoners, Pierre Vallières, Charles Gagnon, Doctor Serge Mongeau, chairman of the Movement for the Defense of Political Prisoners of Quebec (M.D.P.P.Q.), poet Gaston Miron, singer Pauline Julien, and journalist Gérald Godin.

The state is hitting back in anger. All F.L.Q. sympathizers or supporters not in jail shut up and duck. The bourgeois state is taking its revenge for the scare it got. The bourgeois have to be reassured.

On Saturday, October 17, an anonymous telephone call gives the place where the body of Pierre Laporte can be found. Near the St Hubert air-base the police find the body in the trunk of a car. Searches, arrests, dragnets, questionings continue.

Marcel Pepin, chairman of the C.N.T.U., Louis Laberge, head of the F.T.Q. (Quebec Federation of Labour), Yvon Charbonneau, chairman of the C.E.Q. (Quebec Teachers Association), Claude Ryan, editor-in-chief of *Le Devoir*, René Lévesque, leader of the

Parti Québécois, all beg the government to negotiate the release of Mr Cross.

In spite of all that's going on, the municipal elections of Montreal take place on Sunday, October 25. The Civic Party of the Boss of Montreal, Jean Drapeau, exploits the situation to the full. Drapeau accuses F.R.A.P. of being a front for the F.L.Q. The trick works. His Civic Party takes all the seats while F.R.A.P. gets 15 percent of the votes, despite the imprisonment of a number of its candidates and Drapeau's terrorist campaign.

On November 6, Bernard Lortie, alleged member of the Chénier cell, is arrested.

On November 9, Maintenance Minister Jérôme Choquette holds a press conference to tell the underworld it should not fear that the special powers granted the government by the War Measures Act will be used against it. The underworld is reassured.

On November 11, Father Charles Banville, curé of Saint-Paul-de-Matane (Gaspésie), states, "The great majority of the population and the priests of Matane and Matapédia ridings agree with the F.L.Q. manifesto!"

A few days later, the member of the National Assembly for Matane (Gaspésie) advocates the restoration of capital punishment, a compulsory I.D. card, a very strict control of demonstrations, censorship of the press, TV, movies, the cleaning-up of colleges and universities, a strict ideological training for all teachers and professors and compulsory military service.

The police stick up posters of Marc Carbonneau, Jacques Lanctôt, Paul Rose and Francis Simard with a reward of $150,000 for anyone giving information leading to the arrest of these individuals.

On November 25, at the coroner's inquest into the death of Pierre Laporte, Paul Rose's sister, Lise, refuses to testify and cries out how the police stripped and beat her in her cell. The judge condemns her to six months' imprisonment for contempt of court.

The Provincial Police threaten to go on strike over the criticism of their conduct by some of the politicans.

On December 3, an apartment in number 10,945 on rue des Récollets in Montréal-Nord is surrounded. The *Libération* cell holding Mr Cross there negotiates his release and its own safe conduct to Cuba. Jacques Lanctôt, his wife and child, Jacques Cossette-Trudel and his wife, Marc Carbonneau and Yves Langlois leave for Cuba on an R.C.A.F. plane and Mr Cross is set free.

On December 28, Paul Rose, Jacques Rose and Francis Simard are arrested in a farmhouse near St Jean and accused of the murder of Pierre Laporte.

The state apparatus considers it has the guilty ones behind bars and can now start easing the hold of repression while at the same time trying to plaster over the cracks of its public image.

A few hundred 'suspects' are gradually released while the better-known ones are accused of membership in an illegal organization and seditious conspiracy.

It is now the turn of the judicial arm of the state apparatus to fight those who question its order. The accused accuse the judges and Crown attorneys. The judges fight back with contempt of court charges, expulsions, in-camera sessions and adjournments.

With its image tarnished, the judicial apparatus finds a way to free Chartrand and Lemieux on bail, though Paul Rose is prevented from even attending his own trial.

The reigning order is defending itself while the Québécois are thinking things over.

History is in progress.

St-Jean-Baptiste demonstration June 24, 1971.

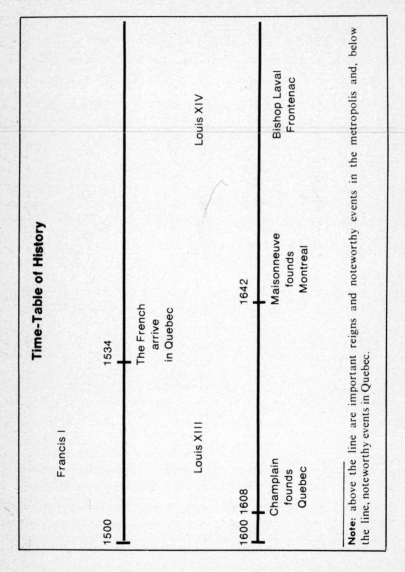

Time-Table of History

Francis I

1500

1534

The French
arrive
in Quebec

Louis XIII

1600 1608

Champlain
founds
Quebec

1642

Maisonneuve
founds
Montreal

Louis XIV

Bishop Laval
Frontenac

Note: above the line are important reigns and noteworthy events in the metropolis and, below the line, noteworthy events in Quebec.

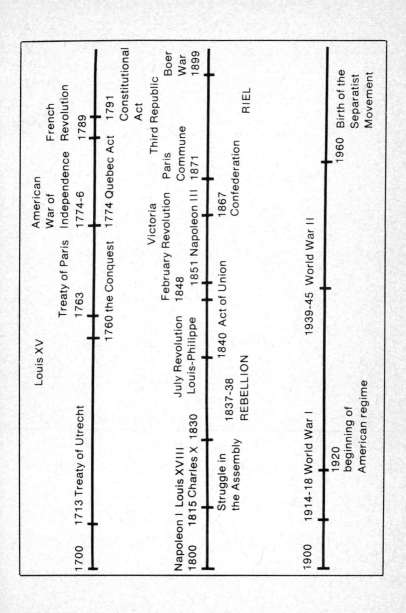

Louis XV

1700   1713 Treaty of Utrecht

Treaty of Paris
1763

1760 the Conquest

American
War of
Independence
1774-6   1774 Quebec Act

French
Revolution
1789   1791
        Constitutional
        Act

Boer
War
1899

Napoleon I Louis XVIII
1800   1815 Charles X 1830

July Revolution
Louis-Philippe

1837-38
REBELLION

Struggle in
the Assembly

1840 Act of Union

February Revolution
1848   1851 Napoleon III

Victoria

1867
Confederation

Paris
Commune
1871

Third Republic

RIEL

1900   1914-18 World War I

1920
beginning of
American regime

1939-45 World War II

1960   Birth of the
        Separatist
        Movement

Publisher's Statement Regarding the C.W. Jefferys Historical Drawings

C.W. Jefferys' historical drawings are the most accurate and comprehensive depiction of our history – truly a national treasure. While preparing *The History of Quebec,* we requested reproduction-quality proofs of some of these drawings from the Imperial Esso Oil Co., which currently has them in its possession.

Initially Imperial Oil agreed as it is obligated by its purchase agreement with the Jefferys estate to make these proofs available without charge for "educational purposes."

Later, Imperial Oil changed its mind, claiming this book is not educational as it reflects "a particular political or social philosophy" – that is, anti-imperialism. Imperial Oil is controlled by the Standard Oil Co. of New Jersey, the original basis of the world-wide multi-billion dollar empire of the Rockefeller interests of the U.S.

Protests and demonstrations across Canada and Quebec by patriotic organizations and individuals lead by the Canadian Liberation Movement resulted in a meeting at Imperial Oil headquarters in Toronto between representatives of Imperial Oil, New Canada Publications and some concerned citizens.

At this meeting, Imperial Oil agreed it would take no action as a result of the reproduction of Jefferys' drawings in this book. Later press reports make it now questionable whether Imperial Oil intends to abide by that agreement.

We have consistenly held that Imperial Oil has no moral or legal right to prevent the reproduction of the drawings in this publication. We have never requested 'permission' to use them. None is needed. However, Imperial Oil's actions have raised an important question: *should a U.S.-owned firm be permitted to deny to the Canadian people our own national heritage?*

In its secret contract of purchase from the Jefferys estate, Imperial Oil is believed to have agreed that at some future time it would turn over the priceless collection (which it bought for only $14,250 – $11 to $15 per drawing!) to a public gallery or museum. In the meantime, it claims to be holding the collection as a "public trust".

Imperial Oil has spent millions reproducing the Jefferys drawings in a campaign to convince the Canadian people that it, as a foreign-owned company, is 'concerned' about the preservation of Canadian culture.

This incident demonstrates that imperialist companies like Esso are interested in preserving Canadian culture only where it helps preserve their profitable interests.

Eric Kierans, former Minister of Communications in the federal Liberal cabinet, has revealed that the largely foreign-owned oil companies in Canada (Esso is the largest) paid a mere $14 million in taxes on a *declared* profit of $350 million in 1970 – according to *their* figures, a tax rate of 4 per cent per annum.

We suggest there is a direct connection between the exploitation of our natural resources by U.S. firms like Esso and the sorry state of *real* Canadian culture – that which tells the truth about our peoples and our struggles, that which aids in our liberation.

Esso uses a small part of its fabulous profits to control and pervert Canadian culture, the better to maintain its ownership and control of Canadian resources. Sooner or later, they will be regained by their rightful owners: the people of Canada.

Under these circumstances, it is our obligation as Canadian liberation publishers to include pertinent C.W. Jefferys historical drawings in *The History of Quebec*.

— *New Canada Publications,
a division of NC Press Ltd.*

239

An Open Letter to W.O. Twaits
Chairman of the Board, Imperial Oil

Your refusal to allow the publication of C.W. Jefferys' historical drawings in *The History of Quebec: A Patriote's Handbook* is a national insult.

This book, soon to be published by New Canada Publications, is the English translation of Quebec's No. 1 best-seller, *Petit manuel d'histoire du Québec* by Léandre Bergeron. In a country where sales of 5,000 copies constitutes a best-seller, this book's sales of over 60,000 copies in only seven months makes it a true publishing phenomenon – and conclusively shows the high regard in which it is held by the people of Quebec.

C.W. Jefferys' drawings are part of the national heritage of the Canadian people. Because of their unparalleled scope and accuracy, they are included in the majority of Canadian history books.

It was precisely for these reasons that the Jefferys estate made it a condition of its sale of the drawings to your company that they be made available free for use in educational books.

You have attempted to justify your refusal on the flimsy grounds that *The History of Quebec* has "a particular political or social philosophy." *All* histories reflect "a particular political or social philosophy" – it's just that some reflect one philosophy and some reflect others.

The History of Quebec tells how U.S.-owned companies such as yours control and rob Quebec and Canada in a systematic fashion. It is obviously no coincidence that your company is majority-owned by the Standard Oil Company of the U.S.A. which is the foundation of the notorious Rockefeller empire that has vast holdings all over the world including about $4 billion here in Canada.

Imperial Oil purchased the C.W. Jefferys drawings with profits made from the Canadian people and is now using them as a means to censor any Canadian history that does not agree with a *certain particular* political or social *philosophy;* namely that of Imperial Oil.

Your recent actions show that national treasures such as the Jefferys drawings must be removed from the private possession of companies like yours to the National Archives or a public museum where they will be freely available to all of the Canadian people.

As persons deeply concerned about the cultural life and rights of the Canadian people, we demand that Imperial Oil immediately grant to New Canada Publications the right to freely reprint any C.W. Jefferys drawing.

MILTON ACORN, *poet, Charlottetown*
ALMA MATER SOCIETY, *University of British Columbia, Vancouver*
PROF. LESLIE ARMOUR, *University of Waterloo, Waterloo*
PROF. HENRY BEISSEL, *Sir George Williams University, Montreal*
LEANDRE BERGERON, *author, Montreal*
MARV BLAUR, candidate, *New Democratic Party, St. Catharines*
JOHN BOYLE, *artist, St. Catharines*
MORDECAI BRIEMBERG, *Simon Fraser University, Vancouver*
PROF. HAROLD BRONSON, *University of Saskatchewan, Saskatoon*
ROBERT BURNS, *member, Quebec National Assembly*
GARY CALDWELL, *lecturer, Trent University, Peterborough*
CANADIAN UNION OF OPERATING ENGINEERS, *Windsor*
CLAUDE CHARRON, *member, Quebec National Assembly*
MICHEL CHARTRAND, *president, Montreal Council, CNTU*
PAUL COPELAND, *lawyer, Toronto*
PROF. JOHN COWAN, *University of Ottawa, Ottawa*
BRENDA CRYDERMAN, *NDP Waffle, Thunder Bay*
GREG CURNOE, *artist, London*
GAIL DEXTER, *lecturer, Ryerson Polytechnical Institute, Toronto*
RALPH ELLIS, *delegate, Hamilton & District Labour Council*
GRAHAM FRASER, *free-lance writer, Toronto*

241

DR PHILIP FRY, *curator, Winnipeg Art Gallery*
BRUNO GERUSSI, *CBC radio personality, Toronto*
GRAEME GIBSON, *novelist, Toronto*
SHIRLEY GIBSON, *general manager, House of Anansi, Toronto*
DAVID GODFREY, *author, New Press, Toronto*
GERALD GODIN, *editor, Québec-Presse, Montreal*
CY GONICK, *member, Manitoba Legislative Assembly, Winnipeg*
PROF. RESHARD GOOL, *chairman Dept. of Political Science,*
  University of Prince Edward Island, Charlottetown
PROF. NINO GUALTIERI, *Carleton University, Ottawa*
CAROL GUDMUNDSON, *vice president, NDP, Saskatoon*
FRED GUDMUNDSON, *organiser, NFU, Saskatoon*
DR. GEORGE HAGGAR, *president, Canadian Arab Federation*
LARRY HAIVEN, *chairman, 85% Canadian Quota Campaign, Tor.*
BRUCE HODGINS *lecturer, Trent University, Peterborough*
MEL HURTIG, *publisher, Edmonton*
C.S. JACKSON, *president, United Electrical Workers, Toronto*
BRUCE KIDD, *sports commentator, Toronto*
PROF. GASTON LAURION, *Loyola College, Montreal*
DENNIS LEE, *poet, Toronto*
RENE LEVESQUE, *leader, Parti Québécois, Montreal*
DR. PHILIP LONDON, *author, Windsor*
BARRY LORD, *art critic, Ottawa*
PROF. A. LUCAS, *McGill University, Montreal*
PROF. IAN LUMSDEN, *York University, Toronto*
A. MAYHEE, *Watson Island Local No. 4, Pulp and Paper*
        Workers of Canada, Prince Rupert, B.C.
PATRICK MCFADDEN, *free-lance writer, Toronto*
TOM MCGRATH, *CBRT&GWU, Vancouver*
PROF. ED MAHOOD, *University of Saskatchewan, Saskatoon*
DR. MARGARET MAHOOD, *psychiatrist, Saskatoon*
PROF. JERRY MALZAN, *University of Waterloo, Waterloo*
PROF. ROBIN MATHEWS, *Carleton University, Ottawa*
Dr. SERGE MONGEAU, *secretary-treasurer, Mouvement pour la*
        défense des prisonniers politiques Québécois
MONTREAL COUNCIL, *Confederation of National Trade Unions*
PROF. STAN MUNOZ, *Sir George Williams University, Montreal*
NATIONAL COMMITTEE for the Canadianisation of Canadian
        Universities
NEW DEMOCRATIC PARTY EDUCATION COMMITTEE, *St. Catharines*
JACK NICHOL, secretary-treasurer, UF&AWU, *Vancouver*
PROF. GRAEME NICHOLSON, *University of Toronto, Toronto*

JACQUES PARIZEAU, *executive member, Parti Québécois, Montréal*
PROF. PIERRE LEMIEUX, *University of Ottawa*
PROF. JOHN RICHARDS, *candidate, NDP, Saskatoon*
JOE ROSENBLATT, *poet, Toronto*
KENT ROWLEY, *secretary-treasurer, Council of Canadian Unions, Brantford*
CLAYTON RUBY, *lawyer, Toronto*
JOHN SEWELL, *alderman, City of Toronto*
PROF. LORENNE SMITH, *University of Toronto, Toronto*
PROF. ROMA STANDEFER, *York University, Toronto*
PROF. JAMES STEELE, *Carleton University, Ottawa*
MEL SWART, *candidate, New Democratic Party, Welland*
EXECUTIVE, LOCAL 199, *United Auto Workers, St. Catharines*
JOHN VARLEY, *past president, Canadian Student Liberals*
PROF. MEL WATKINS, *University of Toronto, Toronto*
PROF. VICTOR WIGHTMAN, *Lakehead University, Thunder Bay*
PETER WILSON, *artist and writer, Toronto*
PROF. W.D. YOUNG, *chairman, Dept. of Political Science, University of British Columbia, Vancouver*
PROF. JACQUES YVAN-MORIN, *Université de Montréal, Montreal*

Organizations are listed for identification purposes only – except where they are listed separately

Canada is a colony. Our trade unions, our natural resources, our culture, our universities, and our industry -- all are controlled from across the border, the largest undefended border in the world, that we "share" with the largest imperialist power in the world.

There are those who, seeing the extent of this colonialism, believe the battle to be lost. We do not see it that way. We see people across the country rising up against U.S. imperialism: workers struggling to forge militant, democratic Canadian unions, farmers fighting U.S. agri-business, students opposing the takeover of the universities by increasing numbers of American professors.

To win this struggle, Canadians need an organization devoted to the cause of fighting U.S. imperialism and willing to make any sacrifice to win. The Canadian Liberation Movement is dedicated to this task.

The Canadian Liberation Movement sees as its task the struggle for an independent socialist Canada: to unite all those classes, strata, national groups and patriotic personalities who can be united to fight U.S. imperialism.

For further information please write:

Canadian Liberation Movement

Box 41, Station 'E', Toronto 4, Ontario

NEW CANADA

New Canada is the anti-imperialist monthly newspaper that reports on the struggles being waged across the country for independence and socialism.

In the year and a half since it began publishing, *New Canada* has exposed the injustices of the U.S. stranglehold and explained how Canadians are fighting back — to win! — in stories like these:

- **Bringing American Imperialism into Canada's Classrooms: a case study of the Ontario Institute for Studies in Education**

- **How the U.S. Unions Run the NDP**

- **Youth Culture: Helping the Very People it Hates**

- **Prairie Farmers Oppose U.S. Agri-Vultures**

- **Why Trinidad Exploded**

- **Locomotive Engineers Fight for Canadian Union**

- **The Heroic Nova Scotia Fishermen**

To: **NC PRESS LTD.,** *Box 6106, Station 'A', Toronto 1, Ontario.*

I want to receive NEW CANADA regularly.

Enclosed please find:

( ) $2.00 for 1 yr. ( ) $3.50 for 2 yrs. ( ) $8 for 5 yrs.
( ) Here is a donation to help you with your work

Name_____
PLEASE PRINT

Address_____

City_____Zone_____